CW00742883

THE
SCARBOROUGH
BOOK
OF
DAYS

ROBERT WOODHOUSE

I am indebted to my wife Sally, for her research and unstinting support, and to Liz Taylorson for her administrative skills. My gratitude goes to: John Woodhouse; Bob Eastwood; Dave Elliott; staff at Middlesbrough, Northallerton and Scarborough libraries.

The Julian calendar was in use until Wednesday, September 2nd 1752. The following day, the Gregorian calendar was adopted, making the date Thursday, September 14th 1752. The dates in this book before and after the shift correspond to the respective calendars.

References for extracts appear in brackets at the end of each entry.

Robert Woodhouse, 2013

First published 2013

The History Press
The Mill, Brimscombe Port
Stroud, Gloucestershire, GL5 2QG
www.thehistorypress.co.uk

© Robert Woodhouse, 2013

The right of Robert Woodhouse to be identified as the Author
of this work has been asserted in accordance with the
Copyright, Designs and Patents Act 1988.

British Library Cataloguing in Publication Data.
A catalogue record for this book is available from the British Library.

ISBN 978 0 7524 7649 0

Typesetting and origination by The History Press
Printed in India

JANUARY 1ST

1934: On this day, an article about the building of wooden barques and schooners was printed in the *Scarborough Evening News*. Written by Douglas J. Boyle, who drew upon information from old insurance papers, it highlighted the role played in the world's carrying trade, by brigs of around 250 tons and barques of about 350 tons. Many of these vessels were constructed on the banks of the River Esk at Whitby or along Scarborough's Sandside, where buildings extended from the Marine Drive Toll House to the Olympia.

The introduction of iron for shipbuilding effectively ended Scarborough's role in the industry, with the construction of fishing yawls, by firms such as Tindall's, marking the final stages. (*Scarborough Evening News*)

———◆———

1973: Jimi Mistry was born in Scarborough, and after schooling at Cheadle Hulme and Cardiff he trained at the Birmingham School of Speech and Drama. His first major television appearance was as Dr Fred Fonseca in BBC Television's *EastEnders* and, in addition to a series of starring roles in films such as *Blood Diamond*, *Exam* and *It's A Wonderful Afterlife*, he has also written and produced a music documentary about Ibiza, with the title *And the Beat Goes On*. Jimi Mistry competed in the BBC series *Strictly Come Dancing* in 2010, where he was partnered with Flavia Cacace until their elimination in week seven. (en.wikipedia.org)

January 2nd

1979: Jonathan Greening, an experienced footballer in the higher levels of English football, was born in Scarborough. His early promise as a creative midfielder saw him begin his career with York City. He made his debut as substitute in a 1–1 draw against Bournemouth on March 22nd 1997 and almost exactly one year later he signed for Manchester United, where first team opportunities were limited. Greening won England under-21 honours during his time at Old Trafford and as substitute he won a UEFA Champions League medal in 1999. On August 8th 2001 a move to Middlesbrough saw him join up with former assistant manager of United, Steve McClaren. He was voted 'Player of the Year 2002/3' and was included in the full England squad (though he did not play). As appearances for Middlesbrough became fewer, he signed for West Bromwich Albion at the end of the 2003/4 season. During his time at the Hawthorns, Greening was club captain for the 2007/08 season and was named in the PFA 'Championship Team of the Year', before he moved to Fulham in August 2009. This was followed by a transfer to Nottingham Forest in July 2011, where he again joined up with Steve McClaren. (en.wikipedia.org/wiki/Jonathan_Greening)

January 3rd

1949: Alfred Rutherford was appointed secretary of Scarborough Cricket Club. A total of seventy-nine applicants were considered for the post, but his experience as a clerk with the County Council, coupled with time as an RAF physical training instructor and then secretary of Thirsk Athletic Club, ensured Rutherford's success.

The post-war era brought record attendances at a range of sporting events, and with support from an enthusiastic, far-sighted committee, Alfred Rutherford's organising ability and commitment ensured a period of growth and prosperity for Scarborough Cricket Club. These improved fortunes were highlighted by publications such as the *Yorkshire Illustrated*, with comments such as:

> The Festival seemed to wake up with a bang! Amenities improved for players and spectators alike. The Festival, instead of swimming along on an even keel suddenly got a jerk from outside, from Alfred! There was a clamour for reserved seats and last year's takings for these (£1,554) were more than double what they were in 1949 (£749).

Structural changes resulted in larger changing rooms, a new bar, dining room and spectator seating, as well as construction of the West Stand which could accommodate 1,700 spectators.

During 1961, Alfred Rutherford left Scarborough to become general manager of Leeds Cricket, Football & Athletic Co. Ltd at Headingley. (Ian Hall & John Found, *Cricket at Scarborough: A Social History of the Club and Its Festival*, Breedon Books Publishing Co. Ltd, 1992)

JANUARY 4TH

1891: Joseph Hunter, one of Scarborough's foremost cricketers, died at the young age of thirty-five after bouts of serious illness. Born on August 3rd 1855, he played for the town in the 1870s and often opened the batting, before making his mark as a wicketkeeper.

In 1878 he was selected by Yorkshire County Cricket Team and featured in a total of ten matches during that season. It was three years before Joseph Hunter gained a regular place in the county team and he continued as first-choice wicketkeeper for a further seven years. His prowess behind the stumps led to him touring Australia in 1884-5, the only Scarborough-born cricketer to play for England, and he averaged over 18 with the bat, made 3 stumpings and took 8 catches.

For almost a hundred years, Hunter held the record number of dismissals in a county match with 9 catches during a match against Gloucestershire in 1887. His record of six dismissals in a single innings was only bettered by David Bairstow (with 7 catches in an innings and 11 in the match) in 1982. Returning to Scarborough's team after his county days, Joseph Hunter totalled almost 1,200 runs with a top score of 60 not out. (Ian Hall & John Found, *Cricket at Scarborough: A Social History of the Club and Its Festival*, Breedon Books Publishing Co. Ltd, 1992)

JANUARY 5TH

1917: William Phillips, one of a considerable number of artists based in Scarborough at the end of the nineteenth century, died on this day at the age of eighty-six. Born in Manchester, he was living in Scarborough during 1881 when he listed himself as an 'artist' in the census of that year. He is also named as an artist in the 1893 Scarborough directory, with his home address given as 102 Long Westgate. William Phillips was buried in Scarborough cemetery. (Anne and Paul Bayliss, *Scarborough Artists of the Nineteenth Century: A Biographical Dictionary*, Anne Bayliss, 1997)

2011: On this day, Helene Palmer, actress and entertainer, died at Scarborough Hospital following a short period of illness. She was born at Bolton-on-Dearne, South Yorkshire on March 5th 1928. During her career as an entertainer in the 1960s and '70s, Helene befriended celebrities such as Pat Phoenix, Lynne Perrie, Freddie Starr and Les Dawson. In 1978 she joined the cast of ITV's *Coronation Street* and made regular appearances as machinist Ida Clough. After being written out of the script in 1988, she reappeared during 1995 and continued in *Coronation Street* for another three years. Combining work in the licensed trade with her media work, Helene Palmer and her husband Alex managed premises in Sewerby and Bridlington during the 1970s and '80s. (en.wikipedia.org/wiki/Helene_Palmer)

JANUARY 6TH

1865: The Wheelhouse Free Almshouses were founded by deed on this day, by George Wheelhouse and Mrs Elizabeth Buckle. New trustees were also appointed by order of Charity Commissioners on February 12th 1907. According to Baines' *Yorkshire Past and Present*, the almshouses are located on Dean Road and are built in the form of a square, with the hall and tower at one end. Completed at an overall cost of £40,000, each dwelling consists of a good porch, living room, bedroom and scullery besides a larder, coal closet etc. Baines' survey, which covered the years up to 1871, concluded that charitable institutions in Scarborough were numerous and well-supported. These included the Amicable Society, founded by R. North Esq. in 1729, established to clothe and educate the children of poor families in the town, the nearby Seamen's Hospital, which was under the superintendence of the Trinity House in Deptford, and a sea-bathing infirmary that had been opened in 1811, through the unstinting efforts of Archdeacon Wrangham, in order to supply free medical services to the poor. A cottage hospital, founded by a Mrs Wright, could also accommodate twenty-four patients. (www.genuki.org.uk)

JANUARY 7TH

1905: During the hours of darkness, heavy seas and an extremely high tide caused Scarborough's North Pier to collapse. Driven coastward in the teeth of a north-west gale, huge waves had battered the North Bay, and backwash from the Royal Albert Drive added to the onslaught that left a trail of twisted metal and floating debris.

The only part of the structure left standing was the pier head pavilion at the seaward end, far below the low-water mark. The pier's demise appealed to local photography companies, such as Thomas Taylor and E.T.W. Dennis, who rapidly produced photographs of the destruction. Such was the popularity of the images, that the initial supply sold out and extra photographs were printed. The owner of the pier at the time was Scarborough's mayor, William Morgan, who had purchased it for £3,500 in 1904, but because of previous storm damage, it could not be insured and the destroyed ironwork was sold for scrap.

A local newspaper stated that, 'The sea was left to wash gleefully over the foundations of what once had to meet the full force of the oncoming waves and was, to all intents and purposes, destroyed for daring to offer resistance.' (Martin Easdown, *Piers of Disaster: Sad Story of the Seaside Pleasure Piers of the Yorkshire Coast*, Hutton Press Ltd, 1996)

JANUARY 8TH

1988: On this day, a telephone kiosk on the Scarborough Station Concourse was listed by English Heritage as being of historic interest. The distinctive square, red-painted, cast-iron structure was one of many made by various contractors, taken from an original design by Sir Giles Gilbert Scott in 1935. Named type K6, it was designed to commemorate the Silver Jubilee of King George V and became the first telephone kiosk to be widely used outside London, with many thousands subsequently positioned in towns and cities throughout the country.

Initially, the K6 was not universally popular, with the red colour providing the main area of debate, so the Post Office allowed a more muted colour of grey with red glazing bars for areas of natural and architectural importance. As demand for K6 kiosks increased, the initial number grew from 19,000 in 1935, to 44,000 in 1950 and 73,000 in 1980, as a result, in 1953, a purpose-built kiosk trailer was designed to allow easier transportation. (www.britishlistedbuildings.co.uk)

2012: On this day, two local teams triumphed in an under-18s Indoor Bowls Tournament held at Eastfield House in Scarborough. A total of ten teams from Yorkshire and the north east took part and Scarborough A won the trophy competition, while Scarborough B were successful in the Plate contest. Eastfield House provides a range of day-care services and the Head of Care, Melanie Padgham, presented the trophies. (*Scarborough Evening News*)

JANUARY 9TH

1945: Four hundred evacuees from London and the Hull area were guests of the Mayor of Scarborough at the Olympia, where a Punch & Judy man provided entertainment and a variety of games were arranged.

Evacuees had begun to arrive in Scarborough during the morning of September 1st 1939, when a trainload accompanied by teachers and helpers disembarked from Hull at the Londesborough Road railway station. Preparations were thorough, and on arrival in Scarborough each child was given a paper carrier bag containing chocolates and potato crisps, along with a tin of bully beef, 1lb biscuits, qt. lb. chocolate or two chocolate crisps, and tins of both sweetened and unsweetened milk.

During the following week, thousands more refugees arrived in Scarborough from Hull, West Hartlepool and Middlesbrough, but by November 10th 1939, 3,696 evacuees had chosen to return home and by April 2nd 1940 a total of 6,000 had left. Another wave of refugee arrivals took place in the later days of July 1944 with a group of 1,250 children from areas of London, where they had suffered attacks from flying bombs and rockets. An additional group of 676 evacuees arrived on August 21st 1944, and it was the following summer before evacuees left the Scarborough area. (Richard James Percy, *Scarborough's War Years, 1939-45*, Sutton Publishing Ltd, 1992)

January 10th

1852: In the early part of this day, high winds from the north-west caused one of the highest tides for twenty years. Coping stones on the Spa walls were swept away and scattered some distance away, while thousands of tons of sand were scoured from the area between the pier and Mill Beck. Coastal fences were badly damaged, as were vessels in the harbour, and as winds strengthened further later in the day the roofs and chimneys of several houses were dashed to pieces. (Keith Snowden, *Scarborough Through the Ages: The Story of the Queen of English Watering Places*, Castleden Publications, 1995)

———•◆•———

1954: The first meeting of the Scarborough Railway Society was held in the garage of Ken Hoole, behind his shop on Newlands Park Drive. Present at this inaugural meeting were Ken Hoole, Brian Webb, Norman Skinner, Fred Rowntree, Ian Lewis, Bill Hardwick and David Bointon. After their third meeting, members of the society moved to the club room of the British Railways Rifle Range on West Parade Road adjacent to Gallows Close Goods Yard. Room hire within a coach cost 5s (25p) per week and during winter months senior members arranged to arrive early in order to light the old cast-iron stove in the centre of the coach. (Robin Lidster, *Scarborough Railway Society 1954-2004: a Brief History to Mark the 50th Anniversary*, Robin Lidster, 2004)

JANUARY 11TH

1979: This day saw the closure of the Cricketers' Room at Scarborough's Grand Hotel, which brought to an end a unique link with the famous annual Cricket Festival. From its official beginning in 1876, the festival grew rapidly in popularity to attract almost every great name in the sport and, through the years, most of the game's amateur players stayed at the Grand Hotel, as well as many of the overseas professionals.

About ten years after the festival got underway, the hotel's general manager decided that his cricketing guests should be allowed greater privacy and allocated a room for their exclusive use. Located beside the old dining room and near the foot of the main staircase, it became known as the Cricketers' Room. It soon displayed photographs of an array of outstanding players, ranging from Dr W.G. Grace and Ranjit Singh, to N.W.D. Yardley and B. Bosanquet, originator of the googly. The Grand Hotel's links with the Festival even extended to the cricket ground, where, during the late 1940s, cricketers took their tea on the field rather than in the pavilion. Food and drink (which, evidently, included whisky when requested) was served on silver trays by staff from the hotel, including the head waiter. (Bryan Perrett, *Sense of Style: Being a Brief History of the Grand Hotel, Scarborough*, Burscough, B. Perrett, 1991)

JANUARY 12TH

1895: Reverend Samuel Edward Fitch died on this day and is buried in Scarborough Cemetery. Born in Cambridge in 1812, he trained and qualified as a doctor, but never seems to have practised medicine, before taking up a career in the Anglican Church. After training at St Bees' Theological College in the Lake District between 1844 and 1846, he was based in Norfolk and then Bedfordshire, where an interest in Celtic and Saxon remains led to him publishing his research in illustrated articles. Revd Fitch then spent time in the Lake District before moving to Scarborough in 1875, where some of his work, including *Legends of Lakeland* (1881) and weekly 'Versified Charades', was published in the *Scarborough Gazette*. (Anne and Paul Bayliss, *Medical Profession in Scarborough 1700 to 1899: A Biographical Dictionary*, A.M. Bayliss, 2005)

———•◆•———

1940: On the evening of this day, Scarborough-based trawlers came under attack from enemy aircraft for the first time. The *Persian Empire* with skipper Thomas Robson and the *Riby*, under Joe Winship's command, were dive-bombed and machine-gunned, but damage was slight. Four bombs were released but fell wide of their target, however, the incident left a compass, dynamo and wireless on the *Riby* damaged. The *Persian Empire* fired its rockets and this seemed to deter the raiders. (www.mistoftime.co.uk)

JANUARY 13TH

1936: The Great Annual Sale of Westbrook Wholesale Cabinet Works Ltd at no. 6 Castle Road was advertised on this day, with the bold statement:

We have only one sale per year. This is a genuine sale. Anyone can afford to buy furniture at these prices. It is not an expense, it is an investment. A few examples are as follows: 250 4ft and 4ft 6in Full Panel Bedsteads, with Vono Fittings 17/6, Oak Drawleaf Dining Tables 37/6 Oak Dining Chairs 11/6 4ft Oak sideboards 37/6 50 only, 5 piece Lounge Suites in various coverings, from £4 Large Meat Safes 15/- 250 only, Feather Pillows, 2/- each to clear Many other items at correspondingly low prices . . . Westbrook Furniture is as good as the best and better than most. It is made on the premises by skilled craftsmen, and we cut the middleman's profit clean out. That is how we can sell so much below ordinary dealers' prices, at the same time giving superior quality and finish. If you are requiring good, sound furniture at lowest possible prices, your decision will definitely be Westbrook, the furnishing specialists.

(Scarborough Evening News)

January 14th

1940: A highly realistic Air Raid Precautions (ARP) exercise took place in the Scarborough area today. A practice warning was given to all key posts, and wardens who were already on duty summoned other wardens to take part. A total of twenty-three incidents were dealt with during the operation, in places including Derwent Street, Morgan Street and Sidney Street, where gas was supposedly present. (Richard James Percy, *Scarborough's War Years, 1939-45*, Sutton Publishing Ltd, 1992)

———— • ◆ • ————

2002: This day marked the launch of a fundraising campaign by the *Scarborough Evening News* which called on its readers to help. The newspaper was adopting the St Catherine's Hospice campaign, which was aiming to complete a new £5.5 million building in the town. Over the next two years the sum of £2 million needed to be raised by members of the public so that the dream could become reality. The hospice had outgrown its thirteen-bed accommodation in Scalby Road, and in 2001 officers of St Catherine's Hospice had acquired 4.5 acres of land in Throxenby Lane. The intention was to construct a twenty-bed hospice and headquarters unit, with more single rooms for patients, with better shower and bathing facilities, as well as a family room for relatives to stay overnight. (*Scarborough Evening News*)

JANUARY 15TH

1921: A report in the *Drapers Record* described the successful Christmas Tableau that was a feature of the Bazaar at Messrs Boyes' Stores at Scarborough . . . Robinson Crusoe and Man Friday were shown on the island with the wreck visible in the distance, and the fact that all the characters were alive added greatly to its interest. Robinson Crusoe was sometimes seen at work in the cave and at other times strolling along the sea shore, and his companions in the form of a talking parrot and even a live dog and goat gave great delight to the children who came in the thousands to see the show. A live teddy bear walking about the store was the cause of great amusement, and no Christmas attraction would be complete without Father Christmas, and this popular gentleman was at home in his chimney corner where he was met with a great reception. It was reported that one little girl, when told to go to bed early on Christmas Eve as Father Christmas would be coming, replied, 'Oh, don't worry, he won't have left Boyes' store yet.' (The tableau was either a walk-in series of settings or a ride such as 'A trip to the Moon'.) (*Boyes Stores: the Story of a Family; Boyes, 1881-1981, a Century of Good Value*, Boyes, 1981)

JANUARY 16TH

1952: One of Britain's finest singers, the contralto Kathleen Ferrier, gave a concert at Queen Street Central Hall on this day, and a review in the *Scarborough Evening News* reported: 'The recital was a wonderful experience and one which must have given unalloyed pleasure to all who were privileged to hear it. From beginning to end Miss Ferrier succeeded in holding her audience enthralled.' She was at the height of her popularity and the audience was completely unaware of her deteriorating medical condition as cancer spread to her bones and caused increasing pain. In the following year, during a concert at Covent Garden, her left thigh fractured and she sang through the pain barrier to complete what turned out to be her final public performance. Two days before she died, Sir John Barbirolli visited her in hospital, where she sang for him parts of Chausson's *Poème de l'amour et de la mer*. He remarked that although her body had deteriorated, Kathleen Ferrier's voice had lost none of its radiance. Sixty years later, the 1952 concert programme was recreated in Scarborough by mezzo-soprano Anna Stephany, winner of the Kathleen Ferrier award, with proceeds going to Macmillan Cancer Support and similar charities. (*Scarborough Evening News*)

January 17th

1905: A meeting of the Scarborough Forty Club on this day held an impromptu discussion on the subject – 'Is the present age an excessively competitive one? The evils of the drink traffic'

Early activities of the Forty Club were associated with the aims of the Scarborough Amicable Society, which was set up in March 1729 'with the intention of clothing and educating the children of the poor of Scarborough', and meetings during the first decade of the twentieth century often included discussions on current social or political issues. (Alan Staniforth, *Scarborough Forty Club & Discussion Group: A Brief History: the '40' Club, founded in 1899*, Alan Staniforth, 2005)

1921: J.V. (Vic) Wilson was born and brought up at Scampston, near Malton, and joined Scarborough's successful cricket team in 1938 as a hard-hitting batsman and fine close-in fielder. These qualities led to a place on the Marylebone Cricket Club touring party to Australia in 1954-55, where he featured as the twelfth man in all five Test matches.

As captain of Yorkshire from 1960-62 he led the county to success in the championship (in both 1960 and 1962) and exhibited a brand of strong discipline, which saw Fred Trueman be sent home for arriving late. In his 658 innings for Yorkshire he scored a total of 20,539 runs at an average of 31.21 per match. (Ian Hall & John Found, *Cricket at Scarborough: A Social History of the Club and Its Festival*, Breedon Books Publishing Co. Ltd, 1992)

January 18th

1935: The North Riding Police Court at Scarborough was the setting for lively exchanges between the chairman and the defendant's solicitor. William A. Bull, a resident of Hull, was charged with taking half a dozen bricks from the roadside at Lebberston on January 11th. The bricks, which were the property of the Corporation Electricity Department, were used in the laying of an electricity cable and had a value of 10*d*. George Frederick Fitzwater, senior assistant mains engineer, explained that the bricks were of a particular type and gave warning to a person digging that they were approaching a high tension cable carrying 11,000 volts. Police Constable Huggins explained how he had found the bricks in the front of the defendant's car and how Bull had immediately expressed his regret for his actions. He had taken them to build up a fireplace and did not think that he was committing a criminal offence. 'I have been a fool' he continued, as he had jeopardised his employment, where he held a position of trust and confidence and handled large sums of money every day. If convicted he would lose the fidelity bond, which was a requirement of that job. (*Scarborough Evening News*)

January 19th

1945: Scarborough lighthouse was brought back into use again at high tide from this date, as wartime restrictions were gradually relaxed. Almost exactly one month later, on February 20th, pleasure craft were allowed to operate to a maximum distance of 2.5 miles from the coastline during daylight hours. Within the town itself, traffic lights operated again from June 1st 1945 and during the same month a one-way traffic flow began on Aberdeen Walk. Further moves towards normality followed later in the year, when Scarborough Castle reopened for public visits on November 17th and the annual charity football match between fishermen and firemen, last held in 1938, was staged on Boxing Day 1945. The final weeks of the year also saw the withdrawal of troops from local billets and the YMCA canteen for forces personnel, located at the South Cliff Congregational Church, was closed for good during December. In spite of these elements of everyday life, there were chilling reminders of the previous war years, with the discovery of two live Mills bombs at Swift's Hotel on Blenheim Terrace and five blast bombs in the garden of 132 North Marine Road. (Richard James Percy, *Scarborough's War Years, 1939-45*, Sutton Publishing Ltd, 1992)

January 20th

1922: John Harwood Hick, the son of a solicitor, was born in Scarborough on this day. After a period of study at the Bootham School in York he became an articled clerk in the family's law firm. During 1941, Hick gave up his legal studies to read Philosophy at Edinburgh University and in the following year he served with a Friends' Ambulance Unit in Egypt, Italy and Greece. Returning to his studies after the war he gained a First at Edinburgh in 1948 and completed a PhD at Oxford, before becoming a minister in the Presbyterian Church at Belford in Northumberland; however, a move into academic circles soon followed.

In 1956, Hick went to America as Assistant Professor of Philosophy at Princeton Theological Seminary, and during the next few years he gained an international reputation through his book *Philosophy of Religion* (1963) and because of a doctrinal disagreement with the hierarchy of the Presbyterian Church. During the mid-1960s, Hick spent time teaching in England and America, as well as writing another significant book, *Evil and the God of Love* (1966). His career as a writer, lecturer and academic continued beyond his retirement in 1992 and he died on February 9th 2012. (*The Daily Telegraph*)

JANUARY 21ST

1967: Andrew Hedley Hornby, prominent businessman of recent years, was born in Scarborough. The family soon moved to the Bristol area where his father was headteacher at Clifton College Preparatory School. Andy Hornby's own education included a degree in English literature from St Peter's College, Oxford, and an MBA from Harvard Business School. After leaving Harvard he joined Blue Circle Industries where he held a range of management posts and then moved on to Asda in 1996. Three years later, at the age of thirty-two, he was promoted to the Asda Management Board, before he joined Halifax as Chief Executive of Retail in November 1999. During 2001, after the merger with Bank of Scotland, he became Chief Executive of HBOS Retail and he was thrust into the forefront of media attention when a government-facilitated rescue by Lloyds TSB took place during autumn 2008. At that time he was also Chairman of the Remuneration Committee. On July 1st 2009 Andy Hornby became Group Chief Executive of Alliance Boots, and after resigning from this post in March 2011 he took over as Chief Executive of Coral. (en.wikipedia. org/wiki/Andy_Hornby)

JANUARY 22ND

1941: Sirens were sounded between 12.10 and 12.57 a.m. on this day, when enemy aircraft flew over Seamer. Five high explosive bombs were released at Rillington, and the German raider then machine-gunned several cottages in the village where a number of windows were broken. The invader also machine-gunned a goods train. Men on the train took cover, as well as a number of workmen who were labouring nearby. The railway line itself was wrecked, and damage was caused to the roofs and windows of eight houses. A nearby farmhouse also suffered damage. (www.mistoftime.co.uk)

2012: Delighted passers-by on Scarborough seafront gathered in large numbers to watch a porpoise that had made its way from the open sea into the harbour. Crowds also spread along the slipway off Sandside as the animal swam up and down. One of the shore-side spectators reported that it had been in the harbour for quite a while and seemed perfectly happy, while a member of the Humber coastguard commented that the porpoise had not caused any disruption. Although it was a fairly unusual occurrence for one to come all the way into the harbour, he added that they can be spotted fairly regularly further out to the sea off Scarborough. (*Scarborough Evening News*)

JANUARY 23RD

1963: One of Scarborough's coldest nights was recorded on this day, with temperatures reaching their lowest mark for eighteen years. Air temperature in the Town Hall gardens went down to 21 degrees Fahrenheit (11 degrees of frost), to equal the figure for December 29th 1961, and there were still 7 degrees of frost at 9.00 a.m. Scarborough's previous coldest night was in January 1945, when the air temperature in the Town Hall gardens dropped to 15 degrees Farenheit (17 degrees of frost). This latest bout of intense cold brought problems for the North-East Electricity Board's Scarborough office, which was inundated with calls from customers about loss of power during the evening. A spokesman stated that as far as was known, the fault was a result of icing on the grid lines near Hull. Power loss occurred about eight or nine times through the evening, with many television viewers worried when they saw the picture suddenly fading and then returning to normal. The Scarborough-Pickering road was reported to be clear and safe, but the Scarborough-Whitby road was still restricted to single-lane traffic in parts. Demand for gas was reported to be 'absolutely fantastic', and Scarborough plumbers were expecting a flood of calls to deal with burst pipes once the thaw set in. (*Scarborough Evening News*)

JANUARY 24TH

1903: Scarborough Forty Club stated on this day:

> . . . that a Smoking Concert be held with the object being to aid the
> distressed . . . that the proceeds be devoted to providing free dinners
> for necessitous children, that the dinner tickets be handed over for
> distribution to the teachers of the various schools and that payment
> be made periodically to the various serving agencies only on the
> presentation to the Treasurer of the numbers of tickets received.

(Alan Staniforth, *Scarborough Forty Club & Discussion Group:
A Brief History: the '40' Club, founded in 1899*, Alan Staniforth, 2005)

———•—•———

1940: On this day, the Scarborough and District Licensed Victuallers
Association organised a ball at the town's Grand Hotel, with proceeds
being passed to the Mayoresses' Comfort Fund. Music was provided
by Jack Elvidge and his band. (Richard James Percy, *Scarborough's
War Years, 1939-45*, Sutton Publishing Ltd, 1992)

———•—•———

2009: Scarborough Rugby Union Football Club played their last
match at the Newby ground before moving to new premises at Silver
Royd on Scalby Road. The club was formed in 1926 at a meeting held
at the Pavilion Hotel, and the team's first match was at Whitby. In the
early years, home games were played at pitches adjacent to Seamer
Road and a Supporters' Club, formed in the 1928/29 season, has
played a major role in guiding progress which has culminated in the
new era at Silver Royd, which boasts one of the best amateur rugby
venues in the country. (www.scarboroughrugby.co.uk)

JANUARY 25TH

1603: An entry in the diary of Lady Margaret Hoby states: 'This day it was told Mr Hoby that a ship was wricked up at Burniston upon his land and thus at all times God bestowed benefittes upon us. God made us very thankful . . .' Lady Margaret had married her third husband, Sir Thomas Hoby, in 1596, and she is said to be the earliest known example of a woman of high rank whose personal diary has survived. She died at the age of sixty-two in September 1633 and was buried at Hackness. This statement in her diary has been interpreted by some observers as indicating the involvement of members of the local gentry in nefarious activities. During the Tudor period, Filey was reported to have three pirates, Bridlington to have seven while Scarborough totalled no less than twenty-two. At that time, the term 'pirate' was applied to unpleasant activities ranging from harrying and capturing shipping to wool smuggling, and in some remote communities it is quite likely that most people were involved to a greater or lesser extent. (Graham Smith, *Smuggling in Yorkshire 1700-1850*, Countryside Books, 1994)

JANUARY 26TH

1919: Bill Nicholson (christened William Edward) was born in Scarborough on this day. Educated at Scarborough Boys' High School, he then worked in a laundry while beginning a career in football, playing for local teams such as the Young Liberals. His talents as an inside forward led to a trial at Tottenham Hotspur Football Club in 1936 and he made his league debut during 1938. The war years saw him enlist with the Durham Light Infantry where he became a physical training instructor. During 1948, Nicholson resumed his career with Spurs and some three years later he won his only England cap, against Portugal, before retiring in 1954 to take up a coaching career. After becoming manager in 1958 he built teams around household names such as Danny Blanchflower, Dave Mackay and Jimmy Greaves and then again around Alan Mullery, Pat Jennings, Martin Peters and Martin Chivers. Playing with great style and panache, Spurs won eight English and European cup competitions before Nicholson unexpectedly resigned in 1974. He was awarded an OBE a year later and returned to Tottenham as a consultant in 1976, before becoming club president in 1991. He died on October 23rd 2004. (www.telegraph.co.uk)

JANUARY 27TH

1936: On this day, newspaper articles reported on dense fog along the Yorkshire coast, which caused 'several mishaps to shipping'. During this episode three vessels ran ashore – there was a collision in the vicinity of Whitby, and the Scarborough lifeboat was launched to go the aid of the *Heatherfield*, which had crashed into rocks. Ninety helpers were called out to haul the lifeboat over a long stretch of sand and it was quickly floated from its carriage. It had only travelled two lengths under engine power when it ran into a sandbank off the mouth of Scarborough harbour. All the crew, apart from the coxswain and engineer, leapt into the waist-deep water while the ninety helpers waded across the water to pull the ropes. After considerable difficulty they managed to re-float the lifeboat, and as it edged northwards the coxswain, John Owston, reported that crew members could not see each other in the fog. An hour and a half later they had almost reached the stranded vessel but could not approach close enough until daylight. After a wait of around two hours, Morse signals from shore-based rescuers indicated that crew members had been removed by life-saving apparatus from the *Heatherfield* and the lifeboat returned to Scarborough. (*Scarborough Evening News*)

JANUARY 28TH

2006: Today, Britain's largest illuminated 'Star Disk', measuring 26 metres in diameter, was officially switched on at 7 p.m. by the Deputy Mayor of Scarborough, Councillor Jim Preston. Constructed on the site of the South Bay Pool, the disk included (in the form of fibre optic terminals) the forty-two brightest circumpolar stars (meaning stars which never disappear below the horizon) as seen in the heavens from Scarborough. It also defines the positions of the sunrise points over the North Sea for various dates in the year. Create, an arts and cultural agency specialising in setting up temporary works of art and related events, initiated plans for this phase of development around the South Bay Pool. Further input was provided by the Scarborough Urban Renaissance of Public Space Group in partnership with Scarborough Borough Council. The event was accompanied by a large public star party, where the major attraction for members of the public was the opportunity to observe Saturn through telescopes and pick out its distinctive ring system and major satellites. By coincidence, or design, the planet was nearest to earth on the day before the event. (forum.popastro.com)

January 29th

1900: A meeting of the Forty Club featured a special talk on the 'Genesis of Crime' by Mr Bowerman, which was illustrated with limelight slides. The audience included about thirty guests in addition to members and the presentation was followed by a musical programme. This is typical of the Forty Club's early meetings, which featured discussion and debate and were complemented by musical programmes, dinners and social evenings, as well as an annual Smoking Concert (first held on March 12th 1900). (Alan Staniforth, *Scarborough Forty Club & Discussion Group: A Brief History: the '40' Club, founded in 1899*, Alan Staniforth, 2005)

———————◆————————

1940: Scarborough's first air-raid warning sounded after enemy aircraft had been spotted in airspace over Cayton Bay, but on this day attacks were restricted to shipping. SS *Stanburn* was sunk to the south east of Flamborough Head, after a Stuka dive bomber suddenly appeared from cloud cover to drop three bombs on the ship. Captain Lewis and twenty-five of her crew died in the attack, leaving only three survivors. During the following months the town suffered tip-and-run raids that caused wide-scale damage to property and important targets such as the harbour, the Admiralty wireless station and army barracks, which were singled out in later attacks. (David Fowler, *God Bless the Prince of Wales: Volume 1, The War Years*, Farthings Design & Publishing, 2008)

JANUARY 30TH

1987: Today, the Windmill on Mill Street in Scarborough was listed with Grade II status. Windmills have stood on this site for over 400 years, but the present structure dates from 1784 when it was completed in red handmade bricks by Thomas Robinson. In 1880, a fierce gale blew down most of the mill's sails, but corn grinding continued until 1927 using power from a gas turbine engine. During the following decades, it fell into disrepair and narrowly escaped demolition in the 1980s before restoration work got underway. The sails have been replaced, and an exterior balcony has been added as part of the mill's most recent era as holiday accommodation. Internal machinery has been replaced by modern furnishings and fittings, but this fine structure still represents an outstanding example of a tower mill. The earliest type of windmill in England was the post mill, where machinery and sails on the central post were rotated to bring the sails into the wind, but by the fifteenth century the tower mill, with grinding machinery mounted in a fixed stone or brick tower, was being introduced throughout the country. The third type of windmill in England was the smock mill, allegedly so-called because of its similarity in appearance to a man wearing a smock. (www.britishbuildings.co.uk)

JANUARY 31ST

1939: On this day, Dr Robert Cuff, surgeon and local medical officer, died in a Scarborough nursing home. Born at Binderton, Sussex, in 1858, he studied at Guy's Hospital, London and was appointed to the Scarborough Sanitary Authority in 1885. Some three years later, Cuff was elected a member of the medical staff of Scarborough Hospital and Dispensary and soon afterwards he was Medical Officer of Health for Scarborough. He was also Medical Officer to the Royal Northern Sea-bathing Infirmary for forty years and chairman of the local branch of the British Medical Association from 1903-5. During his later life, Cuff served as a borough magistrate, a magistrate for the North Riding of Yorkshire and a county councillor. After establishing the Scarborough Convalescent Home for Children, in association with Lady Isa Sitwell, he continued as Honorary Consulting Medical Officer and Senior Trustee. A bout of illness in 1928 saw him head to the south of England, but he returned to Scarborough some two years before his death at the end of January 1939. (Anne and Paul Bayliss, *Medical Profession in Scarborough 1700 to 1899: A Biographical Dictionary*, A.M. Bayliss, 2005)

———◆———

1941: Sixty enrolments were made today, for the Air Training Corps under a new national scheme, which provided pre-entry training for boys intending to join the RAF or Fleet Air Arm. (Richard James Percy, *Scarborough's War Years, 1939-45*, Sutton Publishing Ltd, 1992)

FEBRUARY 1ST

1896: On this day, Colonel John Kendall conveyed Kendall's Hospital by deed and endowed it with £2,074 South Eastern Railway 4 per cent preference stock, vested with the official trustees. The accommodation consisted of eight almshouses in St Mary's Street and, along with other municipal charities in Scarborough, it was administered by trustees appointed by the Charity Commissioners. (www.british-history.ac.uk/charities)

* * *

1924: Samuel North Smith died at the Southlands Boarding House in Scarborough on this day. Born in 1840, he joined his father's building business before taking up a career as an accountant and estate agent. In 1877, he was elected to represent the North Ward as a councillor and was successful in local elections in 1880, 1883 and 1886. During November 1879, Smith was chosen as Mayor of Scarborough, and during his term in office the Lord Mayor of London paid an official visit to the town to reopen Scarborough Spa, which had burned down in 1876.

In October 1881, he was appointed a Borough Magistrate, and in February 1911 he replaced Benjamin Fowler as chairman of Licensing Justices. As well as business interests in the area, Smith held the posts of secretary and treasurer at Falsgrave Wesleyan Chapel. (Anne and Paul Bayliss, *Scarborough's Members of Parliament, 1832 to 1906: Scarborough's Mayors, 1836 to 1906: A Biographical Dictionary*, A.M. Bayliss, 2008)

FEBRUARY 2ND

1857: Consolidated annuities (or Consols) held by the official trustees upon the trust of a deed poll, dated February 2nd 1857, amounted to £325 13s compared with an initial endowment of £300 provided by the Rt Hon. Charles Duncombe, Lord Feversham when Scarborough National Schools opened in 1837. In the early decades of the nineteenth century, before a state system of education was in place, schooling was arranged by the British and Foreign School Society with non-denominational Bible teaching or the National Society for the Education of the Poor according to the Principles of the Church of England. These National or Church schools became the most usual form of popular education in villages or small towns. (www.british-history.ac.uk)

———— • ◆ • ————

1953: On this day, Scalby Station, built in 1885, was finally closed. Certain trains continued to stop there, however, until 1964, for visitors to camping coaches. Built to similar designs as other stations on the Scarborough and Whitby Railway (such as Cloughton, Stainton Dale and Robin Hoods Bay), it had outer walls eighteen inches thick. All of the station buildings at Scalby were demolished in 1974. (J. Robin Lidster, *The Scarborough and Whitby Railway*, Hendon Publishing Co. Ltd, 1977)

February 3rd

1900: Pantland Hick, prominent businessman and local dignitary, died at his home in the Falsgrave area of Scarborough on this day. Born in 1833 to a family of ship owners, he was educated at Scarborough Grammar School before spending time at sea from the age of fourteen. In 1863, Hick retired from overseas travel to join the family shipping company and a decade later he began a long association with local politics. First elected to the town council in 1873, he was re-elected in 1876, 1879 and 1882. The following year he was chosen as mayor (1883-4), before becoming an alderman. Further periods in office as a councillor, between 1886 and 1898, allowed him to make effective use of his experience in the shipping industry. (Anne and Paul Bayliss, *Scarborough's Members of Parliament, 1832 to 1906: Scarborough's Mayors, 1836 to 1906: A Biographical Dictionary*, A.M. Bayliss, 2008)

1947: Local newspapers reported today that demolition of wartime brick-built shelters had got underway, at a cost of £8 10s 0d for each one. As clearance work continued, basement shelters in public buildings were removed and underground areas filled in or covered over, while some of the surface structures continued in use for a time as cycle stores or even chicken sheds. (Richard James Percy, *Scarborough's War Years, 1939-45*, Sutton Publishing Ltd, 1992)

FEBRUARY 4TH

1825: On this day, three ships under construction at Scarborough yards were washed off the stocks and badly damaged. At this time, the port was a major shipbuilding centre, and between 1742 and 1879 almost 42,000 tons of ships were constructed at Tindall's alone, as well as 30,000 tons of vessels at other local yards. The peak year for shipbuilding was 1801, when thirteen were completed. At that time the most popular name for a ship was *Providence*, followed by *Elizabeth* and *Fortitude*. The same storm and high tide caused damage to the Spa. (www.scarboroughsmaritimeheritage.org.uk)

1910: The Oddfellowship at Scalby was reported to be growing in popularity. First established less than five years before, the Loyal Vale of Derwent Lodge of the Manchester Unity of Oddfellows at Scalby had made more rapid progress than its most optimistic supporters had hoped for. Its membership of both seniors and juveniles was not far short of 100 and with officers as energetic as the lodge could boast of, the prospects were thought to be quite bright. The annual tea and concert took place at the Nag's Head today, when a company numbering nearly fifty sat down and then drank loyal toasts to the 'Manchester Unity and the Vale of Derwent Lodge', 'Medical officers' and the 'Host and Hostess'. (*Scarborough Mercury*)

FEBRUARY 5TH

1942: Susan Hill, award winning novelist, children's writer and playwright, was born in Scarborough on this day. She was a pupil at Scarborough Convent School before moving to Coventry with her family in 1958. An early interest in theatre and literature led to an English degree at King's College London and her first novel, *The Enclosure*, was published when she was still a student. Her next novel, *Gentlemen and Ladies*, was published in 1968, and several other titles including *I'm the King of the Castle*, *Strange Meeting* and *In the Springtime of the Year* were all written and published between 1968 and 1974. Among her early successes, Hill won a Somerset Maugham Award for *I'm the King of the Castle* in 1970, the Whitbread Novel Award for *The Bird of Night* in 1972, and the *Mail on Sunday* John Llewellyn Rhys Prize for *The Albatross* in the following year. In 1983 her famous ghost story, *The Woman in Black*, was published and later turned into a celebrated play and film. In 1988, she was awarded the Nestlé Smarties Book Prize (Gold Award) (6-8 years category). During 1996, she set up her own publishing company, Long Barn Books, and since 2004, Hill has written a series of crime novels featuring detective Simon Serrailler. (literature.britishcouncil.org)

FEBRUARY 6TH

1764: Richard Wilson, founder of Wilson's Mariners' Homes on Castle Road in Scarborough, was born on this day. He was christened at St Mary's Church some five months later, on July 8th. The Wilson family had been prominent among Scarborough's seafarers since the mid-1600s and around 1778, Richard began an apprenticeship at sea in one of his father's ships. By the age of twenty he was master and part-owner of two brigantines. On November 7th 1791, he became captain of his own ship, *Cybele*, and then went on to acquire shares in several other merchant vessels that traded between the Yorkshire ports and London. He also built up profitable interests in other land-based enterprises, such as the Cliff Bridge Company. In about 1805, Richard Wilson married Mary Dowker and they lived in a property on St Nicholas Cliff, while he played an increasingly significant role in Scarborough's institutions, including three terms as Senior Bailiff and Chief Magistrate. He was a generous supporter of all local schemes that offered free or cheap education to needy children, as well as provision for retired seagoing men and their wives and widows; it was probably this involvement that led to the foundation of the Mariners' Asylum on July 1st 1837. (*Scarborough Mercury*)

FEBRUARY 7TH

1814: Bartholomew Johnson, a celebrated musician in the Scarborough area, died on this day at the age of 103 years, and was interred in Wykeham churchyard. Born on October 3rd 1710, he moved from his home at Wykeham to nearby Scarborough in order to take up an apprenticeship as a barber and for almost seventy-one years he was one of the town's 'waits' (musicians). Bartholomew Johnson's prowess as a musician, coupled with many commendable personal qualities, ensured that he was surrounded by a large circle of friends, and his 100th birthday (on October 3rd 1810) was celebrated with a jubilee dinner and musical performance at the Freemason's Lodge in Scarborough. A medal was struck as memorial of the event and Lord Mulgrave commissioned John Jackson R.A. to paint a portrait of the venerable centenarian, which was later presented to Scarborough Corporation and put on display in the Town Hall. (William Smith, *Old Yorkshire*, Longmans Green & Co., 1891)

❖

1923: Today saw the opening night production of *Hobson's Choice* staged at Scarborough's Arcade Theatre, with Charles Laughton playing the role of Willy Mossop, the journeyman cobbler who married his employer's daughter. The *Scarborough Mercury* described his performance as 'Ranking with the best of character portrayals'. (Ed. Denis Coggins, *Scarborough in Old Photographs*, Budding Books, 2001)

FEBRUARY 8TH

2000: There were echoes of *Dr Who* along Scarborough's seafront on this wintry day, when a blue police telephone box was moved from the Foreshore and up Sandside, to an area near the West Pier slipway. The change of location was part of the Foreshore redevelopment scheme and the vacant space was earmarked for a 400 sq ft tourist information centre. Hard hats were the order of the day among council workmen, as a crane lifted the 3 ton box from its base, before slings stretched underneath helped to move it to a set of foundations at its new location, where a Scarborough council spokesperson expressed his opinion that the job had been completed exactly according to plan. When it was first positioned on the seafront in 1920, there were a dozen similar boxes in the town, and the award of Grade II listing did not affect its use as a subsidiary police office. It represented one of eighteen similar police boxes in this country with protected status. (Press reports in November 2009 indicated that the box had fallen into disrepair and North Yorkshire Police had funded restoration to its original condition.) (*Scarborough Evening News*)

FEBRUARY 9TH

1879: John Woodall, a member of a prominent family of Scarborough bankers, died on this day. The bank premises of Woodall, Hebden & Co. were located at the corner of Newborough and St Nicholas Street from 1864, in a building designed by Henry Watt. Woodall lived in the nearby St Nicholas House, which was purchased by the Corporation as the new Town Hall in 1898. This Jacobean-style building, with shaped gables and turrets, was probably completed as Woodall's residence during 1846-7, although it incorporates a decorative '1844' within an initialled plaque. (Scarborough and District Civic Society in Conjunction with Scarborough Borough Council, *The Scarborough Heritage Trail, Part 1, The Old Town, 2nd Edition*, 2004)

1940: The WVS (Women's Voluntary Service) for Civil Defence was visited by the Countess of Feversham today. She was the county organiser of the WVS for the North Riding, and called at two hospital supply depots at 42 Filey Road and St Martin's Vicarage. During 1938, the Home Secretary, Sir Samuel Hoare, had established a women's voluntary organisation to provide support in the event of future air raids, of which Lady Reading was placed in overall charge. By the time war broke out in September 1939, the WVS numbered 135,000 and local members provided invaluable service to Scarborough, most notably during the blitz on March 18th 1941. (Richard James Percy, *Scarborough's War Years, 1939-45*, Sutton Publishing Ltd, 1992)

FEBRUARY 10TH

1857: The Annual General Meeting of the Scarborough Dispensary was held on this day in the Town Hall, and it was here that an unexpected procedural difficulty arose over the appointment of a consulting physician. In 1854, Dr W.E. Swaine had resigned from the post and the position remained vacant until this meeting, where the Congregational Minister, Robert Balgarnie, proposed that George Peckitt Dale, one of the original founders of the Dispensary some six years earlier, should be appointed. Dr Dale was already one of the Dispensary's medical officers and the proposal was carried unanimously. It was also agreed that one hour from midday each Thursday should be set aside for him to see patients. The procedural difficulty emerged because Dr Dale had not been appointed at a Special General Meeting. This was arranged for March 16th, when it was determined that the appointment of Dr Dale was valid. The problems escalated when the two other medical officers resigned in protest, and at an adjournment meeting Dr Dale offered to forego his appointment. A solution was reached at another meeting on March 31st 1857, when the posts of Consulting Surgeon and Consulting Physician were abolished and four medical officers were appointed. (Anne and Paul Bayliss, *Scarborough Hospital and Dispensary: The First Fifty Years, 1852-1902*, Anne Bayliss, 2006)

FEBRUARY 11TH

1862: George Pickering Harrison was born in Scarborough on this day. As a teenager, he moved less than ten miles away to the tiny village of Ganton in order to learn the trade of a cobbler. It was there that 'Shoey' Harrison, as he became known, came to the attention of Scarborough Cricket Club and he played the last month of the 1881 season for them as a professional. At the end of the following season he headed the Scarborough bowling averages with a total of 31 wickets at an average of 9.4, and Yorkshire called him into the county team during the following season.

This right-arm fast bowler was an immediate success and bowled unchanged through both innings of the match against Kent at Dewsbury to take 11 wickets for 76 runs as the visitors were dismissed for 65 and 79. Further recognition followed at the end of his first county season with an appearance for the Gentlemen Vs. Players match at Lord's, and over the whole season he had taken 100 wickets at an average cost of 13 runs.

'Shoey' Harrison's cricketing career suffered a serious setback in 1892 when he tore muscles in his right arm and never bowled as fast or accurately as before. Once his playing days were over he umpired first-class cricket matches. (www. espncricinfo.com)

FEBRUARY 12TH

1963: On this day, Scarborough sports outfitter Mr Hugh Cecil Day, owner of Appleton and Day sports shop in Huntriss Row, died at his home above the shop premises. He died after a short illness and left a widow and one son. As the son, brother and nephew of professional golfers he had enjoyed considerable success at the game himself, with achievements including a semi-final placing in the *Yorkshire Evening News* tournament and trying for fifth place in the Dunlop Southport tournament. In 1935, Day moved to Formby in Lancashire, as a golf professional and two years later he was appointed as first professional at the new golf club at Scarcroft, Leeds. In 1945, in partnership with Mr R. Appleton, he took over the business of C.J. Withnell & Son on Huntriss Row, and when the partnership ended in 1954 with Mr Appleton's emigration to New Zealand, Day took over sole management of the business. (*Scarborough Evening News*)

1963: Since late 1959, Scarborough WVS members had regularly forwarded parcels of clothing and food to their adopted refugee family in Hohenecken in the Kaiserslautern area of Germany. On this day they received the latest thank you letter from twelve-year-old Maria Kielan on behalf of her father Francisek, mother Zofia and ten-year-old brother Wladislaw. (*Scarborough Evening News*)

FEBRUARY 13TH

1823: On this day, James Dobson, a local woodman, was met by a hostile mob when he visited Scarborough market. Local smugglers were seeking retribution after informers had given evidence against Billy Mead for smuggling at the end of the previous year and their fury escalated into an orgy of violence. Dobson was badly beaten and rolled in a dog kennel, before he was fastened to a ladder and dragged through the streets. If it had not been for the intervention of a couple of farmers, James Dobson could have been fatally injured. Although he survived, outbreaks of mob violence continued for some time. (www.smuggling.co.uk./gazetteer)

———— ◆ ————

1879: John Woodall, local businessman and dignitary, died on this day at his home, St Nicholas House, which later became Scarborough's Town Hall. Born in 1801, he spent his early adult years at sea, but following the death of his grandfather, also named John Woodall, he became a partner in Scarborough's Old Bank. He was the only member of the old Corporation elected to the new council in 1836 (following the Municipal Corporation Act) and held office as mayor in 1851-52. Though he declined to become a borough magistrate or parliamentary candidate, he was Commissioner of Piers and Harbours, Chairman of Scarborough Water Company and Deputy Lieutenant for the North Riding. (Anne and Paul Bayliss, *Scarborough's Members of Parliament, 1832 to 1906: Scarborough's Mayors, 1836 to 1906: A Biographical Dictionary*, A.M. Bayliss, 2008)

FEBRUARY 14TH

1874: Today, John Haigh, Mayor of Scarborough (1863-4), died at his home in the Crescent after suffering ill health for some time. Born in Halifax in 1802, he became head of a large manufacturing business based there and a magistrate for the West Riding of Yorkshire, before moving to Scarborough in the late 1850s. He was selected as a Justice of the Peace for Scarborough and for the North Riding, as well as serving as a Liberal member of the town council before being chosen as Mayor of Scarborough. Haigh was also chairman of the Cliff Bridge Company that managed Scarborough Spa, and was president of the town's cricket club. (Anne and Paul Bayliss, *Scarborough's Members of Parliament, 1832 to 1906: Scarborough's Mayors, 1836 to 1906: A Biographical Dictionary*, A.M. Bayliss, 2008)

2000: Scarborough's Crown Hotel was purchased today, for just under £2m by an established local company run by the Frank family. This imposing building took shape in the early 1840s after the arrival of the railway link with York in 1841, and in 1847, J.F. Sharpin added a ballroom to the original layout. It was refurbished in 1898 by Hudson Hotels at a cost of £725,000 and flourished during the twentieth century, as a variety of popular sports, such as aqua planing and tunny fishing, brought crowds to Scarborough, along with a demand for conference facilities. (www.crownspahotel.com)

February 15th

1884: A 409 ton screw steamer, the *Glengarry*, sank two miles off Scarborough on this day. She is just one of countless vessels that have foundered off the Yorkshire coast down the centuries. She was bound from Grangemouth to Rotterdam carrying a cargo of refuse chemicals when a south-easterly gale battered her mercilessly in the early hours of February 15th. For several hours, the *Glengarry* ploughed through mountainous seas until a massive wave hit her broadside-on, causing the cargo to shift. Crew members made frantic efforts to heave the chemicals overboard, but her dangerous list could not be corrected and distress signals were raised. Two tugs from Scarborough set out to assist while the rescue services assembled, but the *Glengarry*'s crew were forced to lower the port lifeboat and two men clambered aboard. Immediately, the lifeboat capsized only for the men to be rescued by a yawl, the *Ruby*, but when the ship's engineers took to the jolly boat it also turned over and they were both drowned. As Captain Menzies and the remaining five crew members struggled to launch the starboard lifeboat, a stem trawler, the *Flying Sprite*, was able to manoeuvre alongside and haul the men to safety. Minutes later the *Glengarry* sank to the sea bed. (Arthur Godfrey and Peter J. Lassey, *Shipwrecks of the Yorkshire Coast*, Dalesman Publishing Co. Ltd, 1974)

FEBRUARY 16TH

2010: Scarborough's Skipping Day took place on this day, as it has done on every Shrove Tuesday since at least 1903. This involved people gathering on the town's promenade to skip using long ropes which stretched across the road for up to ten or more people to use. The origins of this event are unclear but it may have begun when fishermen sorted out their nets at this time of year and gave those unsuitable for use to local children. Another theory suggests that it was a display of pleasure and freedom shown by servants and workers, who enjoyed this brief break from the humdrum routine of daily toil. Another custom in Scarborough, dating from at least 1853, involves the ringing of a church bell, the 'Shriving Bell', which was rung at 11 a.m. or 12 noon to give notice to the housewives that they should begin pancake making. Nowadays, the bell is rung by the town's mayor or deputy mayor to begin the skipping celebrations. (www.information-britain.co.uk)

———◆———

1866: Matthew Baynes, an artist, died on this day. He described himself in the Scarborough Directory of 1823 as a 'portrait and animal painter' but also painted landscapes; engravings of his work were used in books such as *Illustrated Memorials of Old Scarborough* (1890). (Anne and Paul Bayliss, *Scarborough Artists of the Nineteenth Century, A Biographical Dictionary*, Anne Bayliss, 1997)

FEBRUARY 17TH

1836: Tragedy struck Scarborough's first lifeboat on this Ash Wednesday, when the *Skelton* overturned, resulting in the loss of ten lives, during an attempt to reach a single-masted sloop named *John*. A storm had raged along the north-east coast since the previous day, leaving shoreline buildings in the Scarborough area badly damaged. As crowds gathered on piers, cliffs and South Sands on February 17th, they could make out the *John* making unsuccessful attempts to enter the harbour. There were plenty of willing hands to help launch the lifeboat on its rescue mission, but just as it reached the battered sloop a series of huge waves caused it to capsize. Ten members of the crew were swept overboard on the seaward side and carried away from the lifeboat, while three others who had strapped themselves to the boat's arm lines were able to cling to its underside. Another of the lifeboat crew, William Mellon, had been swept to the shoreward side, where he clung to timbers as a double line of people waded to his rescue. Although exhausted, he was able to tell his rescuers about the other three crewmen still trapped with the lifeboat and, amid cheers from onlookers, they too were brought ashore by the human chain. (www.scarboroughsmaritimeheritage.co.uk)

FEBRUARY 18TH

1645: Sir Hugh Cholmley, Governor of Scarborough, held the town for three weeks before ordering his forces to retreat into the castle. During the early stages of the Civil War between King Charles I and his parliament, Cholmley was given a commission and ordered to raise a regiment in order to hold Scarborough for parliament. For about five months he fulfilled this role successfully before choosing to change sides, and for some two years, from March 1643, the town was an important Royalist base for controlling coastal shipping.

Following the Battle of Marston Moor in 1644, parliamentary forces pressurised Royalist bases in the north and Cholmley's forces withstood another siege at Scarborough before retreating into the castle. (John A. Goodall, *Scarborough Castle, North Yorkshire*, English Heritage, 2000)

———◆———

1923: Cricketer E.I. (Ted) Lester was born on this day. He first played for Scarborough Cricket Club at the age of thirteen, and his range of shots, including a trademark 'late cut', thrilled spectators and led to appearances for Yorkshire between 1945 and 1956. Following his retirement from playing cricket at the end of the 1961 season he became a highly regarded scorer for Yorkshire. (Ian Hall & John Found, *Cricket at Scarborough: A Social History of the Club and Its Festival*, Breedon Books Publishing Co. Ltd, 1992)

FEBRUARY 19TH

2012: It was reported on this day that a charity auction at Scarborough Rugby Club had raised in excess of £3,000 for a military charity. The money was raised for the Help for Heroes charity and was intended for use by a new rehabilitation centre for soldiers at Catterick Garrison. Organiser Nigel Salt, along with Steve and Jeanette McNamara, reported that the auction had been so successful that there were plans for an even grander event next year. They added that considerable support for their event had been provided by a Scarborough soldier, Tom Lawlor, who lost both legs in an explosion while on foot patrol in Afghanistan.

Among the lots at the auction were an England goalkeeper's jersey signed by David Seaman, a Scarborough Athletic shirt signed by the team and a round of golf for four people at North Cliff Golf Club. Scarborough Rugby Union Football Club is based at Silver Royd in Scalby, since moving from their Newby ground in January 2009. Facilities include five full-sized rugby pitches – two of which are floodlit – three training pitches and the highly impressive J.M. Guthrie clubhouse, which hosts not only rugby occasions, but also a range of community events. (*Scarborough Evening News* and www.scarboroughrugby.co.uk)

FEBRUARY 20TH

1851: A meeting was held today, in the premises of Scarborough's Savings Bank, where members of the town's medical profession discussed plans to set up a dispensary. The origins of the 'Dispensary Movement' can be traced to the Aldersgate General Dispensary in East London. In most cases, Quaker physicians were behind moves to provide medical care for needy people without the means to pay. Initial plans for Scarborough's dispensary were put forward by Dr George Peckitt Dale, who was born in York and practised at Sheriff Hutton before moving to Scarborough shortly before this meeting took place. Five other local men, each with a medical background, were present and proceedings were managed by William Harland (1787-1866), who had been based in the town since 1810 and owned a suite of medicinal baths. During the meeting, Dr Dale successfully presented the case for a dispensary in Scarborough and the minute book stated that:

> The medical gentlemen present do forthwith commence the organisation of a dispensary for the benefit of the sick poor of Scarborough and its neighbourhood, and having completed it, to appeal to the benevolence of the public for pecuniary support.

(Anne & Paul Bayliss and Alan Jackson, *Scarborough Hospital and Dispensary, The First Fifty Years, 1852-1902*, Anne Bayliss, 2006)

FEBRUARY 21ST

1880: Local newspaper, *The Mercury*, published an article on the subject of coastal erosion on this day. A landslip on Scarborough's North Bay prompted this review of land that had disappeared during the last few decades and, among other references, the article quoted the distance from Ladies Well in the castle to the edge of the cliff. In 1800, there were twenty-five yards between the well and cliff edge, but at the time of the article only twenty yards remained. The article also predicted some 'remote epoch' when the 'old rock will be an island'. (*The Mercury*)

———◆———

1976: The first meeting of the Scarborough and District Astronomical Society took place on this day. Organised by its president John Harper FRAS, meetings were initially held at the Osgodby Community Centre on the southern outskirts of Scarborough, before moving to the former North Riding College on Filey Road and then to the town's library. Meetings are now held at East Ayton Village Hall, some four miles from Scarborough, and the organisation has been renamed the Scarborough and Ryedale Astronomical Society. In 2001, Sir Patrick Moore FRAS opened the Society's Astronomy Centre at Low Dalby, where members and community groups make use of two recently built observatories. (www.scarborough-ryedale-as.co.uk)

FEBRUARY 22ND

1917: A Scarborough-based trawler, the *Lord Collingwood*, was sunk by a U-boat, approximately 130 miles north-east of Longstone Drift (Farne Islands), but not before the crew were cast adrift in open boats. Initially they were lashed together with another Scarborough trawler, the *Frolic*, but then decided to part in order to improve their chances of being found. Crew members of the *Frolic* were picked up after thirty hours adrift, but the crew of the *Lord Collingwood* spent almost seven more days on the cold North Sea before they were gathered up by the trawler *Stork* of Dundee on March 1st 1917. (www. scarboroughsmaritimeheritage.org.uk)

❖

2012: Production at the Scarborough coach manufacturer Plaxton, was reported to be stepping up a gear today, with an order from the national transport group Stagecoach. Engineers in Scarborough had been developing the new interdeck Elite, which represented the first through-deck coach to be built in Britain and also offered easier wheelchair access while maximising capacity. Stagecoach had ordered eleven vehicles from Plaxton and these were to be built on a Volvo chassis for delivery in late 2012, or early 2013. They represented part of the company's £600 m investment for almost 400 vehicles in all parts of the country. (*Scarborough Evening News*)

FEBRUARY 23RD

1860: David Hunter, one of Yorkshire's finest cricketers of all time, was born on this day. He was the youngest of five sons of a Scarborough builder and three of them, including David, soon showed considerable cricketing prowess. When older brother Joe took over as Yorkshire wicketkeeper, David began a long and illustrious career with Scarborough Cricket Club; he was first selected for the county against Cheshire at Bradford in 1888. At first, other commitments meant that he could not play regularly, but in a match during the cricket festival of that year, against Marylebone Cricket Club, he took 3 catches and was second top scorer in Yorkshire's second innings, with 21 lbw to W.G. Grace.

During the following season he was established as the county's first choice wicketkeeper and claimed fifty-five victims, as well as scoring 157 hard-earned runs. It was these limitations as a tail end batsman that denied him an England place, but he featured in many notable last wicket stands, including one during his benefit match against Lancashire in July 1897 and another (of 148 runs) against Kent at Sheffield the following season. In total, he played 521 matches for Yorkshire, and on his retirement in 1909 he was presented with an illuminated address and £500. David Hunter died on January 11th 1927. (Ian Hall & John Found, *Cricket at Scarborough: A Social History of the Club and Its Festival*, Breedon Books Publishing Co. Ltd, 1992)

FEBRUARY 24TH

2012: Four men were granted the Freedom of the borough of Scarborough at a council meeting on this day, in recognition of their 'eminent services to the community'. This honour has only been bestowed upon fifteen people since Scarborough Council was given the power to make the award in 1974 and past recipients include playwright Sir Alan Ayckbourn. In addition to the former IBF featherweight boxing champion, Paul Ingle, the honour was also granted to businessmen Andrew and Tim Boyes, who have been at the heart of the Boyes' empire as joint managing directors for more than forty years, and Don Robinson, a former chairman of Scarborough Football Club. A former councillor and Mayor of the town, Lucy Haycock was also made an honorary alderman in recognition of her services to the council between 1983 and 2011. (*Scarborough Evening News*)

———————•◆•———————

2012: The Copper Horse at Seamer near Scarborough was named winner of the 2012 Les Routiers Restaurant of the Year Award on this day. It had previously won the same accolade in 2008. Judges had looked for consistent, exceptional service and hospitality together with a high quality of food throughout the year, and manager Rob Lazenby reported that staff were delighted to receive the award for a second time. (*Scarborough Evening News*)

February 25th

2012: The death was announced of Joyce Craig-Tyler, one of Scarborough's foremost hotel owners in the late twentieth century, at the age of eighty-six. During 1948, aged twenty-three, she had become housekeeper at the St Nicholas Hotel and two years later married Douglas, the son of the hotel's owners. She soon showed an enviable capacity for working extremely long hours at the height of the summer season in both the St Nicholas Hotel and at Mr Tyler Senior's 300-seat restaurant on Vernon Road. During her time off, Joyce would indulge her love of cars and driving, which had seen her own a Jaguar SS during her youth and a two-tone brown Rolls-Royce later in life. The death of her husband in 1969, and then his father just two years later, meant that Joyce was left with extremely difficult business choices, but she successfully maintained a programme of modernisation, along with day-to-day management of the hotel until it was sold in 1985. Retirement allowed her to develop a keen interest in gardening and to continue visits to major sporting events such as Wimbledon and the Grand National. (*Yorkshire Post*)

FEBRUARY 26TH

1907: Scarborough Forty Club held an impromptu discussion today, titled 'Should women have votes? Should barmaids be abolished?' (Alan Staniforth, *Scarborough Forty Club & Discussion Group: A Brief History: the '40' Club, founded in 1899*, Alan Staniforth, 2005)

———◆———

1915: On this day, a deafening, early morning explosion echoed around the quiet streets and lanes of downtown Scarborough. Memories of the bombardment by German battle cruisers less than three months earlier must have flashed through people's minds, but on this occasion the single blast was from the boiler room of Boyes' Remnant Warehouse in Queen Street. Within minutes the shop premises were engulfed in flames, as one of Scarborough's most spectacular blazes spread to adjacent buildings. The adjoining Queen Street Methodist Chapel was almost completely razed to the ground and the raging fire caused considerable damage to other shops and businesses in Queen Street and Market Street, before it was finally extinguished. Undeterred by this dramatic setback, William Boyes rented alternative premises for his business and two weeks later trading resumed. Less than seventeen months after the fire, a completely rebuilt store was opened on July 19th 1916, and in the immediate post-war years W. Boyes & Co. opened a store in Hull (December 1923), before moving into other parts of the north east and North Yorkshire. (*Scarborough Evening News*)

FEBRUARY 27TH

1920: During the First World War, Scarborough trawler men faced a threat from German U-boats and also from enemy mines. Only one of the town's trawlers was sunk in wartime – the *Condor* – which went down with the loss of all crew members in June 1915, but after the end of hostilities, mines continued to pose a threat for many more years. During 1920, three Scarborough trawlers were sunk by German mines and the first of these was the *Strathford*, which was fishing 37 miles east-north-east of Castle Hill on this day.

Owned by the Raincliffe Steam Trawling Company, the trawler was commanded by Samuel Normandale, who came from a family of Scarborough-based trawler skippers and who had completed an active wartime record on-board trawlers. Nine other crew members were aboard when the mine exploded at about 9.50 p.m. and all of the crew, apart from a young deckhand, were married men with children. There were no survivors and as deep sorrow swept through Scarborough, the Fishing Vessel Owners' Association set up a relief fund to support victims' families. (www.scarboroughsmaritimeheritage.org.uk)

FEBRUARY 28TH

1872: Charles Rooke, an eminent chemist and druggist, died in Scarborough today. He had arrived in the town some thirty years before and set up a business manufacturing and selling medicinal products. His company was based in premises on the corner of Hanover Road and Westborough, and from here employees prepared and sold pills and medicines, such as Solar Elixir and Oriental Pills, throughout the country. Charles Rooke also had a keen interest in rocks and fossils, which led to him opening his own museum in Scarborough's Westover Road during 1862. His published writings included *The Handy Pocket-Guide to the Health and Health-Restoring Places* and *Legends of the Lake Geneva*. His eldest son, William, took over the business in the late 1860s, and it was during William's term as Mayor that Charles Rooke died. (Anne and Paul Bayliss, *Medical Profession in Scarborough 1700 to 1899: A Biographical Dictionary*, A.M. Bayliss, 2005)

2012: A Scarborough man celebrated his 100th birthday with his 101-year-old wife at his side, surrounded by family and friends at Priceholme care home in Givendale Road. Originally from the Manchester area, Raymond Moss was a horticulturist until he retired, and he and his wife Lillian had lived independently until five weeks before his birthday. (*Scarborough Evening News*)

FEBRUARY 29TH

1604: An entry in the diary of Lady Margaret Hoby for this day reads 'This afternone Came Mr Teublie from Scarborow and brought Mr Hoby That he was Chossine Burgisse for the Town and Mr Ffrances Ewrie.' Official verification of the election of Sir Thomas Posthumous Hoby and Francis Eure was published some six days after, and a few years later Sir Thomas was elected, on several occasions, as Member of Parliament for Ripon. Lady Hoby (1571-1633) is regarded as the earliest known English female diarist and her record of daily events cover the years 1599-1605 when she lived at Hackness, near Scarborough, with her third husband Sir Thomas.

The diary includes considerable detail of Lady Margaret's spiritual life as well as descriptions of domestic routines. Sir Thomas Hoby, who was given the additional name Posthumous because his father died before he was born, has been described as 'that most overbearing, touchy and resentful of Yorkshire magistrates'. It is claimed that the character of Malvolio in Shakespeare's *Twelfth Night* is based on Sir Thomas, who died on December 30th 1640 and is entombed along with his wife in Hackness parish church. (Ed. Joanna Moody, *The Private Life of an Elizabethan Lady: The Diary of Lady Margaret Hoby, 1599-1605*, Sutton Publishing Ltd, 2001)

MARCH 1ST

1841: A detailed proposal for a railway connecting Scarborough Harbour to a junction with the York and North Midland Railway was put forward on this day. This scheme followed an earlier plan, dating from 1833, for a railway from York to Malton and Scarborough, and subsequent survey by Sir John Rennie in 1840. (Mike Hitches, *Steam Around Scarborough*, Amberley Publishing, 2009)

1900: Construction work on a new goods depot at Gallows Hill in Falsgrave was authorised on this day. Following completion of this scheme, the original goods warehouse and goods shed area were converted into passenger platforms 6 to 9. These four platforms were taken out of service in 1984 and the ground became a car park. The original platform roof over platforms 3, 4 and 5 has been retained and represents a unique example of design work by G.T. Andrews for a station of this size. The railway station has Grade II listed building status; the same rating has been given to the retaining wall and station railings beside Valley Road, along with the restored signal box, which retains 120 levers and signal gantry. (Scarborough and District Civic Society in Conjunction with Scarborough Borough Council, *The Scarborough Heritage Trail, Part 2: South Cliff and Spa, Crescent and Town Centre, North Bay*, 2nd Edition, 2009)

MARCH 2ND

1870: On this day, George Reeves-Smith ended an eventful period as Spa Manager by resigning his post. He had been selected from a total of fifty-six applicants and moved into the newly-completed Spa Chalet from his base in Sunderland in the early days of 1860. However, his stay at the chalet was short-lived, for in May 1863 he applied to 'change his residence in consequence of insufficient accommodation for his increasing family'. This arrangement was approved and included an allowance of £35 in lieu of accommodation. Within a few years Smith was given leave of absence for part of each week to work with the photographer, Oliver Francois Xavier Sarony. During autumn 1869, as a result of Smith 'having received offers which might have deprived the company of his services', Francis Goodricke was appointed secretary and following Smith's resignation he served as general manager for forty years. Smith soon became general manager of the Brighton Aquarium and in 1876 manager of the Royal Westminster Aquarium. (Meredith Whittaker, *The Book of Scarborough Spaw*, Barracuda, 1984)

1886: The Scarborough Dispensary Board of Guardians determined that 'The time has come to add an honorary dental surgeon to the medical staff to relieve the house surgeon of the chief dental work', and on March 29th George Henry Walshaw was chosen as Honorary Dental Surgeon. (Anne and Paul Bayliss, *Scarborough Hospital and Dispensary: The First Fifty Years, 1852-1902*, Anne Bayliss, 2006)

MARCH 3RD

1915: On this day, the *Scarborough Pictorial* newspaper was advertised as *Scarborough's Great Fire Souvenir Number*. It included photographs and reports of a dramatic blaze that destroyed a warehouse operated by the local Boyes family. William Boyes opened a small store in Scarborough during 1881, selling odd lots and remnants from merchants. As the business grew he purchased premises in Market Street and Queen Street that were adapted to become a large store known as the Remnant Warehouse. A sale advertisement displayed outside Boyes' Café in Scarborough during 1903 featured 'Cycle bells, Japanese Bread Boats, Bed Ticks, Tea Cosies and Children's Overalls'. The company prospered under William Boyes Junior, who lived at Chester Villa in Scarborough's Oak Road, before the huge fire left the town's largest and most popular store as a mass of broken walls and twisted girders. New premises were quickly found and the building's clock tower became a local landmark. From 1910, the company began a programme of expansion that eventually led to forty stores opening throughout Yorkshire, the North East and the Midlands. (Colin Waters, *Scarborough: Then & Now*, The History Press, 2011)

MARCH 4TH

1878: Scarborough Queen's Parade Tramway Company Ltd was established on this day. Some five months later, on August 8th, the official opening took place of the North Cliff lift that linked Queen's Parade with the Promenade Pier, but operations were dogged by misfortune from the outset. On the opening day, the cabin broke loose and caused serious damage to the lower station resulting in the closure of the lift for the rest of the year. Regular accidents, mechanical failures and landslips compounded the problems and the cliff lift ceased operation in 1887. (www.hows.org.uk)

———— ◆ ————

1910: John Horne died in Scarborough on this day, after spending many years practising as a doctor in the town. After qualifying in medicine at Edinburgh in 1859, he was appointed in the following year as House Surgeon and Secretary to Scarborough Dispensary with an annual salary of £80. Three years later he took over and built up a general practice, as well as holding consultancy posts at the town's dispensary and cottage hospital, and serving as a magistrate from 1886. Following his retirement in 1901, Dr Horne funded the construction of eight houses for elderly people, which opened in 1909 and continue to be in use today. (Anne and Paul Bayliss, *Medical Profession in Scarborough 1700 to 1899: A Biographical Dictionary*, A.M. Bayliss, 2005)

MARCH 5TH

1903: Today, a meeting of the Scarborough Forty Club held a debate which posed the question, 'Which possesses the greatest power for good; the pulpit, the press or the stage?' It resulted in a first vote of 5, 6 and 3 respectively; the second vote recorded 8 for the pulpit and 5 for the press. (Alan Staniforth, *Scarborough Forty Club & Discussion Group: A Brief History: the '40' Club, founded in 1899*, Alan Staniforth, 2005)

———◆———

1945: Several houses were damaged when an enemy aircraft gunned and shelled the Filey Road area of Scarborough on this day. A high school master, Herbert Freeman, aged thirty-nine, of 8 Cornelian Avenue, suffered serious wounds to his shoulder. (Richard James Percy, *Scarborough's War Years, 1939-45*, Sutton Publishing Ltd, 1992)

———◆———

1955: At the annual meeting of the Spa (Scarborough) Ltd held on this day, the chairman of the company, W.B. Hagenbach, stated that the board would recommend selling to the Corporation if a fair price was offered. As early as the late 1880s, the council had voted to obtain parliamentary powers to take over the Spa and from time-to-time such a move was reconsidered. This statement opened the way for a process lasting almost two years, which finally culminated in the Corporation entering their new property on November 1st 1957. (Meredith Whittaker, *The Book of Scarborough Spaw*, Barracuda, 1984)

MARCH 6TH

1906: On this day, a meeting of the Scarborough Forty Club gathered for a programme under the title 'Holiday Jaunts in Scotland and Ireland'. Reports of proceedings state that Mr Atkinson, secretary of the Forty Club, apologised to Mr Hall for having taken up eighty minutes of the precious time and Mr Hall agreed to deliver his paper 'A Trip to Iceland' on a future occasion. One and all agreed that another jolly evening had been spent. *(Alan Staniforth, Scarborough Forty Club & Discussion Group: A Brief History: the '40' Club, founded in 1899, Alan Staniforth, 2005)*

1965: The last passenger train between Scarborough and Whitby ran on this day. Following a prosperous period in the 1930s, the railway ran at continuing financial loss. During one week in 1964, £160 was spent on staff wages at Staintondale and Cloughton, while income from this section of line (which included the unstaffed Hayburn Wyke Station) totalled just £6. Ventures such as camping coaches were successful, but not enough to bear the losses sustained by the whole line. For the last day of the line a Whitby Moors Rail Tour was hauled by Class K4 3442 The Great Marquess, piloting Class K1 62005, along the length of the line. During the early 1970s, Scarborough Borough Council purchased the track bed for development as a recreational route. (J. Robin Lidster, *The Scarborough and Whitby Railway*, Hendon Publishing Co. Ltd, 1977)

MARCH 7TH

1936: Footballer Colin Harry Appleton was born in Scarborough on this day. He enjoyed a long career as a player, before managing soccer clubs for a further twenty years. His early playing days were at his home town club, but March 1954 saw the beginning of a highly successful spell at Leicester City. Following the appointment of Matt Gillies as manager in November 1958, Appleton formed a formidable half-back line with Frank McLintock and Ian King. After captaining Leicester to their first major trophy (the 1964 League Cup), he was awarded a testimonial as a reward for his services to the club. After short spells at Charlton and Barrow in the late 1960s, he returned to Scarborough as player manager in 1969 and under his guidance the club won the FA Trophy in 1973, 1976 and 1977. This success led to further spells of management with Hull City, Swansea City and Exeter City before retiring from the sport. (en.wikipedia.org/wiki/Colin_Appleton)

———— • ◆ • ————

1946: On this day, the first five tenants moved into prefabs in Commercial Street, Scarborough when the Mayor handed over keys to the properties. The occupants were all ex-servicemen and three of them had formerly lived in bombed houses at this location. (Richard James Percy, *Scarborough's War Years, 1939-45*, Sutton Publishing Ltd, 1992)

MARCH 8TH

1844: A grave in St Mary's Church at Scarborough is the final resting place of William Sibborn Blythe, aged forty-four, who died in a storm at sea on this day. He was on-board a brig named *Betty's Delight* when disaster struck. The inscription on the gravestone features a poignant verse:

> He's safely moored amongst the peaceful dead,
> And from his labours rests his weary head,
> With Neptune's waves many times he's fought,
> Yet the blow was struck when least was thought.

William Blythe's grave is in the area overlooking St Mary's Walk and is set next to the burial place of William Mollon's wife, Elizabeth. Mollon was a noted Scarborough lifeboatman who survived the tragic events in 1836 when ten others were lost; he lived for many years afterwards. (www. scarboroughsmaritimeheritage.org.uk)

❖

1965: The Whitby Bog Hall to Scarborough (Gallows Close) line closed completely today, under the so-called 'Beeching Plan'. Dr Beeching had identified cuts in railway services in his report, *The Reshaping of British Railways*, and although Harold Wilson had declared before the General Election of 1964 that if the Labour Party won they would rescind the proposed closures, one third of the rail network was scrapped. (Stephen Chapman, *Railway Memories No. 19: York to Scarborough, Whitby and Ryedale*, Bellcode Books, 2008)

MARCH 9TH

1960: The Scarborough branch of the British Sub Aqua Club was formed at a meeting in the Newcastle Packet in Sandside on this day. A handful of members of York Sub Aqua Club decided to set up a separate Scarborough Club under chairman Gareth Thomas. In the early days, members carried out shore dives from Marine Drive and sometimes took spear-guns with them for a bout of spear diving, or explosives to blow holes in wrecks so that items such as the propeller, the telegraph, bell or maker's plate could be retrieved. (The use of explosives was banned many years ago.) In 1965, the club purchased its first property, 25 St Mary's Street, and it was adapted as a headquarters and clubhouse, which included compressor equipment, a bar and trophy lounge. An adjacent building was also bought by the club and converted into holiday accommodation before being sold. Since its formation, membership numbers have steadily increased to around eighty people and the club owns two boats of its own, as well as twenty full sets of diving equipment, which is used by trainees in pool training. While most dives are off the east coast the club's favourite location is the west coast of Scotland. (*Scarborough Evening News*)

MARCH 10TH

1953: An unusual case was heard in Scarborough County Court on this day. A Newcastle man, who was unable to visit the town during the previous summer because one of his children had measles, was ordered to pay £32. John Raymond Steel of 210 Westgate Road in Newcastle-on-Tyne had booked accommodation at Parkdene, Vernon Road, for the period from August 30th to September 13th but had cancelled his stay by letter on July 28th. The proprietor of the holiday rooms, Miss Martha Flounders, told the court that she had tried to re-let by answering other newspaper advertisements but had no success. Judge F. Kingsley Griffith reduced the amount awarded to Miss Flounders from 32 guineas to £32, because no gas or electricity had been used during the period in question; he also awarded her costs of the case. (*Scarborough Evening News*)

———— • ◆ • ————

1953: In his annual report to the Watch Committee meeting, Mr I.E. Thomas, the Scarborough Shops Inspector, stated that twenty local traders had been cautioned the previous year. He had reported that they had kept their shops open to serve customers after normal closing hours and sold articles other than those scheduled for Sunday sale, or failed to allow their shop assistants proper intervals for meals. (*Scarborough Evening News*)

MARCH 11TH

1879: On this day, plans were drawn up to upgrade the original engine shed at Scarborough, which had begun operations on July 7th 1845. Also on this date, the construction of a roundhouse was approved, at an estimated cost of £5,393 for the shed and £2,976 for the associated engineering work. Improvements were completed during 1882 and the final cost exceeded the original estimate by £187 13s, with an additional £335 needed for a new turntable. The roundhouse soon fell into a state of disrepair because an eight-road straight shed was built on reclaimed ground in 1890, with the result that the roundhouse was solely used for storing engines, most often during the winter months when less rail traffic was operating.

During the days of the London North East Railway, the allocation to Scarborough Depot totalled twenty-four locomotives and one railcar, and although this number was reduced to twelve during the Second World War, many classes of locomotive returned after the war. In the 1950s, the wall at the east end of the shed building had to be reinforced on account of subsidence and eventually half of the building was demolished, but a new wall on the south side converted the shed into a four road building. (Mike Hitches, *Steam Around Scarborough*, Amberley Publishing, 2009)

MARCH 12TH

1900: The first Annual Smoking Concert of the Scarborough Forty Club was held today. The minutes of meetings held by Scarborough Forty Club make regular mention of concerts and dinners where funds were raised for worthy causes. With E. Nelson in the chair and about 100 guests present, there was an excellent musical programme with toasts to the Queen, the Army and Navy and the Forty Club.

Despite the excitement occasioned by the presence in town of Cronwright-Schreiner (*see* March 13th) there was an excellent attendance and a most enjoyable evening was spent. The meeting dispersed at 10.55 p.m., with everybody voting that it had been 'a jolly good do'.

After the main business had ended:

The members to the number of 28 and five friends adjourned upstairs and partook of the hospitality of Mr & Mrs Garrad (the hotel manager and his wife) at dinner. Later a successful Smoking Concert was held with the proceedings being kept up until 12 p.m.

(Alan Staniforth, *Scarborough Forty Club & Discussion Group: A Brief History: the '40' Club, founded in 1899*, Alan Staniforth, 2005)

— • ◆ • —

1912: The Forty Club held a highly successful 'Ladies Night' at the Balmoral on this day, where there was a large attendance. Mr Witty gave an interesting lecture, followed by songs, and the event was described as 'The outstanding feature of the year.' (Alan Staniforth, *Scarborough Forty Club & Discussion Group: A Brief History: the '40' Club, founded in 1899*, Alan Staniforth, 2005)

MARCH 13TH

1900: A serious outbreak of mob violence spread through Scarborough this evening, after a crowd gathered outside Rowntree's Café in Westborough. Mr Joshua Rowntree had invited friends to an 'At Home' in the café before Mr Cronwright-Schreiner, a British subject from South Africa, gave an address at the old Town Hall on 'The Conditions for Obtaining a Durable Peace in South Africa', 'but as the mob became more hostile guests left by a rear door'. A stone thrown through the café window heralded a bombardment of missiles, and after, mounted police were also stoned, at about 11 p.m. troops of the Royal Artillery and Artillery Militia were brought to the town's police station in readiness. Further bombardment of other Rowntree family businesses led the Deputy Mayor and Town Clerk to consider reading the Riot Act, but at 1.30 a.m. Captain Fell addressed the crowd as his troops were greeted warmly by the rioters. It was some time before the streets were cleared, and in the aftermath of the disorder three men were charged with assaults on police and twenty appeared in court for throwing stones. Although claims for riot damage were received by the town's Watch Committee, the Rowntree family did not pursue compensation. (S. Foord, *Scarborough Records*)

MARCH 14TH

1963: A newspaper report on this day indicated that a major drive to streamline the Methodist church in the Scarborough district was causing considerable heartache among a number of older Methodists. Many Methodists agreed that there were too many churches in Scarborough for present day needs and that some should close, but there were others who remained far from happy about possible closure of the church that they had attended since childhood. Reverend J.E. Christian, superintendent minister of the circuit, issued a statement in which he reported that the quarterly meeting had agreed that the churches were sited wrongly, with too many in the centre of town and not enough on the outskirts. The proposals would involve the closure of the Gladstone Road and St Sepulchre Street churches, along with Jubilee Church and two of the following three churches as well; Seamer Road, Falsgrave and St John's Road Churches. When funds became available the intention was to build a church at Wrensfield Drive to replace the existing dual-purpose hall. Gladstone Road Church, which began as a mission room in September 1881, was said to be nearer to closure than the other buildings; its fate would be decided at the May district Synod meeting at Hull. (*The Mercury*)

MARCH 15TH

1915: A Swedish steamer, the 1,573 ton *Hanna*, was sunk off the coast of Scarborough today, carrying a cargo of coal from Tyneside bound for Las Palmas. During the hours of darkness, the ship's second officer was on watch when he spotted what seemed to be the wash of a torpedo on the starboard side. Soon afterwards, an explosion blasted away much of the stern, killing six of the eight men sleeping in the fo'c'sle (forecastle), and as water rushed in the vessel began to sink. The crew took to the ship's lifeboats and fourteen of them were later landed at Hull by the steamer *Gylier*. This dramatic episode was of considerable significance because the *Hanna* was a neutral vessel, with her name and nationality clearly painted on her side in large lettering, and it was some time after the event before Germany stated its policy of sinking all vessels in the North Sea. During the First World War, eight steamers were the victims of U-boat attacks off the Scarborough coast, adding to the loss of life that resulted from the laying of minefields by German forces and the ever-present threat of weather conditions, such as fog. (Arthur Godfrey and Peter J. Lassey, *Shipwrecks of the Yorkshire Coast*, Dalesman Publishing Co. Ltd, 1974)

MARCH 16TH

1966: A letter was published in the local press on this day, outlining criticisms to do with the opening of Radio 270, which would broadcast from a boat off the Yorkshire coast. It was one of a number of critical letters submitted by residents along the coast, who were far from convinced about the need for this new radio service. Even though the editor of the *Scarborough Evening News* was a shareholder in Radio 270, the letter was published in full.

Mr D.H. Johnson of 53 West Avenue in Filey, began by expressing his surprise that no letters criticising the planned radio station had yet appeared in print, and pointed out that the transmitting frequency of 270 was likely to cause serious interference with the 261 metres of the BBC Home Service. He claimed that pop fans could hear their music on Radios Luxemburg, Caroline and London as well as in countless milk bars and pubs nearby. In reply, Leonard Dale stated that the frequency had been chosen by an electronics expert, and he added that if the Home Service was overpowered by 270, then the BBC needed a more powerful transmitter. (Bob Preedy, *Radio 270: Life on the Ocean Waves*, R.E. Preedy, 2002)

MARCH 17TH

2012: Contrasting styles of music were on offer this evening at two very different venues in Scarborough. Internationally renowned violinist, Ian Belton, appeared in concert at Scarborough Methodist Central Hall, with his cellist wife, Sophie Harris, and his sister, Judith Belton, also playing the violin. They were accompanied by the Scarborough Symphony orchestra. Mr and Mrs Belton performed Brahms' Double Concerto for Violin and Cello and the concert also featured Beethoven's Fifth Symphony. Ms Harris is a cellist with the Duke Quartet, as well as a solo performer, and Ian Belton is a member of the Brodsky Quartet that has played alongside Elvis Costello and Sir Paul McCartney.

Meanwhile, at the town's Futurist Theatre, The Hollies were celebrating fifty years of popular music-making by performing such songs as 'He Ain't Heavy, He's My Brother', 'Carrie Ann', 'The Air That I Breathe' and 'Bus Stop'. In 2011, The Hollies were inducted into the prestigious American Rock 'n' Roll Hall of Fame 'For their impact on the evolution, development and perpetuation of rock 'n' roll'. (*Scarborough Evening News*)

MARCH 18TH

1941: An air raid, which became known locally as the 'March Blitz', began at about 8 p.m. on this day. Enemy aircraft flew over the nearby villages of Flixton, Folkton and The Carrs and dropped large numbers of incendiaries across a wide area of Scarborough. By 9 p.m., when the siren was sounded, the raid was focused on more central parts of the town, and for about four hours high-explosive bombs, parachute mines and thousands of incendiaries known as 'breadbaskets' rained down.

An early casualty of the raid was the printing works of E.T.W. Dennis & Sons Ltd in Melrose Street (which had only just been vacated by staff at 9 p.m.), when incendiaries caused melting metal to form a layer on the floor of the composing room. Soon afterwards, at around 9.30 p.m., a large bomb shattered the brickwork of a row of terraced houses in Commercial Street, and the former Waddington's Warehouse, near the Mere, which was being used by Tonks & Sons to store furniture at the time, was completely destroyed. There were many acts of bravery on the part of civilians and the wartime services during this raid, which left twenty-eight people dead and several hundred injured. (Richard James Percy, *Scarborough's War Years, 1939-45*, Sutton Publishing Ltd, 1992)

MARCH 19TH

2012: The initial phase of building work got underway on the site of a sports village in Scarborough on this day, with teams of specialist contractors carrying out a detailed ground investigation. The results of this work were then passed on to three companies which had been shortlisted by the Scarborough Council, so that they could prepare and submit detailed plans for the sports village. The council's development officers indicated that it was common practice to carry out these preliminary checks, so that ground conditions could be determined before building work began. The completed sports village had a scheduled opening time set for the start of the 2014/15 football season and would incorporate a 2,000 capacity football stadium, an eight-lane swimming pool and a sports centre that had facilities for ball games and racquet sports. Areas of ground at the existing sports centre in Filey Road and at the club's former ground, the McCain Stadium in Seamer Road, would be handed to the chosen developer as part of the agreement to build the sports village. (*Scarborough Evening News*)

———— • ◆ • ————

2012: Work was continuing to transform a former railway route near Hawsker into a picturesque route for walkers, cyclists and horse riders today, with the clearance of an overgrown area and installation of steps and a picnic table. (*Northern Echo*)

MARCH 20TH

2008: Scarborough's new £100,000 seal rescue centre opened its doors to the public on this day. This new facility at the town's Sea Life and Marine Sanctuary was designed to accommodate up to four injured seals at one time, whereas previously the centre could only cope with one. Guest of honour at the grand opening ceremony was Herbie, a nine-month-old seal pup who had been transferred from the Sea Life Centre at Weymouth, to be united for the first time with his father Bubbles and older brother Ed. Other VIP guests at the opening ceremony included pupils from the reception class at St Martin's School, who wore seal masks and had a look inside the new seal pens.

A spokesperson explained that seals can need rescuing for a number of reasons, largely due to being injured or abandoned. Upon rescue, the seal is removed from danger and brought to the centre for rehabilitation with regular monitoring and feeding. The pup is then moved to the resident seal pool to learn how to compete for food and interact with other seals, before being released back into the wild. Seals that are not suitable for release back into the wild are retired at the centre. (*Scarborough Evening News*)

MARCH 21ST

1884: William Keighley Briggs, a notable portrait artist, died at Crown Terrace in Scarborough on this day. Among mourners at his funeral were fellow artists, including Paul Marny, Louis Timmermans and Scarborough-based artist Henri Philippe Neumans, who was married to Briggs' daughter, Frances. Born in West Yorkshire in 1816, Briggs was tutored by the portrait artist John Jackson, and his own work was exhibited at London galleries, including the Royal Academy, between 1849 and 1860.

William Briggs moved to Scarborough in around 1867 and was in charge of Oliver Francois Xavier Sarony's Portrait Painting Department, before moving to W.D. Brigham's photographic studio. A report in the *Scarborough Gazette* in 1881 indicated that Briggs had painted portraits of a large number of the nobility and gentry, including HRH the Prince of Wales. A little more than a year before Briggs' death, his extensive collection of paintings was sold by auction at Scarborough in 1882. (Anne and Paul Bayliss, *Scarborough Artists of the Nineteenth Century, A Biographical Dictionary*, Anne Bayliss, 1997)

MARCH 22ND

2012: A report was submitted on this day, to Scarborough Council's Planning and Development Committee for the lift at St Nicholas Cliff to be converted into a café. The conservation officer's statement indicated that the St Nicholas Lift (more correctly a funicular) had opened at a late stage in the development of such structures (on August 5th 1929), and had undergone alterations in the 1960s, along with the replacement of cars about thirty years previously. It had been out of use for some time and its inevitable deterioration was detracting from the character of the conservation area, as well as affecting the setting of adjacent buildings, such as the Spa Bridge and the Grand Hotel. The council's investment manager believed that it gave an interesting Renaissance perspective and provided a good link between the town and the Spa complex. The Scarborough and District Civic Society gave cautious approval for the work to go ahead, on the condition that the work was fully reversible if funding became available to repair and reopen the lift. Similar statements of support were submitted by local residents and permission was granted, with certain caveats. (*Report to Planning and Development Committee of Scarborough Borough Council*)

MARCH 23RD

1817: Matthew Noble, the son of a stonemason, was born on this day at Hackness. While serving his apprenticeship in his father's workshop, he attracted the patronage of Sir John Johnstone, a local benefactor who financed his move to London, where he was tutored by the eminent sculptor, John Francis. Noble soon rose to prominence as a sculptor in his own right, and from 1845 until his death in 1876, he was a regular exhibitor at the Royal Academy; widespread recognition came after he won a competition to create the Wellington Monument in Manchester (Piccadilly) in 1856. His established position as a craftsman of great merit saw him complete statues of Queen Victoria, the Prince Consort, the Earl of Feversham and other prominent personalities of the nineteenth century. Examples of Matthew Noble's craftsmanship are displayed at museums in London, York, Manchester and India, but fittingly his first work and one of his last are now held at Hackness Hall. (www.genuki.org.uk)

———•◆•———

2000: A plaque was unveiled on the wall of no. 16 York Place today, by Professor Gordon Bell. He was a keen supporter of the works of the artist Henry Barlow Carter, who lived and worked at the premises between 1845 and 1862. (Scarborough and District Civic Society, *Blue Plaques in Scarborough 1974-2010*, 2010)

MARCH 24TH

2012: On this day, a review of the previous twelve months for one of Yorkshire's most prominent businesses, the Scarborough-based Bluebird Vehicles, indicated a year of enviable success. At the beginning of the last financial year, the specialist bus building company had to recruit an additional twenty-five workers when its order book increased. A few months later, the company took a prominent role in promoting the county of Yorkshire at the Lord Mayor's Show in London. A 1929 Leyland Tiger bus that had remained unused for fifty years (apart from its role as part of an allotment shed), was carefully restored by a group of apprentices with help from a retired coach builder. Bluebird Vehicles continued its run of success with the launch of a new product at the Coach and Bus Live 2011 industry event at Birmingham's National Exhibition Centre. The Orion Plus was presented as a fuel efficient alternative for operators on rural and urban routes, and offered seating for twenty-two passengers, with removable seats allowing it to accommodate up to six wheelchairs. At the first ever North Yorkshire International Trade Week, Bluebird Vehicles encouraged local businesses to focus on the potential in the overseas markets, and at Scarborough Engineering Week the company encouraged students to discover more about engineering. (*Yorkshire Post*)

MARCH 25TH

1643: Sir Hugh Cholmeley announced his change of allegiance during the English Civil War on this day, and stated that he would now be holding Scarborough Castle for the King. With his family home at nearby Whitby, Cholmeley had represented Scarborough in the Short Parliament, and in November 1641 had refused to pay ship money. He had been appointed as one of Parliament's commissioners to negotiate with the King at York, but expressed concerns that Parliament's proposals were 'most unjust and unreasonable' and it was with some reluctance that he had agreed to garrison Scarborough for Parliament. On March 20th 1643, Hugh Cholmeley had left the castle, supposedly in order to meet the Governor of Hull, but in fact he rode to York where he accepted the Queen's commission to hold Scarborough Castle for the King. Briefly, this strategically important coastal base was seized by parliamentary troops before Captain Browne Bushell reclaimed it for the King's forces. Sir Hugh Cholmeley was able to return as governor and commissioner for maritime affairs from the Tees to Bridlington, where he and his wife lived 'in a very handsome port and fashion' without 'the worth of a chicken out of the country' or any fee. (Ed. William Page, *The Victoria History of the County of York, North Riding, Volume 2: Wapentakes of: Birdforth, Bulmer, Langbaurgh (West), Langbaurgh (East), Pickering, Lythe, Whitby Strand Liberty, Scarborough Borough*, Constable, 1914-1925)

MARCH 26TH

1879: Captain Thomas Luccock (aged sixty-seven), and his wife Sarah (aged fifty-two), were selected as residents for almshouse no. 11 at Wilson's Mariners Homes on this day. Unfortunately, within a few weeks Sarah's outlandish behaviour had upset and alienated other residents, as her fondness for alcohol fuelled a violent temper and invariably produced a tirade of abusive vocabulary. At a trustees' meeting on May 31st 1880, the warden complained about Mrs Luccock's treatment of her neighbour, Mrs Mary Bone, regarding their shared use of the passage, yard, water tap and closet. The occupants of almshouse no. 10 also complained about Mrs Luccock's indecent behaviour and insolent language, with particular reference to an episode on Boxing Day evening 1879, when an inebriated Mrs Luccock hammered on their door and cursed them at length before spending several hours spread across their doorstep. When she eventually staggered to her feet, she savagely attacked her sleeping husband with a broomstick and a bucketful of cold water. Denying all charges against her, Mrs Luccock claimed her husband often drove her to violence by 'refusing to give her a kiss and cuddle', but the trustees were unimpressed with her defence and ordered the Luccocks to leave almshouse no. 11 within fourteen days. (*Scarborough Evening News*)

MARCH 27TH

1942: On this day, during late evening, a single enemy aircraft flew over Scarborough and dive-bombed a train as it passed the Mere on the south-west side of town. Trains were popular targets, as the pilots could easily spot and follow the locomotives' fires. It is possible that the enemy aircraft believed it was a troop train travelling along the York to Scarborough line. A number of bombs were released, with one falling on allotments adjacent to the line, another on the path running alongside the Mere and one splashing into the water without exploding, leaving its fins protruding above the surface. Blast damage from the bombs shattered all the train windows and caused further limited destruction to properties along Edgehill Road. Many of the casualties were members of the armed forces returning from leave and when the train stopped close to the railway station, twenty-one cases were treated at a nearby first aid post, while six others were taken by stretcher for treatment at Scarborough Hospital. (Richard James Percy, *Scarborough's War Years, 1939-45*, Sutton Publishing Ltd, 1992)

MARCH 28TH

1936: The Odeon Cinema in Scarborough opened on this day, on a site opposite the town's railway station. It was designed by J. Cecil Clavering and Robert Bullivant, with Harry Weedon as architect. Overall, the cost of the single-screen cinema, which included a large café with views across the town centre, totalled £38,700. There was seating for 1,711 patrons, with 946 in the stalls and 765 in the balcony. The official opening was performed by Sir Kenelm Cayley and there was a guest appearance by the Scarborough-born actor Charles Laughton, who was the first British citizen to win an Oscar for Best Actor in *The Private Life of Henry VIII*. Music for the event was provided by the Harry Peel Premiers and the first film to be shown was *The Ghost Goes West*, starring Robert Donat. A special twenty-four-page souvenir programme was provided for the evening's guests. The final film to be shown at the Odeon was *Buster*, on October 21st 1988, and in 1996, after major refurbishment which retained the original front of house areas and façade, it was reopened as The Stephen Joseph Theatre. (artisticdirector.alanayckbourn.net/History-Odeon)

MARCH 29TH

1963: The engines of Scarborough fishing coble the *Hilda II* broke down this morning while she was fishing 4 miles out at sea. Her skipper, Mr Harry Sheader, fired flares and the Scarborough lifeboat *J. G. Graves of Sheffield* was launched. In the meantime, another Scarborough-based fishing coble, the *Premier*, had seen the flares and went to assist the *Hilda II*. She was soon taken in tow, but the lifeboat took over towing operations when she reached the scene. However, a fairly heavy sea and a strong westerly wind made conditions rough and it took the lifeboat forty-five minutes to tow the *Hilda II* back into harbour. (*Scarborough Evening News*)

———◆———

1963: A draft town map for the Scarborough area was published on this day. An accompanying analysis stated that if Scarborough was to retain its current position within the area, then an efficient town centre was vital. The text added that the centre of the town was in danger of becoming obsolete, because the street layout was no longer capable of handling the traffic seeking to use it and many buildings were no longer making the best use of their sites. The population within the town map area was estimated at 51,000; by the end of the period covered by the plan, it was expected to rise to about 54,500. (*Scarborough Evening News*)

MARCH 30TH

2012: The Scarborough annual Mayor's Ball – this year a special Diamond Jubilee Ball – was held at Scarborough Spa, in association with the town's Rotary Club. Central to the evening was the Mayor's gala dinner, but the occasion took on a royal theme when the Mayoress, Jackie Blackburn, donned the Mayoress' Chain. It was presented to the Scarborough Corporation in 1897, after a public subscription had raised funds in order to purchase the chain in celebration of Queen Victoria's Diamond Jubilee. A prime aim of the event was to raise money for the Mayoress' Community Fund, which benefits local groups and organisations throughout the borough – approximately £5,000 was collected from the proceeds of a silent auction and other contributions. The main auction prize, an exquisite diamond necklace specially made for the occasion by David Haywood of Rosh Jewellers, raised an impressive £1,050. Other 'money can't buy' prizes in the auction included a driver's experience on the North Bay Miniature Railway, two tickets to dine on the North Yorkshire Moors Railway Pullman steam train, and a stay at the luxury Crab Manor Hotel in Thirsk. The Mayor of Scarborough, Councillor John Blackburn, and President of the Rotary Club of Scarborough, Nigel Wood, hailed the event as a resounding success. (www.scarborough.gov.uk)

MARCH 31ST

1892: A brigantine, called the *Star of the West*, sank off the coast of Scarborough on this day, carrying a cargo of 348 tons of coal bound for Jersey under Captain H. Saunders and a crew of seven. When she left the Tyne the previous day, several inches of water in the bottom of the vessel were not considered important enough to halt her journey, but as she headed south the water levels rose to 11ft, then 15ft, despite crew members manning the pumps. Orders were given to leave the stricken ship, and at approximately 6 a.m. on March 31st, the crew launched the longboat and watched the *Star of the West* sinking in a calm sea. They were soon taken aboard a Scarborough steam trawler, the *Lord Clyde*, and landed safely ashore. (Arthur Godfrey and Peter J. Lassey, *Shipwrecks of the Yorkshire Coast*, Dalesman Publishing Co. Ltd, 1974)

———— ◆ ————

1947: On this day, the police force in Scarborough ceased to operate as an independent force. From this date, it was absorbed into the North Riding Constabulary as part of the newly-constituted Scarborough Division. By 1865, there were twenty police officers in Scarborough, consisting of a chief constable, two sergeants and seventeen constables; pay for constables was between 18s and 21s per week. (S. Foord, *Scarborough Records*)

APRIL 1ST

1896: Ravenscar Station (known as 'Peak' until October 1st 1897) was reopened on this day, after being closed by the North Eastern Railway Company on March 6th 1895. The closure was in retaliation for the Scarborough and Whitby Railway Company's refusal to build a stationmaster's house at Peak, but it was reopened when an agreement was reached. The station, reached by a long climb at 1-in-41 from the south and 1-in-39 from the north, had a single platform and a goods siding (until about 1908, when a second platform was created along with a passing loop). The station was intended to serve an entirely new coastal resort that was to be developed over 750 acres of land by Peak Estate Co. Ltd, but after completion of the initial stages the whole scheme was abandoned. (Ken Hoole, *Forgotten Railways: Volume 1, North East England*, David St John Thomas, 1984)

———◆———

1974: As a result of local government reorganisation, the new Scarborough Borough Council came into operation on this date. It administers an area stretching from north of Whitby to beyond Filey in the south, and has a population of about 108,000 people. (www.scarborough.gov.uk)

APRIL 2ND

1966: The vessel from which Radio 270 – 'Yorkshire's Own offshore Radio Station' – transmitted programmes was badly damaged in gales on this day. After being fitted out in Holland, the boat had sailed back to Scarborough at the end of February 1966, before it moved into position in the North Sea on Friday April 1st, with fourteen personnel on-board. Severe gale-force winds persisted into Saturday and the mast was swaying dramatically as crew members tightened stays, but it was to no avail and the lightweight aluminium mast snapped and bent over the side. A decision was soon made to jettison the wrecked mast before it made the boat unstable, and it sank to the seabed some 40 miles offshore. Before long, a further decision was taken to return to Scarborough, but when the motor was started it was found that a cable from the mast had become entangled in the ship's propeller and more of the mast section had to be removed. On reaching Scarborough harbour the crew were met by a group of dismayed directors of the broadcasting company and the period of broadcasting from the boat, which had spanned some fifteen months, was at an end. (Bob Preedy, *Radio 270: Life on the Ocean Waves*, R.E. Preedy, 2002)

APRIL 3RD

1940: A Scarborough trawler, the *Silver Line*, was directly involved in wartime hostilities, when a German Heinkel aircraft was attacked by a Spitfire in the airspace above. The Heinkel had already suffered damage in the aerial combat when it flew low over the *Silver Line*, and as bullets from the trawler's Lewis gun struck the fuselage it crashed into the sea. Moving alongside the Heinkel, the trawler's crew evacuated the German airmen, with one seaman pointing a rifle at them. When they reached land, one injured German was taken to Scarborough Hospital, while the others were taken to the local police station to await military officers. (Richard James Percy, *Scarborough's War Years, 1939-45*, Sutton Publishing Ltd, 1992)

◆

2008: Residents at the Knipe Point development in Cayton Bay, near Scarborough, claimed that houses on the site should never have been built. Dramatic cracks and fissures in the ground were threatening to accelerate the rate of clifftop erosion and one local homeowner recalled that original residences were holiday homes built from timber, as the ground was not firm enough to support concrete foundations. These were sold in the 1960s to a Yorkshire property developer who completed adaptations to convert them into full residential properties. (*Scarborough Evening News*)

APRIL 4TH

1947: On this day, the Zylpha Hotel on Scarborough's Albion Road reopened after remaining closed during the war years. The hotel's unusual name was given by a previous owner, Charles Shaw, who had served on a vessel named the *Zylpha* as chief steward. The *Zylpha* was one of the first Q-ships used in the First World War in an attempt to trap enemy submarines. They were also described as 'Special Service Ships', or 'Mystery Ships', and were usually small freighters or old trawlers fitted with hidden guns in a collapsible deck structure. First deployed towards the end of 1914, they enjoyed initial success in sinking enemy U-boats, before Germany's introduction of unrestricted submarine warfare and their use of torpedoes in order to sink Q-ships at longer range. (Richard James Percy, *Scarborough's War Years, 1939-45*, Sutton Publishing Ltd, 1992)

———— ◆ ————

2008: Residents from several properties at the Knipe Point development were evacuated from their homes on this day, as their gardens disappeared over the edge of the cliff. Reports of landslide activity appeared on an almost daily basis in media outlets, as an ancient landslide was reactivated due to a prolonged season of heavy rain. It became widely known as 'The Knipe Point Landslide'. (www.telegraph.co.uk)

APRIL 5TH

1904: The Annual General Meeting of Scarborough Sailing Club was held at Frank Mason's studio on Marine Parade today. At the meeting, J.B. Butterfield retired as Captain and Ernest Dade was once again elected to fill this position (he was the first captain in 1895). Most of the business attended to at the meeting focused on an agreement to send several boats to the Royal Yorkshire Yacht Club (RYYC) Regatta at Bridlington in July. It was also agreed to increase the wages of Ben Grimmer, the boatman, from 12s to 15s per week during the sailing season, as recognition of his continued excellent service. (W.H. James, *Scarborough Sailing Club, Scarborough Yacht Club: A History*, The Walkergate Press Ltd, 1976)

———◆———

1910: Today, a meeting of the Scarborough Forty Club held an impromptu discussion on the subjects 'Do insects display intelligence?' and 'What is the best method of disposing of the carcass of the whale now stranded at Stainton Dale?' (Alan Staniforth, *Scarborough Forty Club & Discussion Group: A Brief History: the '40' Club, founded in 1899*, Alan Staniforth, 2005)

———◆———

2012: On this day, the retirement of a popular local solicitor, Roger Taylor, was announced. Working mainly in the Scarborough area, Taylor visited clients and organised numerous legal workshops for businesses in the area. A farewell buffet lunch was held at the Crown Spa Hotel in the Esplanade to mark his retirement. (*Scarborough Evening News*)

APRIL 6TH

1844: On this day, Joshua Rowntree was born into a family of Scarborough grocers with strong Quaker connections. After attending Bootham School in York, he studied law with companies in both London and York, before joining a Scarborough solicitor as a junior partner in 1866. By this time, he had adopted strong Liberal views and, after returning to his home town, Rowntree played a major role in establishing and improving adult education. His commitment to public service in the town saw him elected as a councillor in 1878 and Mayor from 1885-86, as well as holding office as a borough magistrate, Harbour Commissioner and member of the School Board. After resigning as Mayor, Rowntree was successful in the general election of July 3rd 1886. He continued as Member of Parliament for Scarborough until 1892, during which time he strongly supported women's rights. Following his electoral defeat, Rowntree travelled widely in the Middle East and southern hemisphere and during the Boer War worked tirelessly to promote peace, despite a pro-peace meeting in Scarborough during March 1900 ending in mob violence and rioting. He died peacefully at Scalby on February 9th 1915. (Anne and Paul Bayliss, *Scarborough's Members of Parliament, 1832 to 1906: Scarborough's Mayors, 1836 to 1906: A Biographical Dictionary*, A.M. Bayliss, 2008)

APRIL 7TH

1653: On this day, the Dutch naval commander, Admiral de Witt, sailed into Scarborough Harbour with a total of twenty vessels in pursuit of a convoy of English colliers. Local knowledge of the coastline had enabled the coal ships to take refuge in the shadow of Scarborough Castle's walls, where they were protected by nine men-of-war ships, guns mounted on the pier head and a further six guns stationed close by. The Dutch ships fired twenty guns and then stood off as the collier fleet continued on its way in convoy. This action was set against the Anglo-Dutch war that lasted from 1652-54. Hostilities between the two most powerful navies of that era resulted from a number of causes, including the Navigation Act of October 1651 and the English claim to search Dutch ships for French goods. During the early 1650s, plans were being considered to make changes to the garrison at Scarborough Castle, but the threat posed by Dutch warships meant that all orders relating to the castle were suspended and numbers of personnel were increased. Days later, on April 18th, the collier fleet made it into Scarborough Harbour in the face of a threat from Dutch vessels. (www.british-history.ac.uk/TheboroughofScarborough)

APRIL 8TH

1945: Large crowds gathered to celebrate the centenary of the Methodist Church on Queen Street on this day. The growth in support for Methodism during the 1830s saw preparation of plans for a chapel to be built on Queen Street, and the opening took place on September 8th 1840. On March 3rd 1915 fire destroyed Boyes' Remnant Warehouse and nearby properties in Market Street, along with the church on Queen Street. In 1921, the foundation stone was laid for a new church which opened its doors for worship some two years later. Centenary celebrations for the Methodist Church on Queen Street were scheduled for 1940, but were postponed until this date at the end of the war. (Richard James Percy, *Scarborough in the 1930s and 40s*, Hendon Publishing Co. Ltd, 1990)

———— • ◆ • ————

1945: The Home Guard assembled at the Balmoral Hotel in Westborough today, and presentations were made to the officers. During May 1940, the Local Defence Volunteers were formed, and Captain J.P.S. Kitching was appointed Company Commandant on a temporary base at the Old Hospital on Friarsway. Volunteers acted as fire wardens and were stationed at locations such as Olivers Mount and Falsgrave Park reservoir. From July 23rd 1940, the LDVs would be known as the Home Guard. (Richard James Percy, *Scarborough in the 1930s and 40s*, Hendon Publishing Co. Ltd, 1990)

APRIL 9TH

1898: A football match scheduled for this date may well be termed 'the match that never was'. It was no ordinary match, either, but a replay of the Scarborough and East Riding Cup Final for the 1897/8 season, between Scarborough FC and Leeds. The first match had ended in a 2–2 draw; no extra time was possible due to a rain-sodden pitch, so the local association ordered a replay at Pickering's ground on April 9th. Scarborough refused to play, as they had already arranged a friendly at home on that date against Ossett; they were then 'scratched' from the final after their suggested date of April 23rd was turned down. The County Association's response was to award the cup to Leeds and to suspend Scarborough from playing on April 9th. In retaliation, the Scarborough club – the most senior club in terms of membership and support – withdrew from the Scarborough and East Riding Football Association and instead joined the Cleveland Football Association. (*Scarborough Mercury*)

1900: On this day, at a meeting of the Forty Club the chairman introduced an essayist who, in an interesting paper, had tried to prove that the consumption of alcoholic liquor weakens the brain, impairs the nervous system, damages the digestive system, violates the muscles, shortens life and is detrimental to the happiness and welfare of the community . . . (Alan Staniforth, *Scarborough Forty Club & Discussion Group: A Brief History: the '40' Club, founded in 1899*, Alan Staniforth, 2005)

APRIL 10TH

2012: Edward Bawden's 1931 map of Scarborough was unveiled at the town's public library on this day, by designer and artist Jan Bee Brown. Described during the ceremony as 'a forgotten treasure', it was commissioned by Scarborough hotelier Tom Laughton and displayed in the family-owned Pavilion Hotel, before being moved to the entrance of the children's library in 1961. Over the years it suffered some damage from damp and was attacked by silverfish, which led to the need for careful restoration. Members of the Friends of Scarborough Library group raised the £2,000 required to carry out specialist treatment under project leader Rachel Greenwood, from the North Yorkshire County Council conservation office, who said, 'It really was a privilege to work on something so precious and colourful.' The restored map was enclosed in an oak frame with a Perspex cover to protect it from sunlight and now stands in the foyer to the library's concert room, where it will be viewed by thousands of people each year.

At the unveiling ceremony for the map, Helen Birmingham of Belle Vue Parade Studio gave information on the map's history which she described as 'a priceless treasure' and the ceremony ended with announcements of winners of poetry competitions which were run in conjunction with the restoration. (*Scarborough Evening News*)

APRIL 11TH

1954: On this day, the Scarborough Railway Society made its first visit, since its formation, to the Darlington Works, the Darlington Shed (51A) and, on the return journey, to the York North Shed (50A). When it opened in 1863, Darlington North Road Works replaced Shildon as the main works of the North Eastern Railway, and construction of locomotives here continued until 1964. Overhauls were carried out until April 2nd 1966, after which time the buildings were demolished.

During the lifetime of the works, 2,680 locomotives were built here and closure brought the loss of 2,540 jobs over three years. Darlington (Bank Top) depot replaced previous sheds at Whessoe Road and Parkgate and was extended during 1938-39 with construction of a seven-road straight running shed, a three-road repair shop, a 70ft vacuum-operated turntable and a mechanical coaling plant. The visits to the works and the two major depots would have provided totals of around 300 steam locomotives, in roughly equal quantities, although Sunday was always regarded as the best 'shed bashing' day. (*BR Steam Motive Power Depots: NER* by Paul Bolger, and *Railway Memories No. 2: Darlington & South West Durham*)

APRIL 12TH

1924: George Lord Beeforth (Lord was a family name), businessman and former Mayor of Scarborough, died at the age of 101 and was buried this day in the family grave at Scalby on the north side of Scarborough. Born on Easter Sunday 1823, he was educated at Scarborough Grammar School before taking up an apprenticeship with a local bookseller. With financial assistance from Revd Joseph Skelton, a distant relative, he was then able to establish his own business at premises in St Nicholas Street. According to Beeforth himself, he was a bookseller, printer, stationer, print and music seller, bookbinder and newspaper agent. The building also housed an art gallery and the business prospered. In 1864, Beeforth sold the Scarborough business and operated an art gallery in London in partnership with James Fairless, a Newcastle printer and publisher. In 1889 he returned to Scarborough, and although appointed as a magistrate for the North Riding, he did not become deeply involved in local politics. However, he agreed to a nomination for mayor and he was elected for the year 1893-94. During his final years, Beeforth enjoyed a range of cultural and artistic pursuits in the Scarborough area. (Anne and Paul Bayliss, *Scarborough's Members of Parliament, 1832 to 1906: Scarborough's Mayors, 1836 to 1906: A Biographical Dictionary*, A.M. Bayliss, 2008)

APRIL 13TH

2012: This was the second day of the 2012 Scarborough Literature Festival. It featured a range of events, including a discussion on *Crime in a Cold Climate* with Peter James and Hakan Nesser, a literary lunch with Peter James and talks on writing novels, led by Valerie Wood and Cynthia Harrod-Eagles. In addition, there was a presentation by Yorkshire-born politician and journalist Roy Hattersley about his latest work, *David Lloyd George: The Great Outsider*, as well as a Beginners Workshop and a Poetry Workshop. The four-day event, known as *The Long Weekend*, was in its sixth year and had got underway on April 12th with a talk by prizewinning author, Susan Hill, who was making a return to her home town. With more than fifty books to her credit, including the six 'Serrailler' crime novels, she has won many awards and been shortlisted for the Booker Prize. A whole range of organisations, both national and local, gave help and support, in addition to a £25,000 grant from the Arts Council. The festival's patron, Kate Atkinson, creator of private detective Jackson Brodie and author of *Behind the Scenes at the Museum*, spoke of the weekend as 'a highlight in the literary calendar'. (*Scarborough Evening News*)

APRIL 14TH

2012: Descendants of James Paul Moody, who was born in 1887 at 17 Granville Road South Cliff in Scarborough, unveiled a blue plaque at the property on this day. Wording on the plaque stated: 'James Paul Moody 1887-1912, Sixth Officer RMS *Titanic* was born here 21st August 1887'.

The twenty-four year old was the sixth and youngest officer on-board RMS *Titanic*, which sank on April 15th 1912, and was the person who answered the bridge phone from the lookout and spoke the famous, fateful words, 'Iceberg right ahead!' The blue plaque was provided by Friends of HMS *Conway* – Moody attended the training ship HMS *Conway* from the age of fourteen and later attended King Edward VI Nautical School in London, where he passed his Master's Examination in April 1911. He was last seen by Second Officer, Charles Lightoller, trying to launch a collapsible boat at about 2.18 a.m. He was the only junior officer to lose his life in the disaster. His selflessness has also been marked on a monument in Woodlands Cemetery and on another at St Martin-on-the-Hill Church in Scarborough. (*Scarborough Evening News*)

APRIL 15TH

1908: Work on Scarborough's Marine Drive was completed on this date. It was exactly ten years, ten months and ten days after the foundation stone was laid and for the first time it was possible to travel along the seafront between the Spa and Peasholm. Scarborough's development as a resort during the second half of the nineteenth century had prompted suggestions for such a route as early as 1860 and there was even a subsequent proposal for a tunnel under Castle Hill to link the two bays – this scheme was abandoned when the Scarborough Corporation opposed the parliamentary bill. The first definite plans were made in 1882, when Sir John Coode was approached to draw up a feasibility study for a route to link up with the South Foreshore Road, which had been completed some three years earlier. His conclusion was that such a project was manageable at a total cost of £124,680 and when the scheme was finally completed, more than twenty-five years later, it cost only £20 more than Sir John Coode had originally forecast. Benefits for the local populace were considerable, with the only negative note being the tolls that were levied on pedestrians and vehicles for using the route. (Scarborough and District Civic Society in Conjunction with Scarborough Borough Council, *The Scarborough Heritage Trail, Part 2: South Cliff and Spa, Crescent and Town Centre, North Bay*, 2nd Edition, 2009)

APRIL 16TH

1960: Scarborough's Spa Ballroom reopened on this day, after an extensive programme of refurbishment and alteration at a cost of £26,000. This summer marked the first season of Max Jaffa Concerts at the Spa, which continued until 1986, greatly increasing his own and the Spa's reputations. (www.discoveryorkshirecoast.com/history-and-info)

———◆———

2012: The highly regarded Scarborough photographer and fundraiser, Max Payne, died today at the age of seventy-seven after suffering a heart attack some ten days earlier. He was particularly known for his support of St Catherine's Hospice, for which he raised more than £250,000 through a range of ventures, including his popular photographic calendars. During his lifetime, he received an MBE award and was named as an Honorary Freeman of Scarborough in recognition of his fundraising efforts. Before his death, he was among the first people to donate money towards the cost of staging a spectacular jubilee celebration at Scarborough Castle, and the stunning display of illuminated images that was projected onto the castle's south walls on Monday June 4th 2012 was fittingly dedicated to the memory of Max Payne. (*Scarborough Evening News*)

April 17th

2009: Scarborough was named 'the most English place in the country' after a survey commissioned by local information website locallife.co.uk indicated that it had the most traditional businesses per capita. The categories measuring 'Englishness' were cricket clubs, tea rooms, fish and chip shops, holiday camps and Morris dancing troupes, and the survey showed that Scarborough had a traditional business, organisation or club for every 618 residents. Second on the list, behind Scarborough, was Penwith in Cornwall which includes Land's End, the most westerly point in mainland England. (*The Northern Echo*)

1963: As twelve-year-old Brian Layton lay 100ft down the face of Castle Hill on this afternoon, a fireman was lowered down at the end of a line to rescue him. Stones were worked loose by the dangling rope and hurtled downwards around the head and shoulders of Fireman Mick Major as Brian lay petrified with fear beneath an overhanging rock. With firemen and police officers shouting instructions from 150ft below on Marine Drive, Major took the boy in his arms and began the long haul back to the top of the cliff. In spite of losing his helmet and suffering a gash to the head, Major reached the top some ten minutes later. (*Scarborough Evening News*)

APRIL 18TH

1901: On this day, a meeting of the Scarborough Forty Club debated the question 'Should Women have the Parliamentary Franchise?' but records of this men-only group contain no indication of conclusions reached. The group had been set up in 1899, with membership limited to forty gentlemen and an emphasis on the 'intellectual advancement and entertainment of its members'. Perhaps it is not surprising that the role of women in the home, at work and within society featured at these meetings on a fairly regular basis, as it did on February 26th 1907, with an impromptu discussion 'Should women have votes? Should barmaids be abolished?' (*see* February 26th)

A similar discussion was held on November 19th 1907: 'That the advent of women into public life is detrimental to the best interests of the state' and on this occasion a vote carried the proposition. Ladies were often invited to social activities, as in 1910 when '. . . a party of the Forty Club accompanied by their wives travelled by excursion (train) to Leeds . . . A saloon was engaged and to enliven the journey a piano was carried aboard.' A highly successful 'Ladies Night' took place on March 12th 1912 at the Balmoral Hotel in Westborough, but a subsequent proposal that ladies be invited to the annual dinner was rejected. (Alan Staniforth, *Scarborough Forty Club & Discussion Group: A Brief History: the '40' Club, founded in 1899*, Alan Staniforth, 2005)

April 19th

1938: On this day, the first army recruits arrived at the Burniston Road Barracks at Scarborough for a stay lasting about three months. The plan was to provide 'good food, physical training, remedial exercises and regular hours to fit them to take their place in the Regular Army'. It was the second such physical development centre in the country; the first, which started as an experiment, was at Canterbury and had proved remarkably successful – only 2 per cent of around 800 recruits had failed to make the desired improvement. After the first year at Scarborough, building work would be completed and the centre would be able to 'overhaul' about 300 recruits annually. Local people had no doubts that the sea air at Scarborough would play an important part in bringing them up to standard. (*Scarborough Evening News*)

———— ◆ ————

2012: An ominous shadow appeared over the Scarborough Cricket Club ground in North Marine Road on this day. A hawk-shaped kite was being flown in an attempt to deter pigeons and gulls from roosting and nesting in the North Stand. Scarborough environmental health officers were using this tactic for a couple of weeks as a trial that would be repeated elsewhere in the town if it proved successful. (*Scarborough Evening News*)

APRIL 20TH

1935: John Watson Rowntree, a prominent figure in many aspects of Scarborough life, died at his home on this day. Born in 1854, he attended school locally before transferring to Bootham School in York, after which he returned to his home town and joined the family's grocery business. Election to the town council in November 1889 was followed by defeat in 1892, before a return the following year. He was involved with local politics from 1893, and he was instrumental in different capacities during his time as councillor, mayor and alderman. Other areas of Scarborough life that were influenced by Rowntree include the Adult School Movement, the British and Foreign Bible Society, the District Nursing Association and the town's temperance movement. His pacifist views led to a meeting of the local Peace Society at the Rowntree family's café in Westborough in March 1900, but it resulted in an outbreak of mob violence. A change in political allegiance, from Liberal to Labour, heralded a defeat as parliamentary candidate in 1918, but he continued to work in the family business until shortly before his death. (Anne and Paul Bayliss, *Scarborough's Members of Parliament, 1832 to 1906: Scarborough's Mayors, 1836 to 1906: A Biographical Dictionary*, A.M. Bayliss, 2008)

APRIL 21ST

1953: On this day, the National Federation of Fishmongers craftsmanship competition was held in Scarborough, with competitors from many different aspects of the food industry drawn from a wide area. Mr Arnold Quarmby, of Paddock in Huddersfield, won the title from Mr Frank Wynne who had cycled from Reading to defend it. Mr Quarmby set off back to his workplace of thirty-six years without waiting for presentation of his award, and also making a return journey was 15-year-old Danny Gilbert, winner of the junior championship for preparing fish and dressing poultry. He had journeyed some 500 miles from Truro to take part in the contest. In the fish section, competitors had to split a haddock skin and fillet a lemon sole, fillet a plaice, cut a cod into steaks, fillet a herring, and bone and roll a herring. Contestants in the poultry section had to prepare chickens and rabbits for boiling and roasting. During the competition, Newby's of Westborough were awarded a shield and cheque for the best local fishmonger's window display. The centrepiece of a display by Mac Fisheries of Huntriss Row, was a 28lb royal sturgeon sent from Grimsby and its arrival had coincided with the window dressing display. It had been sold and was to be served at dinner two days later. (*Scarborough Evening News*)

April 22nd

1906: Eric Fenby was born in Scarborough on this day. He soon showed a musical talent that led to his appointment as organist at Holy Trinity Church at the age of twelve. By 1925, he had conducted a work for a string orchestra at Scarborough's Spa Grand Hall and composed a number of musical pieces, but during 1928 he joined Frederick Delius at the composer's home near Paris to work as an amanuensis (copy secretary).

For long periods over the next six years, until Delius' death, Fenby helped the composer to write several of his best known works, and in 1936 he published an account of this exhausting episode in *Delius as I Knew Him*. Fenby's own career as a composer was interrupted by the Second World War, during which he conducted the Southern Command Orchestra before being commissioned to organise Royal Army Education Corps courses in Lancashire. During the post-war years, he established the music department of the North Riding Training College before becoming professor of harmony at the Royal Academy of Music in London between 1964 and 1977. As well as obtaining honorary doctorates from the universities of Jacksonville, Bradford and Warwick, he was an OBE. Eric Fenby died at Scarborough on February 18th 1997. (www. en.wikipedia.org/wiki/EricFenby)

APRIL 23RD

1836: A special general meeting of the Scarborough Cliff Bridge Company was held on this day, following one of the most destructive storms to have struck this area of England's east coast. During the extreme weather conditions, the Scarborough lifeboat capsized on a mission to assist a vessel in the South Bay and ten of the fourteen crewmen were drowned. Reports of this serious loss of life overshadowed details of damage to the Spaw and adjacent bridge. However, it was made clear that there was no chance of repair work being completed for the imminent summer season, as the remaining stonework would have to be removed before re-construction could get underway. The Cliff Bridge Company itself was in a similarly parlous position with debts amounting to around £2,600 and few tangible assets. And so, despite the strenuous efforts of Robert Cattle, Sheriff of York, to organise and revive business, the company ceased trading almost exactly ten years after its establishment on November 1st 1826. (Meredith Whittaker, *The Book of Scarborough Spaw*, Barracuda, 1984)

APRIL 24TH

1849: An unusual freak of nature, which occured on this day and put paid to a sea-going vessel near Scarborough, was recorded in the *Annals of Yorkshire*, published in 1869:

On Tuesday morning 24th April at an early hour, a small vessel belonging to Boston, being off Robin Hood's Bay near Scarborough, was struck by an electric fire-ball or meteor which descended not more than a yard from the place where the crew were standing, and so sudden was the conflagration, that the poor men had only sufficient time to get into their boats and leave the unfortunate vessel; the ship's papers and other articles of value, the men's clothes and everything, in short, but life, was lost. Another Boston vessel, being near at the time, took the men on-board and landed them at Scarborough.

The prime cause of shipwrecks on the North Yorkshire coast was north-east gales, which left the ships' captains with the unenviable choice of riding out the storm or attempting to enter a small harbour. Other reasons for ship losses include fog, collisions with other vessels, enemy action, general sea unworthiness and even spontaneous combustion of cargo such as coal, cotton or jute. (*Annals of Yorkshire, Vol. 1* compiled by John Mayhall)

APRIL 25TH

1557: On this day, Thomas Stafford seized control of Scarborough Castle and proclaimed himself to be 'Protector of the Realm'. This dramatic move was fuelled by his outrage at the marriage of Queen Mary to Philip of Spain and his scheme involved raising a popular revolt against the Queen. One version of events suggests that Stafford took the castle by trickery, while others indicate that he and his accomplices simply strolled into the castle precincts and took control of the gates. Whatever the circumstances, the earls of Shrewsbury and Westmorland recaptured the castle within six days and Stafford was taken prisoner. From Scarborough he was taken to London, where he was put on trial, convicted of high treason and hanged, drawn and quartered at Tyburn on May 28th. Stafford's accomplices received brutal treatment at Scarborough, for after their execution each man's body was boiled and tanned for public exhibition. One outcome of the plot was that in future the governor of Scarborough was required to live in the castle to help ensure its security. (John A. Goodall, *Scarborough Castle, North Yorkshire*, English Heritage, 2000)

———◆———

1879: On this day, St Michael's Chapel in Wheatcroft opened, with Revd R.H. Parr installed as vicar. (*History, Topography and Directory of North Yorkshire, Part II* by T. Bulmer and Co.)

APRIL 26TH

1946: A group of 184 personnel from the Royal Naval School of Music left Scarborough Station this day, on the 12.35 a.m. train travelling to Deal in Kent. The Mayor was in attendance to bid them farewell; an indication of the high regard that was felt in the town for these servicemen. They were billeted in Scarborough during August 1941 and had played an active role in a range of activities, including 'Savings Week', a war-time initiative which promoted thrift and savings in general. In fact, the town had taken on a cosmopolitan appearance during the early stages of the Second World War, as troop trains pulled into Londesborough Road railway station and military vehicles and equipment passed along the streets.

Many premises throughout the town were requisitioned for use as billets, including hotels, guest houses, cafés, the Spa building and the Floral Hall, while local schools were relocated to country estates in the Yorkshire Dales. The Initial Training Wing of the RAF was based at the Grand Hotel, and more RAF personnel occupied St Nicholas Hotel and the Teacher Training College on Filey Road. Servicemen from the Royal Signals were billeted in premises on the North Cliff, and the Royal Hotel and Olympia Ballroom were popular social settings. (Richard James Percy, *Scarborough's War Years, 1939-45*, Sutton Publishing Ltd, 1992)

APRIL 27TH

1745: A press report from this day stated:

They write from Scarborough that Her Majesty's ship 'The Jamaica', sloop off that place, gave chase to a French privateer … shot away her main yard and soon after took her. 'The Jamaica' put several of her hands on-board the privateer and both went in quest of two privateers which were heard off Flamborough Head. The captain of the privateers says that the night before there were seven privateers between Flamborough and Cromer and 'The Gibraltar' and 'Shoreham' will sail immediately from Hull in quest of them.

(*Newcastle Courant*)

<hr>

1900: The Fifth Annual General Meeting of Scarborough Sailing Club was held at the London Inn on this day. Albert Strange chaired the meeting and George Ramsbottom presented the Secretary's report and balance sheet, which showed membership at a record level and a substantial balance in the bank. He expressed regret that only two races had been sailed in the previous year because of the weather. (W.H. James, *Scarborough Sailing Club, Scarborough Yacht Club: A History*, The Walkergate Press Ltd, 1976)

<hr>

2012: Penguins that had to be given anti-depressants after being terrorised by intruders at Scarborough's Sea Life and Marine Sanctuary Centre in Scarborough in May last year, laid their first eggs since the incident today - a total of eight penguins laid eggs. (*Northern Echo*)

APRIL 28TH

2007: Scarborough Football Club played their last game on this day and recorded a 1–0 win at Hucknall Town. The subsequent events of the next few weeks saw the club in the High Court (see June 20th) after a 128-year run that began when members of the town's cricket team organised matches at the cricket ground in North Marine Road. An early move to the nearby Recreation Ground was followed by another switch, this time to the Athletic Ground in Seamer Road during 1898. They remained there until 2007; the stadium was re-named as the McCain Stadium as part of a sponsorship arrangement in 1998. Before the club became professional in 1927, it competed in the Northern League. As members of the Midland League they became champions after just three seasons, with a record points total. They also reached the FA Cup Third Round before losing 2–1 to Grimsby Town. Continued success during the post-war years saw Scarborough among the founding clubs of the new Northern Premier League in 1968, and the 1970s saw them win the FA Trophy three times at Wembley Stadium. Between 1987 and 1999, Scarborough played in the Football League Fourth Division, before a decline in fortunes culminated in the final match at Hucknall Town. (Wikipedia. org/wiki/Scarborough_F.C.)

April 29th

1729: The Scarborough Corporation issued an order today, relating to the Spa. It imposed a charge of *6d* for a half anker of water (an anker was 8 1/3 imperial gallons) with free supplies to local inhabitants for their own consumption. It also stated that 'Money arising thereby to be employed in building a house of correction, a workhouse and a gaol.' An earlier scheme, in 1699, had seen the Corporation construct a cistern with linking pipework and drains, in order to regulate supply of water from the Spa. (Meredith Whittaker, *The Book of Scarborough Spaw*, Barracuda, 1984)

———◆———

1932: Scarborough's North Bay Miniature Railway enjoyed such a successful opening year that a second locomotive was delivered on this day. The *Triton* was ready to go into service some two weeks later at Whitsuntide and a return trip that had taken seventeen minutes, with only the *Neptune* in service during 1931, was reduced to ten minutes, with 8,677 passengers carried on Whit Monday. (Michael Gorbert, *Scarborough's North Bay Miniature Railway Golden Jubilee: 50 Years On, 1931-1981: A Biographical Dictionary*, A.M. Bayliss, 2008)

APRIL 30TH

1996: The Stephen Joseph Theatre opened on this day, following conversion work of the local Odeon cinema that cost £5.2 million. A reshaped internal layout included two auditoria – The Round, a 404-seat section in the round, and the McCarthy, a 165-seat end stage/cinema – as well as a restaurant, shop and full front of house and backstage facilities. Stephen Joseph had seen theatre-in-the-round in America and decided to establish it in Britain. With no suitable venue in London, he turned his attention to the Yorkshire coast, and in 1955 he set up the country's first theatre-in-the-round company on the first floor of the public library, with the aim of encouraging new writers.

Although Stephen Joseph died in 1967 at the age of forty-six, his theatrical aspirations were continued, and in 1972 Alan Ayckbourn was appointed artistic director of the company. His term of office lasted until 2009, during which time 239 new plays, written by 87 writers, were performed here. The majority of Ayckbourn's own plays were premiered at the theatre and over half of these have transferred to London's West End or National Theatre. He was awarded a CBE in 1987 and a knighthood some ten years later. (www.sjt.uk.com)

MAY 1ST

1869: Scarborough North Pier opened to the public for the first time on this day, with an entrance fee of 1*d* for a casual stroll and a charge of 10*s* for an annual angling permit. Building work, which totalled £12,135, included the construction of a small shelter on the pier head, for staging band concerts and serving refreshments, and seating along both sides of the pier decking. In 1864, an early proposal to construct a pier close to the harbour in the South Bay was abandoned because of fears that it would pose a danger to shipping. This subsequent scheme was instigated by a local banker J.W. Woodall. In 1865, he set up a limited company with the intention of constructing a 1,000ft pier in the North Bay and employed Eugenius Birch as the designing engineer, with construction work in the hands of J.E. Dowson. On September 14th 1866, the first pile was driven onto the beach and work was due for completion by the end of the following year, but Dowson's death delayed construction work, which was eventually taken over by Head Wrightson and Co. of Stockton-on-Tees. (Martin Easdown, *Piers of Disaster: Sad Story of the Seaside Pleasure Piers of the Yorkshire Coast*, Hutton Press Ltd, 1996)

MAY 2ND

1868: John Wilson Carmichael died in Scarborough on this day, after spending much of his working life as an artist in Tyneside and in London. Born in Newcastle-on-Tyne in 1799, he developed a career as a Northumbrian painter, but following highly successful exhibitions of his work at the Royal Academy in 1835 and the British Institution in 1846, Carmichael moved to London. Further success in the capital led to the *Illustrated London News* commissioning him to carry out coverage of the Crimean War (1854–56), and although he completed landscapes and architectural paintings, John Carmichael is most celebrated as a marine artist. He published books on marine painting in 1859 and 1864, but a period of ill health, following the death of his son, led to him taking up residence in Scarborough during 1863. Shortly before his death, he was working on forty sepia views of north-east England, between York and Berwick-on-Tweed. (Anne and Paul Bayliss, *Scarborough Artists of the Nineteenth Century, A Biographical Dictionary*, Anne Bayliss, 1997)

1901: Scarborough's Forty Club regularly debated subject matter relating to drink, and on this date the question under discussion was 'Is Drink the Cause of Poverty?' Reports indicate that most members spoke in support of the proposition and as a result no vote was taken. (Alan Staniforth, *Scarborough Forty Club & Discussion Group: A Brief History: the '40' Club, founded in 1899*, Alan Staniforth, 2005)

MAY 3RD

1910: On this day, John Horne MD posted a codicil (supplement) to his will at York, amounting to £200 in his lifetime and a legacy of £300, which were to be invested with Scarborough Corporation. Less than a year earlier, on June 19th 1909, he had conveyed land to trustees, for the building of eight homes 'for the benefit of aged, deserving persons born in Scarborough or resident there for thirty years'. (www.british-history.ac.uk)

———•◆•———

2012: The BBC's *Antiques Roadshow* was filmed on this day at Scarborough's Grand Spa Hall, during which a total of 1,600 items were brought by members of the public for valuation. Two items in particular were given top-end valuations by antique experts – a collection of Bamforth postcards, valued at tens of thousands of pounds, was brought to the Grand Hall by the great, great grandson of Douglas Tempus, who was one of the artists for the original postcards, and a similarly high valuation of £6,000-£7,000 was placed on a racing suit worn by James Hunt when he won the 1976 Hockenheim race. The day's filming was to be divided into two programmes for the autumn/winter series of 2012/13. (*Scarborough Evening News*)

MAY 4TH

1904: Following a final inspection by the Board of Trade officials, approval was given for tram services to begin at Scarborough on this day. The tramway system had cost £96,000 to construct, and it wasn't until two days after the inspection that services actually got underway at 3.30 p.m. At the official opening ceremony the Mayoress declared the system open and the general manager, a Mr Edmundson, drove the first tramcar. (Chris Goode and Ross Hamilton, *Trams by the Sea: Brief History of the Tramways and Early Motor Buses in Scarborough*, United Automobile Services Ltd, 1981)

———— • ◆ • ————

1941: The calm of this Sunday evening was shattered by heavy bombing of the countryside around Burniston, Cloughton, Harwood Dale and Staintondale. It seems likely that the intended targets were within Scarborough's urban area, but that the enemy aircraft missed their intended targets because the radio beam they were following had been distorted. Thankfully, the only casualty was at Brompton, where a couple had been trapped in their home; although his wife survived, the male householder suffered fatal injuries. (Richard James Percy, *Scarborough's War Years, 1939-45*, Sutton Publishing Ltd, 1992)

———— • ◆ • ————

1964: A direct result of Dr Beeching's 'Axe' was the closure of all intermediate goods yards between Scarborough and Whitby, except for Robin Hood's Bay, which retained its goods shed and yard, along with its signal box and up and down platforms. (Stephen Chapman, *Railway Memories No. 19: York to Scarborough, Whitby and Ryedale*, Bellcode Books, 2008)

MAY 5TH

1884: Sir George Sitwell began his political career on this day, when he was adopted by the Scarborough Conservatives as their parliamentary candidate. Later in the same year, he contested two by-elections in the town without success, but in 1885 he defeated the Liberal candidate at a general election. His period of office lasted only until the next general election in July 1886, but in 1889 Sitwell bought a controlling interest in the *Scarborough Post*, which became a mouthpiece for local Conservatives. He was again elected in the general election of 1892, but after defeat in 1895 and an unsuccessful campaign in 1900 he defected to the Liberal Party during 1908.

George Reresby Sitwell was born in London on January 27th 1860. In addition to the family seat – Renishaw Hall in Derbyshire – the family's Scarborough residence was 'Woodend' in the Crescent. He used an extensive collection of family papers to compose a biography of his ancestor, William Sacheverell, as well as other books and papers. During 1909, Sitwell purchased and then restored the ruins of Castello di Montegufoni near Florence as a family home. His wife died in 1937 and five years later, Sir George moved to Switzerland where he died on July 9th 1943. (Anne and Paul Bayliss, *Scarborough's Members of Parliament, 1832 to 1906: Scarborough's Mayors, 1836 to 1906: A Biographical Dictionary*, A.M. Bayliss, 2008)

MAY 6TH

1910: A newspaper report from this day claimed that:

Boxing tournaments are in the nature of a novelty in Scarborough ... and ... boxing is a sport which has not been developed as so many sports have been ... but many members of the Local Territorial Rifles have made use of facilities in the gymnasium at the Drill Hall, North Street and in order to popularise the sport and not with any object of making any money out of it a boxing tournament was promoted to extend over two nights. There was a good attendance at the drill hall and excellent sport was witnessed. All the essentials of a tournament of this description were provided ... A regulation ring, raised a few feet above the level of the floor was placed in the centre of the hall and an uninterrupted view of the contest was obtainable from all parts of the floor ... The feature of the programme was a six round contest for a purse between Cpl Jones of the 18th Hussars and Trooper Littlemore of the 30th Hussars. It was a fine even contest in which an excellent knowledge of the sport of boxing was displayed. Cpl Jones was declared the winner by a narrow margin on points.

(*Scarborough Mercury*)

MAY 7TH

1878: On this day, the president of the Scarborough Dispensary, Arthur Duncombe JP, presented a Christian cross mounted in a leather box to the matron, Mrs Barker. It had been sent by the president of the Fishing Association of Fécamp, along with a letter of thanks addressed to 'Madame La Superiore de l'Hospice de Scarborough', for the care and support that their fishermen had received. On an earlier occasion, in 1866, an outbreak of cholera aboard a Fécamp fishing lugger had led to treatment in the workhouse infirmary, and again the president of the Fishing Association of Fécamp had sent a letter of thanks along with a plaque inscribed with details of the event to Scarborough Poor Law Union. (Anne Bayliss, Paul Bayliss and Alan Jackson, *Scarborough Hospital and Dispensary: The First Fifty Years, 1852-1902*, A.M. Bayliss, 2006)

2001: Today marked the opening race of the season at Scarborough's Oliver's Mount road-racing circuit. The circuit's steep wooded slopes, with numerous twists and turns posed any number of hazards for riders. A landslip caused by heavy rain covered parts of the start / finish area before the season started, and clearance work had to be completed and new fences put in place before the event began. (www. oliversmount.com)

MAY 8TH

1945: VE Day was not only a time for celebration but also for quiet reflection and appraisal. The threat of attack from enemy aircraft was at an end after twenty-one air raids and five machine-gun and cannon attacks on Scarborough. A total of 47 deaths and a further 137 injuries were the result of bombs and mines, while more than 3,000 of the town's buildings were destroyed or damaged. Gradually, everyday life began to return to normality, which included the de-requisitioning of hotels, mainly during 1946, though owners' plans for reopening were hampered by a shortage of linen and soap. (Richard James Percy, *Scarborough's War Years, 1939-45*, Sutton Publishing Ltd, 1992)

———— •◆• ————

1999: Scarborough FC were involved in this dramatic final Saturday of the 1998/9 soccer season. The team's survival in the Football League depended on Carlisle United achieving a draw against Plymouth Argyle and as this match entered injury time with a score of 1–1, the public address system at Scarborough's ground was playing the song 'All Right Now'. All this changed in the ninety-fifth minute of Carlisle's match however, as their goalkeeper, Jimmy Glass, volleyed a close-range shot into Argyle's net, condemning Scarborough to relegation. (wikipedia.org/wiki/Scarborough_Town_F.C.)

MAY 9TH

2008: Scarborough's Rotunda reopened on this day, following a complete refurbishment supported by the Heritage Lottery Fund, the Scarborough Borough Council and contributions from the private sector. The programme of work included essential repairs to stonework, covering the domed roof with replacement lead and constructing an extension at the front of the building, which incorporated a new entrance area, offices and toilets. Replacement of the existing spiral staircase with a new one allowed installation of a central lift shaft which gave access to each of the building's three floors. The total cost of the project amounted to £4.4 million and incorporated a centre for the study of geology for Yorkshire, along with the Dinosaur Visitor Centre.

The Rotunda, which has Grade II listed building status, was completed in 1829 using designs suggested by William Smith, the 'Father of English Geology'. His pioneering work determined that geological strata could be identified and correlated by studying the fossils they contain. Smith was employed by Sir John Johnstone of Hackness Hall as his land steward, and it was Sir John who donated Hackness stone to build the Rotunda. Displayed within its walls are over 5,500 fossils and some 3,000 minerals, collected from locations along the Yorkshire coastline between Redcar and Flamborough. (Scarborough and District Civic Society in Conjunction with Scarborough Borough Council, *The Scarborough Heritage Trail, Part 2: South Cliff and Spa, Crescent and Town Centre, North Bay*, 2nd Edition, 2009)

MAY 10TH

1947: On this day, a direct rail link was opened from the Hull–Seamer line to the recently opened Butlin's Holiday Camp, some two miles outside Filey. The camp was opened on June 2nd 1945, but one of the requirements stipulated when granting permission for the camp was the completion of this line, at an estimated total cost of £98,000. The station included two platforms at 900ft long, and the official opening was performed by Lord Middleton, Lord Lieutenant of the East Riding of Yorkshire, at 10.00 a.m. Other official guests included Mr Geoffrey Kitson, Director of LNER, Sir Charles Newton, chief general manager of LNER, Mr Ian Anderson OBE MC, Chairman of Butlin's Ltd and Mr W.E. Butlin, managing director of Butlin's Ltd.

Following the official ceremony, the first train was a service to York, although trains had actually used the line since the previous Saturday and a special train had travelled from London bringing news reporters. During the evening of the opening, an orchestral concert was held in the Viennese Theatre. Following this ceremonial opening, trains usually ran on Saturdays between the camp and places such as Manchester, Leeds and Newcastle, while occasional trains brought day-trippers on weekdays. (Mike Hitches, *Steam Around Scarborough*, Amberley Publishing, 2009)

MAY 11TH

1644: On this day, Scarborough Castle was furiously bombarded after the Royalist commander, Sir Hugh Cholmeley, rejected proposals of cease fire from Sir John Meldrum. While an initial onslaught focused on the castle gateway, another attack was mounted on the southern end of the wall towards the sea, and it was during this episode that Meldrum was seriously injured in a fall. The stonework of the keep tower started to split under the attack and as lumps of stone were thrown at advancing parliamentary troops, Meldrum was eventually fatally injured in his thigh. He was replaced by Sir Matthew Boynton and the siege was ultimately ended several weeks later by famine and illness among Royalists. (Keith Snowden, *Scarborough Through the Ages: The Story of the Queen of English Watering Places*, Castleden Publications, 1995)

———•◆•———

1998: Local newspaper, the *Scarborough Evening News*, announced a discovery on this day. A research team from Cambridge University had uncovered evidence of a community of Stone Age hunters at Starr Carr, about 8 miles from Scarborough, between Seamer and Flixton. This community is thought to be more advanced than any other in Europe at that time and prompted comparisons with Jericho and the Middle East, which are traditionally considered to be the cradle of civilisation. During that era, Britain was still linked to mainland Europe and land to the east was mainly marsh. (www.interludeshotel.co.uk)

MAY 12TH

2012: Scarborough Rugby Union Football Club staged the Bill Beaumont Cup match between Yorkshire and Lancashire today, at their Silver Royd ground on Scalby Road. It was the main attraction of a whole day of action that also featured a curtain-raiser between a Yorkshire XV and an International XV at midday. A crowd of 2,023 spectators watched a hugely entertaining county championship match, which saw the two teams level at half-time with the score 21–21. The deadlock was soon broken in the fiftieth minute with Lancashire left-winger, Oliver Brennand, scoring a try in the corner. Brennand went on to score a third and fourth try, leaving the game beyond Yorkshire's grasp at 47–21. At that point ten tries had been scored, but before the final whistle was blown, Yorkshire's man of the match, Dan Solomi, from the Wharfedale club, added a great individual effort in the seventy-first minute. Lancashire responded with two more tries to run out as winners by 54–33. A highly successful series of events was rounded off with a White Rose Dinner. (www.scarborougheveningnews.co.uk)

MAY 13TH

1951: Selina Scott, journalist and television presenter, was born in Scarborough on this day. She studied at Lawrence Jackson School in Guisborough, before reading English and American Literature at the University of East Anglia. After a two year spell with the *Sunday Post* in Scotland, where she became a reporter with Grampian TV in 1978 and presented news items from locations, such as a North Sea oil platform and the summit of Cairn Gorm, Scott helped to launch *News Tonight*. Within months, Scott moved to national television as a newsreader on ITV's *News At Ten*, and in January 1983 she joined BBC's *Breakfast Time* programme, with Frank Bough and Nick Ross. After presenting programmes such as *The Clothes Show* and *Wogan* (as guest host) she joined the US Channel CBS, but returned to the United Kingdom to present Sky TV's election night coverage in 1992 with Sir David Frost. During 2003, she based herself on a farm in North Yorkshire where the wool from her Angora goats was used to create mohair garments, and, in addition to presenting a range of countryside and heritage-based programmes, she wrote her autobiography, *A Long Walk in the High Hills: the Story of a House, a Dog and a Spanish Island*. In March 2012, she was awarded an honorary PhD from the University of Hull for services to journalism. (en.wikipedia.org/wiki/Selina_Scott)

MAY 14TH

1927: A Sentinel railcar was brought into service on the Scarborough–Pickering line by the LNER on this day. The Jersey Railway's use of Sentinel railcars some four years earlier had attracted considerable interest, due to their economic running costs. This amounted to a saving of £600 a year in coal costs, and following successful trials on the York–Harrogate and Newcastle–Whitby–Scarborough services, the LNER ordered two Sentinel railcars at a cost of £3,875 each for services in East Anglia during 1924. Additional orders for railcars to operate in north-east England and between Scarborough and Pickering were placed in 1926. By 1928, the LNER had ordered fifty more railcars, of which forty were Sentinels. They performed impressively on the steep gradients of the York–Whitby and York–Scarborough lines, as well as achieving 55 miles per hour on level stretches. The popularity of railcars was furthered by moves to economise because of growing competition from road transport and publicity stemming from the British Empire Exhibition of 1924, but before long rising repair bills made them uneconomical. Regular use also left their appearance tarnished and before the formation of British Railways in 1974, all railcars had been withdrawn from service. (Mike Hitches, *Steam Around Scarborough*, Amberley Publishing, 2009)

MAY 15TH

1883: A notice bearing this date was posted by the Contractor's office of Scarborough and Whitby Railway, with the offer of a £1 reward. It read:

> Whereas, some evil disposed person or persons, have, between the hours of 5 p.m. on Thursday, the 10th inst. And 6 a.m. on Friday the 11th inst. wilfully placed a pair of Bogie Wheels on this railway, near Scarborough Cemetery. NOTICE IS HEREBY GIVEN, that the above REWARD will be paid to anyone giving such information as will lead to the conviction of the offenders.

(J. Robin Lidster, *The Scarborough and Whitby Railway*, Amberley Publishing, 2010)

———•◆•———

1917: On this day, Dr George Barkley died at his home in Scarborough, after spending the later stages of his career working in the general practice in town. Born and brought up in Ireland, he studied medicine there before working in Cumberland in the late 1870s as the medical referee at several ironstone mines. A move to Yorkshire in the early 1880s saw him based in Sheffield and Huddersfield, before finally settling in Scarborough at 58 Castle Road. His work in the town spanned the years 1890 to 1910, when he retired owing to continued ill health. (Anne and Paul Bayliss, *Medical Profession in Scarborough 1700 to 1899: A Biographical Dictionary*, A.M. Bayliss, 2005)

MAY 16TH

1991: A letter published in the *Scarborough Evening News* on this day, from Jack Binns of Chatsworth Gardens, pointed out that:

> Scarborough has only three Grade One listed monuments, namely King Richard III's House in Sandside, Queen Victoria's statue in Town Hall Garden and the Butter Cross. The first has been misused, the second is disgracefully dirty and the last is now virtually forgotten, totally neglected and an embarrassment to heritage guides. The Butter Cross is Scarborough's last surviving medieval street cross. The Corn, Rede and Haldane Crosses have long since gone and the market cross in St. Helen's Square after which Cross Street is named, was taken down 200 years ago. The Butter Cross dated from the fourteenth century and was associated with Scarborough's Saturday market, the old name for Princess Street. When the Old Brass Top Hotel building was demolished and a new building line brought forward the Butter Cross was hidden behind it at the top of West Sandgate. There has been much talk recently in the Town Hall and elsewhere about preserving and promoting Scarborough's rich historical inheritance but it would be encouraging if more than breath was expended.

Happily since then aspects of the town's heritage have been preserved and promoted. (*Scarborough Evening News*)

MAY 17TH

1889: William Roxby Beverley, who died on this day, had maintained close links with Scarborough as he pursued a career as an artist. Born in Scarborough in 1811, when his father was managing the town's Theatre Royal as part of a family-owned northern circuit of theatres, he soon displayed talent as a scene painter. During the 1840s, this work saw him return regularly to Scarborough, and as well as working on projects in provincial theatres, William Beverley was a scenic artist at Covent Garden. His work with watercolours comprised mainly landscapes and seascapes, and between 1865 and 1880 a total of twenty-nine of his pictures, including several Scarborough settings, were displayed at the Royal Academy. Other major venues to show his work include the Victoria and Albert Museum, the British Museum, and Leeds City Art Gallery which, according to an obituary in the *Scarborough Gazette*, was also owned by people in the Scarborough area. (Anne and Paul Bayliss, *Scarborough Artists of the Nineteenth Century, A Biographical Dictionary*, Anne Bayliss, 1997)

1943: New ration books were issued for the people of Scarborough on this day and had to be collected from Scarborough's Christ Church schoolroom. The new books included personal points and coupons in addition to the usual rationing and points' allocation. (Richard James Percy, *Scarborough's War Years, 1939-45*, Sutton Publishing Ltd, 1992)

MAY 18TH

1942: A ceremony took place on this day at All Saints' Church schoolroom in Falsgrave. Twelve-year-old Margaret Willis was awarded the Gilt Cross of the Girl Guides Association by Viscountess Downe, the County Commissioner. Margaret had shown outstanding bravery when her home at no. 63 Commercial Street was badly damaged in an air raid on March 18th 1941. Just before 9.30 p.m., a large bomb had reduced terraced properties in the roadway to a spreading heap of rubble, which resulted in the Willis family being trapped under their own stairs. Rescuers did not reach them until about 6 a.m. the next day, and throughout this terrifying ordeal Margaret had stayed calm and positive in offering support and comfort to other members of her family. Sadly, her baby sister was fatally injured during the incident and both her parents lost a leg. Other casualties of the raid were Squadron Leader J. Walker and his wife, whose bodies were discovered two days later in a gas-filled room of their home; an incendiary device had fallen on the house and burnt through a gas pipe. Although the gas supply had originally been turned off at the mains connection it was inadvertently turned on again with tragic results. (Richard James Percy, *Scarborough's War Years, 1939-45*, Sutton Publishing Ltd, 1992)

May 19th

1962: On this day, four overnight trains transported the array of equipment, animals and performers that comprised Bertram Mills Circus from Hull to Scarborough. Three of the trains arrived at Gallows Close for unloading and the other made its way to Londesborough Road. The founder of this highly popular circus, Bertram Mills, was born in London on August 11th 1873 and spent his early working life in the coach-building business, before staging The Great International Circus at Olympia in London, between December 1920 and January 1921. This first production was a huge success and Mills lifted the status of circuses enormously. In 1930, he launched a tenting circus which operated (apart from the years of the Second World War) until 1964 and following Bertram Mills' death on April 16th 1938, the business was run by his two sons, Cyril and Bernard. The first big top, made in Germany, seated 3,000 patrons, and from 1933 the Bertram Mills Circus began to move by rail. The circus toured the provinces on a three-year cycle and included acts such as 'Rudolph Matthies and his tigers', 'Power's Wonder Elephants' and 'The Great Wallendas' high wire act. (www.circopedia.org)

MAY 20TH

2010: Scarborough's Open Air Theatre was officially reopened today by HM the Queen and HRH the Duke of Edinburgh after it had been closed for a number of years. The original opening took place in 1932, with the Lord Mayor of London performing the ceremony, and as its popularity increased, large scale musicals were staged, consisting of casts of up to 200 people. The house attendance record dates from August 1952 with an audience totalling 8,983, but an unofficial figure of 11,000 was claimed during the 1960s for a recording of *It's a Knockout*. A production of *West Side Story* was the last musical to be performed here in 1968 and during 1977, the dressing rooms and stage set building on the island were demolished and the seating removed. It was in 2008 that planning permission was granted for a major restoration scheme as an integral part of the North Bay Project and after the council gave its backing for redevelopment in October of that year, work got underway on the site in 2009. The completed theatre contains 6,500 seats, which ranks it as the largest operating open-air theatre in Europe. (www.thescarboroughnews.co.uk)

MAY 21ST

1945: Scarborough's Spa buildings reopened on this day, on July 6th 1940 after closure following a concert. The outbreak of the Second World War in 1939 ended a whole range of events and gatherings at the Spa which had taken place during the immediate pre-war era, and included concerts in the Grand Hall by Alick MacLean and his orchestra until 1936, when he was replaced by Kneale Kelley, conductor of the BBC Theatre Orchestra as well as the Scarborough Cavalcade.

During the 1930s there were few internal alterations to the Spa buildings, but outside a bandstand (dating from 1875), that had become known as the North Orchestra, was demolished in 1931, and the entrance to the spa wells was blocked off and replaced by a simple concrete structure. Consumption of Spa waters remained popular, with several hundred drinks dispensed each day, albeit enriched with fruit juice to disguise the unpleasant taste. Wartime regulations placed the Spa out of bounds to members of the general public and barbed wire fences spread along adjacent beaches and cliffs. Troops were billeted at larger premises throughout the town, including the Spa, and barriers were constructed at entrances to the town, with the Spa Bridge forming part of a coastal defence system. (Richard James Percy, *Scarborough in the 1930s and 40s*, Hendon Publishing Co. Ltd, 1990)

MAY 22ND

1484: Following his coronation, King Richard III made a tour of northern England. He visited Scarborough on this day, and again between June 30th and July 11th. An order dated May 28th related to payment of £40 due to a Scarborough merchant, Thomas Sage, and down the years it has been suggested that Richard III's House at Sandside belonged to the same Thomas Sage, who is known to have owned property in that part of the town. (www.scarboroughmaritimeheritage.org.uk)

———◆———

1831: Henry Vandyke Carter was born on this day, and was baptised at St Mary's Church in Scarborough on July 8th. Following a period of study at St George's Medical School between 1849 and 1852, he became a demonstrator in human anatomy and soon showed his artistic ability by producing illustrations for the medical reference work *Gray's Anatomy*. After gaining his MD in 1856, Henry Carter joined the Indian Medical Service some two years later, and up to his retirement in 1888 he illustrated his own medical research projects. In 1890 he returned to Scarborough and during that year he was appointed honorary surgeon to the Queen. Henry Carter died in Scarborough on May 4th 1897. (Anne and Paul Bayliss, *Scarborough Artists of the Nineteenth Century, A Biographical Dictionary*, Anne Bayliss, 1997)

MAY 23RD

1931: Scarborough North Bay Railway, a miniature railway connecting Northstead Manor Gardens with Scalby Mills, was opened in a ceremony on this day at 2 p.m. The locomotive *Neptune*, was officially handed over by the Chairman of the North Side Development Committee, Alderman Whitehead, to the Mayor of Scarborough, Alderman J.W. Butler. During its first season, this short route attracted 400,000 passengers and, apart from a short break during the Second World War, it has operated continuously since its opening day, with the addition of a second locomotive, the *Triton*, in 1932 and the *Poseidon* and the *Robin Hood* in 2006. All of the locomotives, which were modelled on LNER Pacifics, were built by Hudswell Clarke and are steam outline diesels. The railway was one of a number of attractions that were intended to boost visitor numbers to the North Bay. In addition to the single platform terminus at the Burniston Road entrance to the Northstead Manor Gardens, there were two staggered platforms with a passing loop at Beach and an island platform terminus, serving Scarborough Sealife Centre, at Scalby Mills. Operations on the line were taken over by the North Bay Railway Company in 2007. (www.bbc.co.uk/news/uk)

MAY 24TH

2000: On this day, the sixtieth anniversary of the Dunkirk evacuation, the *Coronia* made a memorial cruise from Scarborough to Whitby. The vessel was unable to join the flotilla of 'little ships', which set sail from south coast ports, and instead sailed on this day with 100 passengers on-board, including BBC Radio presenters and Scarborough's Special Events Group. It was an emotional occasion as the *Coronia* set sail, flying the flag of 'Dunkirk's Little Ships' and headed north on a fine day with a calm sea. Greetings were received from the Imperial War Museum, HMS *Belfast* in the Pool of London, the Royal Navy, Royal Air Force and the Royal Signals, as well as coastal stations throughout the country, in acknowledgement of this special anniversary of the part that the *Coronia* played in the dark wartime days of 1940. (Tom Machin, *Scarborough's Coronia*, HPE Print, 2008)

———— • ◆ • ————

2012: Members of Scarborough's Westborough Methodist Church held a three-day Flower Festival starting on this day, as part of their 150th Anniversary celebrations. Henry Fowler, a local shipowner, offered land near the railway station for a chapel and William B. Stewart was the chosen architect. Building work was completed by local firms following the laying of its foundation stone on November 16th 1860 and it opened for worship some eighteen months later. (www.westboroughmethodist.org.uk)

MAY 25TH

1849: Anne Brontë, youngest of the three Brontë sisters from Haworth in West Yorkshire, arrived in Scarborough on this day, along with her elder sister Charlotte and an old school friend, Ellen Nussey. After leaving Haworth on May 23rd, they had made an overnight stay in York to buy items of clothing, such as bonnets, combs, silk stockings, dresses, gloves and a ribbon for the neck and, before heading towards the coast the following day, they paid a visit to York Minster. Anne was in the final stages of her last illness (tuberculosis) and thanks to a legacy of £200 from her godmother she was able to stay at her favourite lodgings at no. 2, The Cliff, (where the Grand Hotel is now located), and meet accommodation costs for herself and her two companions. According to her writings, Anne was in a happy mood during the journey to Scarborough and her spirits were lifted further by the sight of the town's expanse of sea and sands. The following day they took a ride along the beach on a donkey cart and a trip across the bridge that spanned the ravine. Refreshments included dandelion coffee, a glass of lemonade and half a dozen oranges costing just 2s and 7d. (Juliet Barker, *The Brontës,* Abacus, 2010)

MAY 26TH

1963: Mary Nightingale, newsreader and television presenter, was born on this day at Scarborough. After graduating with a Bachelor of Arts Degree in English from Bedford College, University of London she began her career in journalism as a presenter and writer on *World Business Satellite* for TV Tokyo. Her experience in this area continued with the BBC World Service's *World Business Report*, covering economic and corporate news that included interviews with analysts and economists, as well as live two-way links with overseas correspondents. During the early 1990s, Nightingale co-presented *Carlton Country,* a factual series about life in the countryside, and introduced the *Holiday Programme* on BBC One, before moving into sports coverage for ITV; notably the 1995 Rugby World Cup in South Africa. During the following year she presented BBC Two's *Ski Sunday*. Returning to news coverage in the late 1990s, she co-presented *London Tonight* with Alastair Stewart and was sole presenter of Carlton's lunchtime news bulletin, *London Today*. In 2001, Nightingale was promoted to presenter of ITV's *News at 6.30* – she was also a member of the ITN team that covered the 2001 General Election. In 2002 and 2004 she won the Newscaster of the Year Award and continues to present ITV news programmes. (en.wikipedia.org/wiki)

MAY 27TH

1981: The first official Scarborough Spa Express, sponsored by British Rail, ran on this day to celebrate the reopening of the town's Spa building. It would continue to run during the summer months, on two days of each week. Regular steam operations had stopped on most British Rail routes by 1968 but a few years later, in the early 1970s, it was specified that preserved steam locomotives were allowed on particular lines, including the stretch between York and Scarborough. After 1982, the Scarborough Spa Express was re-routed from York to run via Harrogate and Leeds, before returning to York and then eastwards to Scarborough. This schedule operated until 1988, after which there were only occasional rail tours to the resort, but in 2002 West Coast Railways arranged for the Scarborough Spa Express to run three times a week during July and August. In 2010, track problems on the Harrogate Loop resulted in a transfer of operations to the Wakefield Circle route. Perhaps the town's best-remembered express train was the *Scarborough Flier*, which was operated by LNER from July 1927 to September 1963, with a brief suspension from September 1939 until June 1950, as a result of the Second World War. (en.wikipedia.org.uk)

MAY 28TH

1864: In 1864, Mary Ann Fryer, by will dated May 28th of this year, bequeathed £387 14s consols (with the official trustees), the dividends amounting to £9 13s 8d, to be applied by the vicar and churchwardens of St Mary's Church in the distribution of coals and blankets among deserving poor of Scarborough Parish. Fryer also bequeathed £385 1s 9d consols (with the official trustees), the dividends amounting to £9 12s 4d to be applied by the trustees in the distribution of coals and materials for clothing amongst necessitous widows and families of deceased fishermen at Scarborough.

St Mary's Church stands on the ridge between the town's north and south bays, a short distance to the west of the castle barbican on Castle Road. Although much altered since the first phase of the building was completed in the late twelfth century, it originally included three high towers and a large aisled choir, but bombardment from artillery at the castle during the English Civil War saw destruction of parts of the building. Restoration work took place in the late 1660s, which was followed by removal of the galleries and box pews between 1848 and 1850, and the completion of the Lady Chapel Project in 1994. (www.british-history.ac.uk/TheboroughofScarborough)

MAY 29TH

1915: During the afternoon of this day, six trawlers from Scarborough's fishing fleet moved out of the harbour and headed in a northerly direction, towards the fishing ground to the north east of Cloughton Wyke. Fishing operations got underway later in the day, but during the night a loud explosion echoed across the North Sea. Without radio contact skippers of the vessels ordered a swift return to their home port and three trawlers arrived in Scarborough early the following morning, another berthed safely later in the day and a fifth on Monday, May 31st. There was no sign of the sixth vessel, the *Condor*, and at first it was thought that the trawler may have headed to Whitby, but this hope proved to be unfounded and a subsequent search of the *Condor's* last known position proved fruitless.

On June 3rd a patrol vessel came across the *Condor's* waterlogged lifeboat off Flamborough Head, and further searching led to the discovery of a lifebuoy bearing the ship's name and registration number – SH 12. Five oars in the boat had been lashed together, and at a court of enquiry it was later concluded that the boat had sunk with the *Condor*, before resurfacing some days later. (www. scarboroughsmaritimeheritage.org.uk)

MAY 30TH

1925: The ballroom at Scarborough Spa opened today, with Major Cecil Taylor acting as master of ceremonies. Dancing sessions took place twice daily from this day, with music provided by Hilton Cullerne's Dance Orchestra. A notice stated 'evening dress optional, but desirable'. Various changes and additional buildings had been planned since the formation of a limited liability company known as the Spa (Scarborough) Ltd in 1920 and a number of these schemes, including plans for a cliff lift, had been proposed by the board's architect, Frank Tugwell. Many proposed changes involving the Grand Hall building were dropped, but under Tugwell's direction, and with FW Plaxton as contractor, work on the ballroom progressed rapidly – one of the bricklayers claimed to have laid a record number of 849 bricks in one hour.

Once completed, the ballroom proved to be too small, but otherwise it was an outstanding success and capacity was extended in the following year. The total cost amounted to more than £40,000 and this outlay was met by the issue of debentures at 6 per cent. (Meredith Whittaker, *The Book of Scarborough Spaw*, Barracuda, 1984)

MAY 31ST

1977: Joel Ross (born Joel Hogg) was born in Scarborough on this day. He went on to develop a career as a British radio and television presenter, and at the age of sixteen, in 1993, he presented the evening show and *Nothing but the 90s* on Yorkshire Coast Radio (based in Scarborough). He moved further north two years later to present shows on Minster FM, TFM and Metro FM, along with presenting travel reports on various stations. In 1996, Ross moved to Viking FM where he worked on a number of afternoon and evening shows before teaming up with Jason King (known as JK) on the breakfast programme. Their on-air partnership proved to be highly successful and led to two Sony Radio Academy Awards in 2005; gold for Breakfast Show of the Year and silver for Entertainment Show. Between 2004 and 2007 JK and Joel hosted a number of programmes on BBC radio and television channels, and on September 25th 2005, Ross won the accolade of Channel 5's Britain's Worst Celebrity Driver. In January 2006, they won a 'celebrity pairings' edition of *The Weakest Link*, raising £12,900 for a children's charity. Since 2008 media engagements have taken them to Australia and Ireland, as well as various television and radio stations in the United Kingdom. (en.wikipedia.org/wiki/JoelRoss)

JUNE 1ST

1845: An advertisement appeared in *The Times* on this day, to announce the opening of a new hotel:

CROWN HOTEL, ESPLANADE. Contiguous to the SALOON, SPA, CLIFF BRIDGE, PLEASURE GARDENS, SCARBOROUGH. J. F. SHARPIN respectfully informs the Nobility and Gentry that he has entered upon the above new anti extensive Establishment which he is having fitted up in a superior manner with entirely new furniture, and purposes being ready for the reception of visitors on the 10th of June next. The hotel's situation is exceedingly beautiful embracing from the rooms, balcony and adjoining pleasure grounds extensive view of the ocean and the romantic scenery of the eastern coast. The number of apartments exceeds 120, consisting of various suites of dining, sitting and lodging rooms, including a magnificent drawing room sixty feet long. The interior arrangements are very complete, and have been formed with giving (as much as would be consistent with a public establishment) the convenience and comfort of a private residence. Hot, cold and shower baths have been fitted on the most approved plan and can be had on the shortest notice, are easy of access and will be available also to the visitors of the adjoining neighbourhood.

(www.crownspahotel.com)

JUNE 2ND

1899: At a meeting of the House Committee at Scarborough Hospital and Dispensary today, a new fire escape, costing £8 and manufactured by Newman of London, was exhibited to members who had agreed to purchase it. It seems that the equipment unwound and did not remain rigid, as the matron expressed concerns that the window ledge impeded its operation, but the manufacturer was able to resolve this difficulty. Photographs of the building in the early 1900s include a small, fixed metal fire escape on the frontage, that links attic rooms in the main block with a second floor balcony. (Anne Bayliss, Paul Bayliss and Alan Jackson, *Scarborough Hospital and Dispensary: The First Fifty Years, 1852-1902*, A.M. Bayliss, 2006)

———— • ◆ • ————

1984: A 13-pounder anti-aircraft gun was airlifted into position on the harbour wall at Scarborough today, by a helicopter of D Flight 22 Squadron Royal Air Force. It had been mounted on SS *Hornsund*, which sank about 2.5 miles off the harbour on September 23rd 1917, after being struck by a torpedo. In October 1982, the gun was hauled 100ft to the surface from the seabed by members of Scarborough Sub Aqua Club with assistance from local fishermen. (www.flickr.com/photos)

JUNE 3RD

1872: On this day, construction work started near Scarborough cemetery in relation to the fourth proposal for the railway line between Scarborough and Whitby, which had been granted royal assent in 1871. By August 1873, the first 7 miles from Scarborough were ready for ballast and for the track to be laid, but at the Whitby end of the line some of the land, which had already been staked out, had not yet been purchased. Further complications followed, due to problems caused by an Act of May 26th 1873 which authorised junctions at either end of the line and a tunnel at Scarborough, as well as a lack of funds all contributing towards work coming to a halt by 1877. (*The Scarborough and Whitby Railway* by J. Robin Lidster)

1946: Penelope Alice Wilton was born in Scarborough on this day. She attended convent school in Newcastle-on-Tyne, before embarking on a successful stage career. Wilton also appeared on television as Desdemona in *Othello* and Regan in *King Lear* as part of the BBC Television Shakespeare project. She became widely known for her role as Ann in the situation comedy *Ever Decreasing Circles*, which ran for five years in the late 1980s. Further television appearances include *Dr Who* in 2005, *Stolen Earth* in 2008, and the current series, *Downton Abbey*. In 2004, she was awarded an OBE for services to drama. (en.wikipedia.org)

JUNE 4TH

2012: The 'Battle of Peasholm' took place on the lake at Scarborough's Peasholm Park today, as it has done during the summer months for more than eighty years. Lasting about thirty minutes, twenty-foot-long replica boats feature in the recreation of a sea battle, and, until 1929, when electricity was introduced, all boats were manpowered. (In recent years only the larger boats have needed to be steered by council workers.) Model boats featuring in the early years included First World War battleships named Dreadnaughts, Q-ships, the *Orantes* – a passenger liner – and a U-boat, but after the Second World War the fleet was replaced with new vessels that re-enacted the Battle of the River Plate. British boats were HMS *Ajax, Achilles* and *Exeter*, while the German battleship was the *Graf Von Spee*; the line-up was completed by the Royal Mail liner the *Asturias* and a submarine. In about 1960, aircraft featured in the combat and more ships were soon added to the fleet, including HMS *Jervis Bay, the British Pride* and the *Ark Royal*. (www. peasholmpark.com)

JUNE 5TH

1950: Passenger and goods traffic was withdrawn from the Scarborough–Pickering line from this date – except for shipment of freight, mainly stone, from Thornton-le-Dale to Pickering, which continued until 1964. The line had a largely uneventful history, aside from a train breaking through gates at one of the many level crossings and a barrage balloon's trailing cable getting caught in telegraph wires in 1942, which halted traffic on the line. (K. Hoole, *A Regional History of the Railways of Great Britain. Volume 4, the North East*, David & Charles, 1974)

———— • ◆ • ————

2012: Scarborough town crier, Alan Booth, featured in a BBC TV programme broadcast on this day, about people who have met the Queen. In fact, he has met Her Majesty three times, with the first occasion twenty-five years ago during town crier championships on the Isle of Wight. The second was at Scarborough's Open Air Theatre in May 2010 and the third occasion was during April 2012, when he received Maundy Money at York Minster. The television programme featured an interview with Mr Booth about Her Majesty's visit to reopen the refurbished Open Air Theatre, when he had the task of introducing her to an audience of 7,000 spectators. (*Scarborough Evening News*)

JUNE 6TH

1757: Insurance policies with this date, held by Scarborough residents with the Sun Fire Insurance Company, include:

No. 157759: James Cooper, master mariner and shopkeeper:
on his house, shop, tenement and wash house in the Market
Place, bsts (brick or stone, tiled or slated) £400
household goods and stock in trade £600
Total £1,000 (payment) £1-0-0.

No. 157761: Christopher Phillipson, gent
on his house in Cook Row intended for his own dwelling house,
bsts (brick or stone, tiled or slated) exclusive of all manner of
outhouse or adjoining buildings £200
Total £200 payment 4 shillings.

(*Scarborough residents in the records of the Sun Fire Insurance Company* by Anne Smith).

———◆———

2012: American musical legend Dionne Warwick, whose songs include 'Say a Little Prayer' and 'Walk on By', appeared at Scarborough's £3.5 million Open Air Theatre. She was the first of three big name acts arranged to perform there for the summer season by Scarborough Council. (*Yorkshire Post*)

JUNE 7TH

1993: The dramatic finale to events at Scarborough's Holbeck Hall Hotel came on this day, when surviving sections of the building slid off the cliff and collapsed into the sea. Built in 1879 as a private residence, its ownership had passed in recent years to the company, English Rose Hotels, but the unstable nature of this stretch of coastline posed a real danger. Some six weeks before the building's demise, cracks had appeared in the tarmac footpaths across the cliff top and on June 3rd a landslip began below the hotel. A period of heavy rain accelerated the rate of slippage, that left the 60-metre-high cliff cut back by 70 metres and formed a semi-circular promontory, some 200 metres wide, projecting from the base of the cliff. Experts pinpointed classic rotational failure where a layer of sandy, silt-like clay rested on a low cliff of Scalby mudstone and Moor Grit (sandstone). During lengthy litigation the collapse was blamed on poor maintenance of the slope by Scarborough Borough Council, but eventually the court ruled that it was not responsible for the causes of the landslip itself and therefore not at fault for the hotel's collapse. (www.bgs.ac.uk)

JUNE 8TH

1908: Scarborough Londesborough Road Station was opened on this day. It was built specifically as an excursion station, due to limited capacity at Scarborough Station. A through platform measured almost 300 yards in length, while a shorter bay platform was 250 yards long. There was also an exceptionally large covered circulating area which, down the years, was used for a variety of purposes including a parade ground during the First World War, a wet weather rehearsal area in the 1930s and an army supply depot in the Second World War. (K. Hoole, *A Regional History of the Railways of Great Britain. Volume 4, the North East*, David & Charles, 1974)

———— • ◆ • ————

1946: A Victory Day Drum Head Service was held on the south Foreshore today, to commemorate the end of the war a year previously. Large crowds assembled on the sands opposite the Olympia along with members of the council, the Mayor, the 3rd Battalion, Green Howards and representatives from other branches of the armed forces. A massed choir was conducted by Mr A. Keeton and musical accompaniment was provided by Mr E. Robinson on the Hammond organ. A large wreath was loaded onto the lifeboat which was then put out to sea and, to the sound of the 'Last Post', the garland was gently lowered into the water. (Richard James Percy, *Scarborough in the 1930s and 40s*, Hendon Publishing Co. Ltd, 1990)

JUNE 9TH

1893: A week-long series of 'Extraordinary Attractions' starting on this date were advertised on a handbill for Scarborough's People Palace and Aquarium. The continuous and varied programme lasted for nearly ten hours, from 12 noon to 9.15 p.m., with appearances from artistes such as soprano vocalist Miss Madge Morgans, king of the step dancers J.H. Roberts, and the conjuror 'Professor Devono'. The Peoples Palace and Aquarium cost £110,000 to construct, and opened in 1875 to designs by Eugenius Birch, with the whole entertainment complex set completely underground. Covering an area of more than 3 acres, not only was it unique in terms of Scarborough's attractions, but it was also claimed to be the most magnificent marine palace in the world. It was made up of 40,000 cubic yards of masonry and brickwork, with architectural designs reflecting Indian and Arab temples and palaces. In addition to grottoes, a theatre, concert room, picture gallery, baths, monkey house and refreshment rooms, there was also a *monstre* tank that contained 72,000 gallons of water, and in which Captain Webb posted a non-stop swimming record of seventy-four hours in the early 1880s. This amazing complex was converted into an underground car park during the late 1960s. (Ed. Robin J. Lidster, *Yorkshire Coast Lines: A Historical Record of Railway Tourism on the Yorkshire Coast*, Hendon Publishing, 1983)

June 10th

1845: Scarborough's Crown Hotel opened its doors for business on this day. It formed the centrepiece for the Esplanade's Regency-style terrace, and design work was carried out by local architect John Gibson – the town's first purpose-built hotel building had been completed about a year earlier, in May 1844, to a Greco-Roman style. Some twenty years earlier, in 1824, a local newspaper had stated '. . . [We] should like to see a Crescent arise of uniform buildings of white stone, elevated on the margin of the cliff . . . ' It may well have been the views across Scarborough's South Bay to the North Sea, as well as the fine appearance of the hotel, that led twenty-four-year-old John Fairgray Sharpin to take out a twelve-year lease on the premises. He placed advertisements in quality newspapers of the south of England offering holiday accommodation for family groups, which could well include eligible daughters, young children with nannies and family servants. These advertisements also recommended guests to attend musical concerts at the Spa Saloon, which was easily accessible from the hotel. As the hotel's popularity grew, visitors arrived not only by horse and carriage but also by rail following the opening of the York–Scarborough line in 1845. (www.crownspahotel.com)

JUNE 11TH

1893: George Peckitt Dale died on this day and was buried in Scarborough Cemetery. After receiving an education at University College London, and a period as a general practitioner in Sherriff Hutton, near York, he moved to Scarborough, where he built up a practice at Falconer's House, 20 Huntriss Row. Dr George Dale was also Senior Surgeon to the Scarborough Dispensary and Royal North Seabathing Infirmary, and in 1883 he became the first surgeon for diseases of the ear and eye at the Kings Cliff Hospital. Apart from his medical commitments, Dr Dale was a committee member of the Cliff Bridge Company, a Director of Scarborough Gas Company and Chairman of Scalby Water Board, as well as serving as a magistrate for the North Riding of Yorkshire. (Anne and Paul Bayliss, *Medical Profession in Scarborough 1700 to 1899: A Biographical Dictionary*, A.M. Bayliss, 2005)

***

1924: Cricketer Charles William (Bill) Foord was born on this day. He played an important role in the fortunes of Scarborough Cricket Club in the post-war years, as a player, coach, spectator and committee member. A brisk right arm fast-medium bowler and right-hand batsman, he is one of only three cricketers to take 1,000 wickets for the club, and played regularly for the First XI until 1971. (Ian Hall & John Found, *Cricket at Scarborough: A Social History of the Club and Its Festival*, Breedon Books Publishing Co. Ltd, 1992)

JUNE 12TH

1891: The Scarborough Corporation bought the Scarborough Valley Bridge Company and the Valley Bridge on this day. It had first opened on July 1st 1865, at an overall building cost of £28,163. The project was delayed by difficulties in raising the necessary funds and by a lobbying group, who wished to see the bridge in a different location in order to bypass the area now known as Plantation Hill. Despite this, parliamentary approval was granted in legislation dated June 23rd 1864, and building work soon got underway with girders salvaged from a collapsed road bridge over the River Ouse at York. Tolls on the completed bridge ranged from *6d* for omnibuses, to a halfpenny for pedestrians – these payments continued after the Corporation's take-over, until 1919. Details of engineers and contractors who worked on the project are included on a bronze plaque mounted on the wall on the landward side of the bridge. A comparison of the two structures spanning the valley shows a distinct contrast in design styles, with the elegance of the Cliff Bridge being completely different from solidity of the Valley Bridge. (Scarborough and District Civic Society in Conjunction with Scarborough Borough Council, *The Scarborough Heritage Trail, Part 2: South Cliff and Spa, Crescent and Town Centre, North Bay*, 2nd Edition, 2009)

JUNE 13TH

1871: Harry Watson was born in Scarborough on this day and studied at the town's School of Art, receiving tuition from Albert Strange. Success in competitions at the school between 1888 and 1892 saw him rewarded with a North Riding of Yorkshire scholarship to further his studies at London's Lambeth School of Art and the Royal College of Art. From the mid-1890s, Harry Watson probably spent most of his time in London, though he did make regular visits to Scarborough until about 1925, and during these stays on the Yorkshire coast he forged a close link with the Staithes Art Group. Watson's paintings featured mainly figures or landscapes of Scotland and Wales, using both oils and watercolours; they were exhibited at many galleries between 1894 and 1934. Later in his career he taught life drawing at the Regent Street Polytechnic in London and his book *Figure Drawing* was published in 1930. Harry Watson died in London on September 17th 1936. (Anne and Paul Bayliss, *Scarborough Artists of the Nineteenth Century, A Biographical Dictionary*, Anne Bayliss, 1997)

1945: A ceremony in the upper schoolroom of Jubilee Chapel on Aberdeen Walk at Scarborough saw the town's mayor bid farewell to eighty cadets from Hull Trinity House School, who had been billeted here since the start of the war. (Richard James Percy, *Scarborough's War Years, 1939-45*, Sutton Publishing Ltd, 1992)

JUNE 14TH

1958: On this morning, workmen were putting the finishing touches to resurfacing work on the track at Oliver's Mount in readiness for the afternoon's race meeting. One report stated that 'The slowest vehicles ever to use the track, on which machines have reached more than 100 miles per hour, were out. They were two 10-ton rollers being used by the Scarborough Corporation workmen to "iron out" the track for the weekend's racing'.

The first motorcycle meeting at Oliver's Mount took place in September 1946 over a course covering two miles and 780 yards, and its numerous twists, turns and gradients soon earned it the unofficial title of 'the miniature mountain course'. Within a year of that initial meeting, improvements were made by widening the road and enlarging the car park, as well as the relocation of the start/finishing line to its current position at the lower level of the circuit overlooking the Mere.

Course improvements continued during the 1950s, including the major resurfacing work in 1958, and a further programme of complete resurfacing followed during the summer of 1973. In 1991 the Auto 66 Club took over control of the Oliver's Mount venue and maintained the emphasis on safety improvements at one of Europe's most challenging road-racing circuits. (www.oliversmount.com)

JUNE 15TH

1856: An advertisement in the *Scarborough Gazette* stated that Peter Skeolan was opening his Coloured Photographic Institution at 27 St Nicholas Street, Scarborough, on this day. He had moved from Manchester and offered to take a portrait at a 'moderate price' in a 'superior style of execution', during a season that lasted until November. For the 1857 summer season, he moved to the Scarborough Public Rooms in Huntriss Row, but at the end of 1858 he moved to Cheltenham and later Leeds and Harrogate. (Anne and Paul Bayliss, *Photographers in Mid-Nineteenth Century Scarborough: the Sarony Years, a History and Dictionary*, A. Bayliss, 1998)

1893: A 'Grand Sacred Concert – Instrumental and Vocal' was to be held at 8 p.m. in the Peoples Palace and Aquarium on this day. According to a handbill that was discovered at Scalby Station when the buildings were demolished in 1974, the concert featured 'Instrumentalists: The Viennese 1st Original Ladies Orchestra and Vocalist Miss Madge Morgans' at the underground venue, which opened during 1875 at a cost of £110,000. (Ed. Robin J. Lidster, *Yorkshire Coast Lines: A Historical Record of Railway Tourism on the Yorkshire Coast*, Hendon Publishing, 1983)

JUNE 16TH

1951: The first day of a Test match got underway at Scarborough's Marine Road ground on this day, when teams of women cricketers from England and Australia took to the field. The Scarborough club had greatly improved its facilities during the immediate post-war years, and it was only the second time on their tour that the tourists were able to take a shower after the game.

A crowd of 6,000 people watched the opening day's play as England's experienced opening pair put on 95 runs for the first wicket, before the team's captain, Myrtle MacLagan, was caught for 56. By mid-afternoon the England score stood at 130–1, and by the close of the first day's play, wickets tumbled to leave the score at 260–8. The following morning England's lower order added another 23 runs to their score, before being all out for 283; by the end of play on the second day the tourists were all out for 248. On the third and final day, England struggled to reach 115–6, until an eighth wicket partnership helped to set the visitors a target of 214 for victory in just 135 minutes. They made no attempt to force a win and ended on 111–2 to leave teams, officials and spectators well-satisfied with the outcome. (Ian Hall & John Found, *Cricket at Scarborough: A Social History of the Club and Its Festival*, Breedon Books Publishing Co. Ltd, 1992)

JUNE 17TH

2010: Tributes were paid on this day to a former owner of the *Scarborough Evening Press*, as family, friends and acquaintances of Lady Whittaker made arrangements for a service of thanksgiving later in the month. She was in her mid-nineties when she died in early June, and Lady Whittaker's son, Paul, spoke of his mother's work with the British Red Cross and the Women's Royal Voluntary Service, both of which she joined during the Second World War. Her support for both organisations continued for more than half a century and she was awarded an MBE in recognition of her service to the WRVS. She also spent numerous hours at Park Lodge, Scarborough's children's hospital. Lady Whittaker married Sir Meredith Whittaker in 1939, when he was managing director of Scarborough and District Newspapers, and she supported him as non-executive director of the company which was owned by the Whittaker family from 1882 to 1986. Until the early 1960s the family lived at Scarborough before they moved to High Dalby, where Lady Whittaker remained until the early 1990s. After making her home in Priestman's Lane in Thornton-le-Dale, she spent her later days in Redcar. (www.fileymercury.co.uk/news/local)

JUNE 18TH

2012: The Olympic torch arrived in Scarborough on this day during a country-wide journey ahead of the London Olympic Games. The town's Day of Olympic celebrations started at 12.28 p.m. in Columbus Ravine, when the torch was carried from the junction with Victoria Park Avenue past Peasholm Gap and along the North Bay Promenade. A lunchtime stop and special show was staged at the Open Air Theatre, before the torch continued its journey along Burniston Road, Royal Albert Drive, Marine Drive, Sandside, Foreshore Road, Valley Road, Ramshill Road and Filey Road as far as the junction with Queen Margaret's Road. The ceremony ended at that point at 2.14 p.m., before the torch was carried to Filey. Local people acted as torchbearers, including teacher Kelly Williams, who was originally from Scalby, who carried the torch through Whitby before joining the Olympic Indoor Volleyball competition at Earl's Court as a squad member. Swimmer Ellie Wallis of West Ayton carried the torch through Scarborough before a Tesco worker at the Westwood Store, Paul Drake, took it through to Filey. (*Scarborough Evening News*)

1944: The Princess Royal visited Scarborough on this day, and took the salute at the town's railway station as members of the armed forces marched past. (Richard James Percy, *Scarborough's War Years, 1939-45*, Sutton Publishing Ltd, 1992)

JUNE 19TH

1912: Peasholm Park at Scarborough was officially opened today by the town's mayor, Mr T.H. Good, who appeared along with members of the corporation in full regalia. They marked the occasion by sailing around the lake in new boats which represented the very latest designs in rowing skiffs and canoes. The park was developed on land formerly known as Tucker's Filed, and construction of the man-made island and lake got underway as late as December 1911. Following the purchase of this ground by the Corporation the project for gardens in a Japanese style was moved rapidly forward by the Borough Engineer, Mr Harry W. Smith. While excavating the lake, workers found remains of Northstead Manor on the north-west side of the island, and later features of the park included a waterfall, pagoda, tree walk and miniature golf course. Chinese and oriental statues were purchased by the Corporation from Kirby Misperton Hall, near Pickering. Between 1923 and 1932, Peasholm Park was the main location in Scarborough for fetes, galas and firework displays, and in 1924 terraced seating was completed to accommodate large crowds. (www.peasholmpark.com)

———— • ————

1930: Scarborough's public library was opened by the town's corporation on this day. A modern extension was added in 1936. (Scarborough and District Civic Society in Conjunction with Scarborough Borough Council, *The Scarborough Heritage Trail, Part 2: South Cliff and Spa, Crescent and Town Centre, North Bay*, 2nd Edition, 2009)

JUNE 20TH

2007: Scarborough FC was 'wound up' in the High Court on this day, after accumulating debts of £2.5 million. For several years before this momentous date, the club had battled against mounting financial difficulties and disappointing results on the field. Although the club's final game was a 1–0 victory over Hucknall Town on April 28th 2007, Scarborough finished twentieth in the Conference North League and even if they had survived until the next season, the team would have been relegated to the Northern Premier League. Future hopes were linked to a proposed move to a new stadium on the edge of the town for the start of the 2009/10 season, which would be financed by the sale of the McCain Stadium to a housing developer, but difficulties arose due to a covenant on the ground that limited its use to sporting activities. The club was given an eight-day stay of execution on June 12th, but the 'winding up' order soon followed. The supporters' trust then formed a club known as Scarborough Athletic, which was awarded a place in the Northern Counties East League, while the Scarborough FC's Centre of Excellence, Football in the Community scheme and youth team moved to George Pindar Community Sports College. An adult team was formed from this nucleus and played in the Teesside League from August 2008. (www.seadogsfans.co.uk)

JUNE 21ST

1871: On this day, Robert Tindall, five-times Mayor of Scarborough during the 1840s, died at his family home, White House in Longwestgate, Scarborough. Born in 1790 to a prominent Quaker family with considerable shipping interests, it was believed that for about a century following the 1750s, Tindall's yards constructed around 200 vessels, ranging from 200 to 1,000 tons. In addition to running the Sandside-based business, members of the Tindall family were also prominent in politics; Robert served as chairman of the building committee for the Rotunda Museum in 1828 and president of Trinity House in St Sepulchre Street during 1832. Following the Municipal Corporations Act of 1835, he was elected as a Liberal councillor in 1836, before serving five annual terms of office as Mayor between 1840 and 1850. He was also an alderman for six years from 1863 and member of the Piers and Harbours Commission. During 1866, Tindall bought Kirby Misperton Hall, near Pickering, and spent increasing amounts of time there, but returned to his Scarborough home shortly before his death. (Anne and Paul Bayliss, *Scarborough's Members of Parliament, 1832 to 1906: Scarborough's Mayors, 1836 to 1906: A Biographical Dictionary*, A.M. Bayliss, 2008)

———◆———

1936: Following a British Legion service in the Spa Grand Hall, as part of the North Riding County Rally, a soldier ceremonially laid a wreath on the sea. (Richard James Percy, *Scarborough in the 1930s and 40s*, Hendon Publishing Co. Ltd, 1990)

June 22nd

1936: Scarborough Townsmen's Association arranged a 'House Party' programme of events in the summer of 1936, and on this day the Royal Corps of Signals based at Burniston Road Barracks put on a most impressive display. Heavy rain threatened to bring an early finish to the day's events, but several hundred spectators braved the elements to watch the band of the Royal Corps of Signals provide musical accompaniment as horsemen and motorcyclists performed a large figure-of-eight manoeuvre past the central position. (Richard James Percy, *Scarborough in the 1930s and 40s*, Hendon Publishing Co. Ltd, 1990)

———— ◆ ————

1972: Boxer Paul Andrew Ingle was born in Scarborough on this day. As an amateur he competed for Great Britain at the 1992 Summer Olympics held in Barcelona. After turning professional some two years later he became known as 'The Yorkshire Hunter' and showed considerable promise. On April 10th 1999, he challenged Naseem Hamed for the WBO featherweight title but lost on a technical knockout. However, he soon followed this with victory over IBF title holder Manuel Medina, and in his next bout stopped Roy Jones in the eleventh round. Defeat to Mbulelo Botile on December 16th 2000 resulted in surgery to remove a blood clot from his brain and immediate retirement from boxing. (en.wikipedia.org)

JUNE 23RD

1902: Royal assent was granted on this day, for the construction and operation of a tramway system in Scarborough. The Scarborough Tramways Act authorised completion of three miles twenty-three chains of double track, along with three miles twenty-three chains of single track with construction work to be completed within two years (apart from the stretch along Marine Drive where only one year was allowed). Ownership and construction work was vested in Edmundson's Electricity Corporation who already held tramway business interests in the Redruth and Glossop areas, but adequate provision was also made for the financial interests of the Scarborough Corporation. If net profit from the new tramway system exceeded costs by 5 per cent, then the Corporation could draw 50 per cent of the surplus.

Scarborough Corporation was also entitled to invest in tramway company debentures and ordinary shares. In addition, provision was also made for the Corporation to take over the tramway from November 1st 1915, following six months' notice, or at a later date in 1926 or 1939. Construction work got underway on October 12th 1903 and some seven months later it was largely complete, although only 2.97 miles of double track and 1.81 miles of single track were actually brought into operation. (Chris Goode and Ross Hamilton, *Trams by the Sea: Brief History of the Tramways and Early Motor Buses in Scarborough*, United Automobile Services Ltd, 1981)

JUNE 24TH

1732: A levy of a halfpenny for 'every chalder of colas laden on-board any ship, hoy, bark or other vessel at the port of Newcastle-on-Tyne, or at Sunderland, Blyth, Seaton Sluice, Cullercoates and other members of that port' was payable from this date, until June 24th 1763, to the Scarborough bailiffs and burgesses. The duties were to be collected at the Custom Houses of Newcastle and Sunderland and sent en bloc, less a collector's charge. Local duties were similarly authorised until June 24th 1783 and the combined effect was to allow Scarborough's Harbour Commissioners to meet the expense of improvements for 'receiving in distress of weather, ships navigating to and along the northern coasts'. (www. scarboroughsmaritimeheritage.org.uk)

—◆—

1936: Miss Marie Panther was crowned 'Rose Queen' on this day during the Procession and Crowning of the Rose Queen. It was part of the Battle of Flowers which was arranged by the Townsmen's Association at Scarborough's Spa building and the crowning was carried out by Lady Patricia Latham. Musical accompaniment was provided by the band of the Royal Corps of Signals, and the Braemar Girl's Pipe Band. (Richard James Percy, *Scarborough in the 1930s and 40s*, Hendon Publishing Co. Ltd, 1990)

JUNE 25TH

1919: A schooner, named *Melba*, registered at Newcastle-on-Tyne, was at the centre of a dramatic rescue by the Scarborough lifeboat on this day. Conditions were dry with a strong northerly wind as the *Melba* was towed by a tug to Carnelian Bay and dropped anchor, but onlookers from the shore could clearly see that each successive wave was dragging the vessel ever closer to rocks on the shoreline. As darkness began to fall, the *Melba*'s crew hoisted the ensign halfway to the peak and ignited a red flare over the quarter rail. Their signal was immediately spotted by the lifeboat station and within a few minutes the lifeboat was launched. Riding on crests of the waves and then dropping into troughs, the lifeboat disappeared from the view of watching crowds on the pier and foreshore. Before long, the rescue craft came back into view and as it entered the calmer waters of the harbour there were loud cheers when it was revealed that all eight members of the *Melba*'s crew had been saved. (www.scarboroughsmaritimeheritage.org.uk)

2011: Armed Forces Day drew a crowd of 17,000 people to watch an aeronautical display by The Blades team and joint sea exercise involving HMS *Explorer*, the Scarborough Lifeboat and the RAF Sea King helicopter, as well as a seafront parade. (www.scarborough.gov.uk)

JUNE 26TH

1940: After earlier alerts during the first few months of 1940, Scarborough suffered a dramatic and destructive air raid on this day. At around midnight, a single enemy aircraft flew over the area and dropped bombs and incendiaries close to the main road at Burniston. A total of nine bombs caused varying degrees of damage to five properties along the roadside, leaving one house, the Sunnyside, completely collapsed. Three adults and five children, including three evacuees, were trapped under debris and it was only because of the bravery of a special constable and a volunteer war worker that they were led to safety through a hole in the wall. Neighbours living nearby had similar escapes from serious injury, including a mother and new-born baby, who were showered with glass as they lay on their bed. The most remarkable stroke of good fortune happened at a property close to the local garage. A bomb blast brought down a large roof timber, which was prevented from falling to floor level and endangering the occupants when it lodged on a family Bible on the edge of the sideboard. The only injuries sustained in the raid were at Boundary Cottage where a male householder suffered injuries to his back and fingers. (Richard James Percy, *Scarborough's War Years, 1939-45*, Sutton Publishing Ltd, 1992)

JUNE 27TH

1868: The North Eastern Railway Programme of Tourist Ticket and Excursion Arrangements for the 1868 season advertised:

WEEKLY EXCURSIONS to Scarborough, Filey, Bridlington and Whitby commencing on Saturday 27th June. Third Class Return Tickets Fare There and Back Five Shillings. Children under Twelve half fare. The Company will not be responsible for luggage, only 56lbs weight of which will be allowed to each passenger.

(Ed. Robin J. Lidster, *Yorkshire Coast Lines: A Historical Record of Railway Tourism on the Yorkshire Coast*, Hendon Publishing, 1983)

———•◆•———

1890: Prince Albert, the Duke of Clarence, opened the new Royal Albert Drive on this day. The Royal visit was celebrated by a banquet at the Royal Hall, and a Gala with a fireworks display at Scarborough Spa. The town was decorated for the occasion but the cost of festivities, which amounted to £463, resulted in adverse comment. The overall cost of purchasing land, building the seafront promenade and laying out the gardens totalled £43,000. (S. Foord, Scarborough Records)

———•◆•———

1908: On this day, the Alexandra Gardens were officially opened following improvements some nine years after the Scarborough Corporation had bought the land. The recent scheme was prepared by Borough Engineer and Surveyor, Harry W. Smith, and it included two crown bowling greens, three tennis courts and an open space for entertainment. (www.scarboroughcivicsociety.org.uk)

JUNE 28TH

1893: Correspondence from Major General F. De Winton, Royal Equerry at Marlborough House and dated from this day, was received in Scarborough with regard to two wards at Scarborough Hospital and Dispensary. The formal opening of this building was planned as a celebration of the Royal Wedding and it was hoped to name and equip wards in honour of the Royal couple. His reply stated:

> Sir, I am desired by His Royal Highness the Duke of York to thank you for your letter of the 27th and to express his warm approval and that of Her Serene Highness the Princess May of the scheme adopted by the borough of Scarborough referred to in the resolution of which you send a copy. I have the honour to be, Sir, your obedient servant.

Celebrations for the Royal marriage began at the Town Hall, before a procession of civic and religious dignitaries assembled and walked to the parish church of St Mary to attend a service led by choirs from six Scarborough churches. After the service, the group continued to the new hospital where John Dale, Mayor and President of the hospital, performed the official opening. (Anne Bayliss, Paul Bayliss and Alan Jackson, *Scarborough Hospital and Dispensary: The First Fifty Years, 1852-1902*, A.M. Bayliss, 2006)

JUNE 29TH

1871: Royal assent was given on this day for a fourth proposal to construct a direct railway line between Scarborough and Whitby. Covering some 20 miles of North Yorkshire coastline, it ran from Gallows Close at Scarborough, ending with a 1-in-6 downhill incline to Gideon's timber pond at Whitby, on the south side of the River Esk. Terms of the Act authorised the Scarborough and Whitby Railway to build suitable wharfs and landing places, and the first turf for the route was cut on June 3rd 1872. Work progressed slowly, and before long the company ran short of money and by the late 1870s there was a danger that the whole scheme might be abandoned. The ailing project was revived through the enthusiasm and capital of W.H. Hammond of Raven Hall at Ravenscar, and the line was completed. Original plans were based on a totally independent line, with a natural ridge separating Scarborough station from the North Eastern Railway (NER), and the River Esk forming a natural barrier at Whitby, but at a late stage in the building work it was decided to link up with NER at both ends. This was achieved with a tunnel at Scarborough and a 915ft-long viaduct over the Esk at Whitby. (K. Hoole, *A Regional History of the Railways of Great Britain. Volume 4, the North East*, David & Charles, 1974)

JUNE 30TH

1845: The section of railway between Seamer (two miles outside Scarborough) and Bridlington was authorised under the York and North Midland Railway (Bridlington Branch) Act. Permission was also given to raise capital of £87,000 (50 per cent of which could be obtained through a share issue). (Mike Hitches, *Steam Around Scarborough*, Amberley Publishing, 2009)

———◆———

1859: An editorial was published in today's *Scarborough Gazette*, with an appeal for new subscribers to support the town's dispensary. It reported that '. . . In Scarborough, with its fifteen or sixteen thousand inhabitants, this year's subscriptions to its Dispensary only amount to barely £80 . . .' and pointed out that '. . . this is the only institution in the town where the poor, not absolutely in receipt of parish relief, can obtain advice, and medicines gratuitously . . . ' before appealing to '. . . our fellow townsmen not usually in the rear in a good cause to remedy this anomalous state of things . . .' There was no direct request for support from visitors, as the Dispensary, unlike the Seabathing Infirmary, was entirely a Scarborough charity and it was probably significant that a fundraising campaign was already underway to provide resources for a new Northern Seabathing Infirmary. (Anne Bayliss, Paul Bayliss and Alan Jackson, *Scarborough Hospital and Dispensary: The First Fifty Years, 1852-1902*, A.M. Bayliss, 2006)

JULY 1ST

1899: Charles Laughton, actor, screenwriter, producer and director, was born in Scarborough on this day. After attending Stonyhurst College he served in the First World War, before starting work in the family hotel business. After taking part in amateur theatricals in Scarborough he became a drama student at RADA in 1925, and made his first professional stage appearance in a comedy, *The Government Inspector*, at the Barnes Theatre on April 28th 1926. A series of classical roles soon followed before he made his debut in the United States on September 24th 1931. Laughton had also taken film roles in this country during the late 1920s, and in 1932 he appeared in his first Hollywood movie, *The Old Dark House*, with Boris Karloff. He won an Academy Award for his performance in *The Private Life of Henry VIII* and appeared in six Hollywood films during 1932. This success established Charles Laughton as a leading performer in costume and historical drama parts, but during the next thirty years he appeared in widely varying roles, as well as directing plays such as *The Caine Mutiny Court Martial* in 1954 and making spoken word recordings and television appearances. Charles Laughton died on December 15th 1962. (en.wikipedia.org)

July 2nd

1880: The Holy Trinity Church in Scarborough, was consecrated on this day, and the first incumbent was Revd R.V. Dunlop. Many of the building's walls were made from grey Hackness stone and the overall style was thirteenth century. Reverend Dunlop died during 1881 and, in addition to a tablet on the south aisle, a parish room was built in his memory on an adjacent site. (*Ed. T.F. Bulmer, History, Topography, and Directory* of North Yorkshire, T. Bulmer & Co., 1890)

1975: Her Majesty Queen Elizabeth II and Prince Phillip paid a visit to the Scarborough area on this day, as part of celebrations for an important anniversary of the Duchy of Lancaster. It represented the first visit by a reigning monarch since Richard III in 1484. After arriving at Scarborough railway station, the royal visitors were driven in a limousine along Northway, Columbus Ravine and Burneston Road at the start of a tour that included Scalby, Brompton and Pickering. The royal route continued from Scarborough to Station Road at Scalby before finally arriving at Scalby Lodge Farm, where Duchy tenants were invited to the reception in a marquee. A strict timetable dictated that the royal visitors arrived at 10.25 a.m. and left thirty-five minutes later for an engagement at Home Farm in Brompton. (www.scalbyfair.co.uk/history)

JULY 3RD

1933: Glorious weather favoured the opening ceremony, performed by Scarborough's Mayoress, of the luxurious holiday camp for members of the National Association of Local Government Officers at Cayton Bay, on this day.

A news report added that the location of the camp and immediate surroundings were ideal, and supported the claim that it was the best of its kind in Britain:

> Of outstanding beauty are the rock gardens below the wood and adjacent to the beach bungalow. This particular part of the 94 acres which has been acquired is a veritable sun trap and the blaze of colour presented by the mass of vari coloured blooms artistically arranged leaves an impression which will linger in the memory for a long time.

The large gathering of people who attended the opening ceremony went on to attend a tour of the camp and there was a unanimous opinion that it would add to the amenities of the neighbourhood. Mr C.G. Brown, President of NALGO, oversaw the proceedings, and along with thanking the Mayoress for performing the opening ceremony, he also thanked the Borough Engineer for the considerable practical interest that he had taken in the camp. (*Scarborough Evening News* and *Daily Post*)

JULY 4TH

1938: Scarborough's North Bay Pool was officially opened on this day by the town's Mayor as an additional attraction on the resort's north side. At the ceremony a musical programme featured Munn and Felton's Band, and huge crowds gathered to see the 'wonder pool'. At nightfall, the pool was floodlit with forty-two underwater lamps while the adjacent area was illuminated with concealed lighting units. During the 1980s, the pool was extensively refurbished and renamed as a 'Waterscene'. (Richard James Percy, *Scarborough in the 1930s and 40s*, Hendon Publishing Co. Ltd, 1990)

———◆———

1940: A series of dramatic events followed the discovery of a naval mine in the nets of the trawler *Connie* on this day. Once landed, the mine was taken by a Mr Dunwell in his van through the town streets to the Corporation Depot in order to be weighed. Unsurprisingly, he was told to remove it and when he received the same response at Mattie Webster's scrapyard in William Street, it was dumped on the sands. It is unclear why the mine exploded on the beach, but a nine-year-old boy was fatally injured in the ensuing blast and thirteen other people also suffered injuries. Areas along the Foreshore and Eastborough were littered with broken glass from nearby windows. (Richard James Percy, *Scarborough's War Years, 1939-45*, Sutton Publishing Ltd, 1992)

JULY 5TH

1846: Jane Hall died on this day, aged seventy-two. Hall had been an inmate of the Scarborough workhouse for fifty years. She was never married, but her four children were brought up at the expense of the Union; three of them died and were buried at a nearby cemetry. The fourth, a daughter, now forty five-years of age, regularly lived in the house and has also had four children, three of whom died. It is calculated that those two generations of one family cost the Union not less than £1,000. (*Yorkshire Annals*)

———— •◆• ————

2012: The world premiere of Alan Ayckbourn's play for pre-school children, *The Ten Magic Bridges*, took place at the Stephen Joseph Theatre in Scarborough today. The play is spread over ten parts, and after the young Princess Elysia has wandered away from the safety of the castle, it is only with the help of the audience and her faithful 'Clever Cat' that she is able to cross the ten magic bridges in order to return to her home. (thetenmagicbridges.alanayckbourn.net)

JULY 6TH

1875: The Scarborough Spa Cliff Lift opened on this day, to provide an easily accessible route between the town's Esplanade and The Spa. Proposals for a hydraulic tramway were put forward as early as 1867, and plans by Richard Hunt, proprietor of the Prince of Wales Hotel, were approved in 1872. The tramway was completed at a cost of £8,000 and represents the first passenger cliff tramway in Europe. During the early years, the journey lasted three or four minutes for landing and transit, covering 91 metres on an incline of 1-in-3, and by 1876 reports indicate that the lift was carrying as many as 3,500 passengers each day. In 1888, the lift carried 250,000 passengers and numbers reached a peak of 1,200,000 during the immediate post-war year of 1945-46. During 1993, Scarborough Borough Council bought the lift from its owners and some four years later operations were modified for the lift to become completely automatic. In 2001, work was completed at the Esplanade station to make the lift accessible to all passengers and during 2002 more than 231,000 journeys were completed. The success of Scarborough's cliff lift saw many other resorts construct similar tramways. (Scarborough and District Civic Society in Conjunction with Scarborough Borough Council, *The Scarborough Heritage Trail, Part 2: South Cliff and Spa, Crescent and Town Centre, North Bay*, 2nd Edition, 2009)

JULY 7TH

1845: On this day, Scarborough Railway Station opened to mark the completion of work on the line from York. A train made up of thirty-five coaches and hauled by two locomotives, the *Hudson* and the *Lion*, arrived in Scarborough after a journey of about three and a half hours, with stops at Castle Howard, Malton and Ganton. To mark the occasion, all shops closed in Scarborough and a crowd estimated at between 10-15,000 gathered to watch the arrival of the first train, which was greeted by long speeches and a fair amount of junketing. The original station building was designed by G.T. Andrews, with a wrought iron and glazed roof measuring 348ft in length and 88ft in width, set some 30ft above the rail tracks. (www.forgevalleyrailway.co.uk)

———◆———

1943: The Scarborough Amateur Operatic Society performed *The Pay of the Pied Piper* at the town's open-air theatre on this day. Restrictions on stage lighting, owing to blackout regulations, was overcome by the cast's colourful costumes. A cast of 250 took part and of these more than 200 were local children. (Richard James Percy, *Scarborough in the 1930s and 40s*, Hendon Publishing Co. Ltd, 1990)

July 8th

1927: Thick fog shrouded the Yorkshire coastline on this day, as a small coaster, the *Westowrie*, passed Scarborough on a southerly course for Yarmouth carrying a cargo of stone from Inverkeithing. Suddenly, at about 6.45 a.m., another steamer, the *Lambeth*, loomed out of the gloom on a collision course with the *Westowrie* and, although Captain Allen immediately sounded her siren, the *Lambeth* struck his vessel with a deafening crunch. The ships collided almost stem to stem, but rapidly separated and disappeared amid the fog. The *Lambeth* stopped engines as her crew peered into the swirling mist but, with no sign of the other vessel, the journey to her destination on the Tyne got underway again. The *Lambeth* had suffered slight damage to her bow, but the *Westowrie* was in a much worse state, with holes in her bows letting in water. Captain Allen and his five crewmen were forced to abandon ship and were later picked up by a passing steamer, the *Chartered*, heading for Newcastle. (Arthur Godfrey and Peter J. Lassey, *Shipwrecks of the Yorkshire Coast*, Dalesman Publishing Co. Ltd, 1974)

———————◆———————

2006: An article on this day reported: 'Scarborough has a pretty, bustling harbour, like a village on the sea and it has the Grand Hotel which Hitler told his bombers to leave alone because he had earmarked it as his Reich Chancellery after the invasion . . .' (*Daily Telegraph*)

July 9th

2012: A group of five sandcastles were completed on this day, on Scarborough's South Bay beach by sand sculpture experts from the organisation Sand in Your Eye. Pride of place was taken by the dramatic features of Scarborough Castle which, along with the other four depicted castles, is in the care of English Heritage. They were sculpted at the launch of a sandcastle-building competition being arranged by English Heritage during the summer season of 2012.

The primary aim of the competition was to encourage a revival of the traditional holiday pastime of building sandcastles. English Heritage has ninety-eight castles in its care throughout the country and competitors were invited to build a replica sandcastle, which would then be photographed and posted to the English Heritage competition site. Facebook followers voting for their favourite picture would choose a weekly child and adult winner, with a prize of free family entry to an English Heritage castle of their choice.

When the competition closed at the end of August the best overall junior entry received a party for themselves and eleven friends at an English Heritage castle with food, games and party bags provided. The best adult entry won a stay at a nominated castle or a castle ghost tour. (*The Scarborough News*)

JULY 10TH

1759: John Wesley recorded in his diary for this day that, 'We took horse at half an hour past three, and rode over the huge mountains to Scarborough. I began to preach near the main street at seven. The congregation was large and some of them wild enough but in a short time all were quiet and still.' (John Wesley, *The Journal of John Wesley [2 Volumes]*, Charles H. Kelly, 1904)

＊

1882: The first copies of the *Scarborough Evening News* rolled off presses on Aberdeen Walk on this day. Closely-typed pages contained no pictures, and the newspaper faced competition for sales from five other publications in a town with only 30,000 residents. Advertisements covered the front page to highlight goods offered by hatters, watchmakers, shoemakers and saddlers, along with attractions, such as 'The Scarborough Aquarium, the most magnificent in Europe'. The inside pages carried news of the bombing of Alexandria and incidents that resulted in the occupation of Cairo by British troops. There was also a message from the proprietors, which read:

> As Scarborough is the most popular and fashionable health and pleasure resort in the north of England, it is believed that there is a demand for a Daily Evening Paper giving a full service of the day's telegraphic news.

Some early editions ran to six pages at a cost of just one halfpenny and eventually the newcomer took over the other daily newspaper, *The Post.* (*Scarborough Evening News 14th July 2007*)

July 11th

1484: This day marked the final phase of King Richard III's tour of northern England following his coronation. In 1485, King Richard III gave a charter to Scarborough, which made Scarborough a county and a custom port separate from Kingston-upon-Hull. This development gave the town trading rights over a wide area. (www.scarboroughsmaritimeheritage.org.uk)

———◆———

1863: The Church of St Martin-on-the-Hill on Scarborough's South Cliff was consecrated on this day. Most of the cost for the building was met by Mary Craven, and Hull architect, George Bodley, was chosen to carry out design work. He employed William Morris and the Company of Red Lion Square, London, to complete the church's interior design and decoration, and they installed magnificent stained-glass windows by craftsmen such as Dante Gabriel Rossetti, Burne-Jones, Ford Madox Brown and William Morris himself. (Scarborough and District Civic Society in Conjunction with Scarborough Borough Council, *The Scarborough Heritage Trail, Part 2: South Cliff and Spa, Crescent and Town Centre, North Bay*, 2nd Edition, 2009)

July 12th

1880: Consecration of the Church of England sections of Manor Road Cemetery took place on this day, and an additional area was consecrated on August 27th 1909. Most of the cemetery, which was originally known as New Cemetery, had opened on land to the west side of the public road and a religious service was held by Nonconformists on the evening of July 19th 1872. According to Joseph Brogden Baker, in his *History of Scarborough* written in 1882, the enlarged cemetery 'Is much frequented especially on Sunday afternoons, as a place of resort.'

The increase in deaths from smallpox epidemics in 1871 and 1872 led to calls for a mortuary chapel, but in April 1876 it was reported that work on the chapel and a bridge had been postponed, due to the high price of iron and other materials. A new chapel was completed during 1901-02 and consecrated on December 9th 1902. The northern sector of the cemetery was laid out between 1928 and 1938, and additional Church of England sections in this area were consecrated on August 15th 1932. (www.scarborough.gov.uk)

JULY 13TH

1822: An entry in the diary of John Cole for this day, records that he bathed in the sea for the first time and enjoyed a trip in a pleasure boat. He had moved to Scarborough during the previous year to pursue business as a bookseller, and added that the tattooed head of George, a New Zealand chief, was being displayed in the town. (www.scarboroughsmaritimeheritage. org.uk)

———— ◆ ————

1865: Voting in the General Election spanned three days (July 11-13th), and at Scarborough there were scenes of great excitement as candidates were pelted with eggs and other missiles by a gathered mob. Bonnetting, hooting and drunkenness in a few cases led to skulls being broken by police, and one man was seriously injured by a policeman's staff. At the close of the poll Mr J. Johnstone (Liberal) had 932 votes, Mr Dent (Liberal) 674 and Mr Cayley (Conservative) 441, but the candidates could not be heard over the noise of the crowd when offering thanks. (*Annals of Yorkshire*)

———— ◆ ————

1916: Scarborough lost two more trawlers to U-boat attacks on this day when the *Florence*, SH 144, and the *Dalhousie*, SH 72, were targeted about 10 miles off Whitby. Crew members of both vessels managed to row their own boats to the safety of Whitby. (www.scarboroughsmaritimeheritage.org.uk)

JULY 14TH

2005: A plaque was unveiled on the wall of Scarborough Library in Vernon Road by Sir Alan Ayckbourn, to mark the fiftieth anniversary of the founding of the Theatre in the Round. When it was opened in 1955 by Stephen Joseph it was situated on the first floor of the building and represented the UK's first theatre-in-the-round. Stephen Joseph, son of Hermione Gingold and publisher Michael Joseph, has been described as 'An innovator with a vision who believed that the enclosed stage was a barrier to intimacy between actors and audience'.

Following his school days, Stephen Joseph studied at a drama college in London and then worked in broadcasting and television, before joining the Royal Navy in 1939. His service as a gunnery officer saw him being awarded with a DSC, and during the post-war years he became a teacher, before taking up studies for a master's degree at Cambridge. During a visit to the United States, he came across an example of theatre-in-the-round and decided to establish this form of theatrical presentation in his home country. Circumstances brought him to Scarborough, and the first performance at the Library Theatre, *A Circle of Love*, took place on July 14th 1955. (*Blue Plaques in Scarborough 1974-2010*, Scarborough and District Civic Society, 2010)

July 15th

1978: A One Day International cricket match was staged at Scarborough Cricket Club's North Marine Road ground on this day, when England and New Zealand competed for the Prudential Trophy. This form of cricket allows each side 55 overs of batting and the England team, captained by Mike Brearley, put together a total score of 206, with Graham Gooch as top scorer, with 94 runs. Gooch and his teammate, Ian Botham, had made their debuts in One Day Internationals in a previous match at Scarborough on August 26th 1976.

In reply, the New Zealand side, which included household names such as Richard Hadlee and Lance Cairns, reached 187 from their allocation of 55 overs, leaving England as winners by 19 runs. Graham Gooch was named 'Player of the Match' and his team won the second and final match of the series two days later at Manchester, by the convincing margin of 126 runs. Cricket was first played at the North Marine Road ground, initially known as Queen's, in 1863, and Yorkshire have played there since 1878. Well known for its end of season Scarborough Festival, it was named 'Ground of the Year' by *The Guardian* newspaper, after the 2010 season. (www.espncricinfo.com)

JULY 16TH

1860: On this day, a rock garden was opened on Scarborough's North Cliff, with a sea frontage of one quarter of a mile. Architect of the 10 acre project was Josiah Forster Fairbank who included a Moorish Temple at the Rutland Gardens entrance. Beneath the dome of the temple a winding staircase led down to gardens and an assembly hall, where circuses and theatrical performances could be staged in front of up to 3,000 people. An audience of 2,000 attended the first evening's show, but the venue's popularity was short lived and the last entertainment at the Rock Gardens, in 1862, took the form of a Brass Band Concert, featuring 360 musicians from seventeen bands. At the end of the contest all the band members combined to play Meyerbeer's *Coronation March*. (S. Foord, *Scarborough Records*)

1885: The Scarborough and Whitby Railway was opened on this day, and was operated by North Eastern Railway for 50 per cent of the gross profits. Construction of the line, which was first proposed in the late 1840s, had to overcome the problems posed by steep inclines and a rugged coastline. (*The Scarborough and Whitby Railway* by J. Robin Lidster)

1941: Wartime regulations had only allowed members of the public on Scarborough's beaches between 6 a.m. and 9.30 a.m., but an agreement with the authorities on this day improved access to 7.30 a.m. to 9.30 a.m. and 4.30 p.m. to 8 p.m. (Richard James Percy, *Scarborough's War Years, 1939-45*, Sutton Publishing Ltd, 1992)

JULY 17TH

1933: Newspaper reports on this day, described:

A considerable amount of activity at the Falsgrave Yachting Pond after six weeks suspended animation owing to lack of water in the pond. When it became known that pumping operations had commenced and the tide was turning fast, the skippers were filled with pleasant anticipation of renewed contests in nautical skill. One ardent skipper who was present when pumping began could not resist the impulse to take first advantage for a sail and brought out his boat before there was depth enough to float her. Soon, however, the rising tide lifted her clear and she dashed away in the strong breeze as if dancing with delight to be active once more. The yachts presented a charming picture as they glided gracefully along carrying their full suits of sails . . . Several boats were sailed but then rain began to fall accompanied by distant peals of thunder and further contests became impossible . . . This was very disappointing as considerable practice is necessary to make up for lost time if club members are to meet with the desired success at the meeting with the Hull team. In the heats which were raced there were some interesting results, most notably by a junior member with his boat *Scorpion*.

(*Scarborough Evening News*)

JULY 18TH

1954: Sonya Leydecker was born in Scarborough on this day. She was educated at the town's Convent of the Ladies of Mary before taking up a career in law. She currently holds the post of Global Head of Dispute Resolution at London law firm, Herbert Smith LLP, where she specialises in banking litigation, contentious regulatory work and professional negligence, primarily for accountants. Leydecker's wide-ranging remit has seen her acting on behalf of financial institutions and professional firms involved in domestic and international litigation, in particular those under investigation by bodies such as DTI inspectors, the Inland Revenue, the New York District Attorney and the US Department of Justice. The 164th edition of *Who's Who*, which was published in December 2011, for the first time included an eight line entry compiled by Ms Leydecker. (*Scarborough Evening News*)

———•◆•———

2012: On this day, Yorkshire Water announced that a floating barge was to begin testing work off Scarborough and Bridlington, to collect sediment and rock samples along the route of three storm overflow pipes. The project was part of a £110 million scheme along the area's coastline, and assurances were also given that the local beaches would remain open to the public during any investigative work. (*The Scarborough News*)

July 19th

1827: The sounds of church bells ringing and cannon fire marked the opening of Scarborough's Cliff Bridge today. During the previous year, a group of gentlemen from York and Scarborough had formed the Cliff Bridge Company with the aim of improving access to the Spa. A ninety-nine year lease on adjacent land, along with £4,500 raised from an issue of £10 shares, enabled work to get underway and the foundation stone was laid on November 29th 1826. By the time of opening, the overall cost had reached £9,089, but this did not affect the joyous procession that crossed the bridge. Workmen, gentry and shareholders were followed by the Royal Mail stagecoach, with a sailor balancing precariously on top. People using the bridge were charged *6d*, and during alterations in the 1880s toll houses were erected. A staged take-over of Spa properties by the Scarborough Corporation saw purchase of the bridge in 1951 and, with the abolition of tolls, the toll houses were demolished. (Scarborough and District Civic Society in Conjunction with Scarborough Borough Council, *The Scarborough Heritage Trail, Part 2: South Cliff and Spa, Crescent and Town Centre, North Bay*, 2nd Edition, 2009)

1861: 'The Town of Scarborough was thrown into a state of gloom and sorrow in consequence of the upsetting of a boat returning from Flamborough whereby the lives of ten gentlemen, all visitors, were lost.' (*Annals of Yorkshire, Vol. II* by John Mayhall, 1866)

JULY 20TH

1812: Fears of invasion by French forces during the Napoleonic era led to the establishment of both permanent and local militia forces in Scarborough. Members of the local militia spent a month each year learning how to march, manoeuvre and fire a musket, in case beacons gave warning of an imminent invasion. During midsummer, the Fifth North York Militia completed their twenty-eight days of training and on this day crowds gathered in Scarborough to watch a review by Lieutenant General Cheney. In spite of a heavy downpour, the ranks completed almost all of the designated manoeuvres before shouldering their muskets, and General Cheney announced that they had been trained well by Colonel Fothergill. Later in the day, officers were entertained to a 'very handsome dinner' at the Town Hall, in the company of nobility, officials and local gentlemen. The four weeks of training apparently caused no disruption to everyday life in Scarborough and there was not one complaint about the behaviour of the militia men. Town bailiffs reported that they were 'Peaceable, sober and soldier-like'. In the following summer, the annual training was completed by June 7th, and General Cheney informed the Duke of York that the local militia men had performed exceedingly well. (Prudence Bebb, *Life in Regency Scarborough*, William Sessions, 1997)

July 21st

1917: On this day, a 3,099 ton steamer, the *Trelyon*, became a wartime loss in the South Bay off Scarborough after the vessel was struck by a violent explosion. It had probably made contact with a mine some 3 miles north of the town, but remained afloat in spite of the huge blast and was taken in tow by local steamers. The decision was made to beach the *Trelyon* at White Nab, the most southerly point of Scarborough's South Bay, and for the next three months the stricken vessel remained there. During this time, large areas of the sea became covered with timber that had formed the *Trelyon*'s cargo from Archangel and local fishing boats spent periods of time gathering amounts of the wood and then landing them in the nearby Scarborough harbour.

On October 3rd 1917, tugs towed the wreck to the harbour mouth which caused great concern to the Harbour Commissioners. The *Trelyon* measured some 323ft in length and now posed a serious hazard to vessels entering and leaving the harbour, but it was some time before the Board of Trade organised a detailed salvage operation. It was almost five years before the wreck had been dismantled sufficiently to meet the requirements of the commissioners. (Arthur Godfrey and Peter J. Lassey, *Shipwrecks of the Yorkshire Coast*, Dalesman Publishing Co. Ltd, 1974)

JULY 22ND

1645: On this day, Sir Hugh Cholmley, commander of Royalist forces at Scarborough Castle, was forced to negotiate terms and honourably surrender the garrison. There was added significance as this date marked his forty-fifth birthday, and reports indicate that it was a thoroughly dispirited line of troops that left the castle, with many soldiers so weak that they had to be carried out in sheets or supported on either side by comrades. It is thought that women within the castle precincts had threatened to stone Cholmley unless he capitulated.

Sir Hugh and Lady Cholmley made good their escape by boat, as reported in *The Moderate Intelligencer* of July 23rd 1645:

> We heare likewise that Scarborough is also yeelded into our hands, Sir Hugh hath none other conditions for himself, but with his wife and children passe beyond seas. This is excellent good newes, and is a very terrible blow to the enemy.

Parliamentary supporters offered up prayers of thanksgiving, and the Cholmley family paid a high price as their 'great house' at Whitby was ransacked and other possessions confiscated. (Keith Snowden, *Scarborough Through the Ages: The Story of the Queen of English Watering Places*, Castleden Publications, 1995)

JULY 23RD

1990: Brunswick Shopping Centre was opened in the centre of Scarborough on this day. Included within the premises were thirty-one stores, and the overall design of the building, which included a bow front, was intended to blend with the period architecture around the town. (en.wikpedia.org/wiki)

———•◆•———

2010: A Gala concert was held at Scarborough's Open Air Theatre on this day. HM Queen Elizabeth II had reopened the venue in May as part of a £330 million regeneration programme for the resort. This grand occasion in the mid-summer season, which featured Jose Carreras and Dame Kiri Te Kanawa, marked a return to earlier decades at the setting, where the audience were seated on the shore of the lake and the stage was located on an island. First opened in 1932, the Open Air Theatre attracted large audiences including regular sell-out concerts by the Scarborough Operatic Society, with musicals such as *The King and I*, *Annie Get Your Gun* and *Hiawatha*. Musicals ended in 1968 after *West Side Story* (apart from a YMCA production in 1982) but for eleven years the Open Air Theatre staged television's *It's a Knockout* events. After becoming derelict from 1986, it was restored at a cost of £3.5 million. (www.scarborough.gov.uk)

JULY 24TH

1867: Scarborough's Grand Hotel was opened on this day, and its architect, Cuthbert Brodrick, described it as 'The largest and handsomest hotel in Europe'. It also represented Europe's largest brick building, with more than six million bricks, as well as some 40,000 cubic feet of stone used in its construction, and the total building costs passed £100,000. The magnificent exterior was matched by an interior of similar grandiose design, with a main hall set between two arms of the principal block which were surrounded by a series of tall, stately arches. Public areas were covered by 11.5 miles of carpet, and under the management of M. Augustus Fricour (formerly of the Hotel Mirabeau in Paris) communications were maintained by twenty-two speaking tubes that spread throughout the building, as well as nine more in Fricour's office. The opening of the hotel was celebrated by a banquet with around 200 invited guests, which was held in the Coffee Room, and upon departure each guest was presented with a beautifully illuminated copy of the menu. (Bryan Perrett, *Sense of Style: Being a Brief History of the Grand Hotel, Scarborough*, Burscough, B. Perrett, 1991)

———— ◆ ————

1914: Today, fourteen trains transported employees of Bass, Ratcliffe and Gretton Limited to Scarborough for their annual outing, where 225 coaches filled 2 miles of sidings. (Ed. Robin J. Lidster, *Yorkshire Coast Lines: A Historical Record of Railway Tourism on the Yorkshire Coast*, Hendon Publishing, 1983)

JULY 25TH

1885: Edward James Harland, a British shipbuilder born in Scarborough on May 15th 1831, was awarded a knighthood in this year, and on this day he received a baronetcy. After gaining an education at Edinburgh Academy, he served an apprenticeship at Robert Stephenson & Co. engineering works at Newcastle-on-Tyne and then moved to Glasgow where he became head draughtsman at J&G Thomson, marine engineers. In 1854, Edward Harland moved to Belfast and it was there that he formed the company of Harland and Wolff in 1861. (www.gracesguide.co.uk)

1904: Frederic Flint, homeopathic practitioner and staunch Congregationalist, died on this day, after living and working in Scarborough for the last thirty years of his life. Born at Canterbury in 1842, he took up a career in homeopathic medicine while based at Birmingham and after a brief period in Norwich, he moved to premises in Nicholas Parade at Scarborough during 1874. In the same year, he married May Bower, and all of their six daughters and three sons were born in Scarborough. In 1887, Dr Flint moved to premises in Vernon Place where he and another homeopathic practitioner, Dr Alfred Ross, built up a large practice. He was also a keen supporter of the missionary movement, as well as total abstinence. (Anne and Paul Bayliss, *Medical Profession in Scarborough 1700 to 1899: A Biographical Dictionary*, A.M. Bayliss, 2005)

July 26th

1928: Scarborough's new Valley Bridge was officially opened on this day by Mrs Wilfred Ashley, wife of the Minister of Transport. Other members of the civic party included the chairman of the committee responsible for the work, Sir Meredith T. Whitaker, and the Mayor of Scarborough, Alderman E.H. Mathews MBE. Reports indicate that the official party was preceded by a group of local schoolchildren performing the traditional Cornish Furry Dance, while the Minister of Transport and his wife followed behind at a rather more sedate pace. (Ed. Bryan Berryman, *Vintage Scarborough*, Hendon Publishing Co., 1976)

———— • ————

2012: A feature in the *Scarborough News* reported a fear, on the part of coastal experts, that the town's Esplanade and Spa Theatre could suffer the same fate as the Holbeck Hall Hotel (in early June 1993). Councillors are preparing a business case for a £16.6 million rock armour scheme in front of the Spa, after the project was approved some three months earlier. A ground investigation revealed high levels of water penetrating slopes above the Spa, which are causing mudslides and large cracks. (*The Scarborough News*)

July 27th

1925: On this day, a London and North Eastern Railway excursion handbill advertised a day trip from Darlington to Scarborough. It departed at 7.00 a.m. and returned from Scarborough at 8.10 p.m., with stops at more than a dozen stations on the route. Price for a return ticket from Darlington to Scarborough was 8s 11d (45p). (Ed. Robin J. Lidster, *Yorkshire Coast Lines: A Historical Record of Railway Tourism on the Yorkshire Coast*, Hendon Publishing, 1983)

———◆———

1964: The final passenger train from Helmsley was a day excursion to Scarborough on this day. Passenger services in this part of North Yorkshire had been in decline for some time before the Second World War brought an increase in both passengers and goods traffic. Further reductions in the post-war era meant that the only passenger trains after 1953 were special excursions, which ended on May 3rd 1964 with a 'Special Rambler's Daffodil and Primrose Diesel Excursion'. During the early 1960s other special trains ran from the area, unusually from Helmsley, taking Sunday school outings to Scarborough on a regular basis, but also much further afield to London, Largs and King's Lynn. Following closure of the Thirsk and Malton line on August 10th 1964, track lifting started at Kirbymoorside in March of the following year. (www.disused-stations.org.uk)

JULY 28TH

1903: Scarborough Town Hall was officially opened on this day, by Princess Henry of Battenberg. The Princess also unveiled a statue of Queen Victoria in the adjacent garden and a Roll of Honour, which was inscribed with details of Scarborough Volunteers who served in the South African War. The building was probably completed during 1846-47 and it was home for John Woodall and his family, who was succeeded by his son, John W. Woodall, in 1879. He offered the house and adjacent gardens to the Corporation in 1898 and at a meeting on April 5th of that year, the decision was made to buy the property. Mr John Woodall, who was a partner in the banking firm of Woodall and Woodall, was also a member of Scarborough Council from 1863 to 1889 and four times Mayor of the borough. His favourite hobby was cabinet making and some of his beautifully crafted woodwork can be seen in St Nicholas House. The Corporation paid £33,000 for purchase of the building and grounds and the cost of conversion to a Town Hall amounted to £18,555. This involved extending the east end to provide a Council Chamber, Robing Room, Mayor's Parlour and one Committee Room. (S. Foord, *Scarborough Records*)

JULY 29TH

1963: At least eight Glaswegian visitors left Scarborough on the previous Saturday night thinking that local police were wonderful. According to a press report of this day, the visitors were stranded in the seaside town when they missed their coach; however, the local constabulary were able to arrange a 'lift' in another coach to Edinburgh. The Scottish group had gone to William Street car park at 9.30 p.m. to catch their coach but found it had left twelve hours earlier. They had misread their tickets, which said 9.30 a.m., and as soon as they discovered their mistake they went to the police station to explain their predicament. Quite a few coaches were still in the car park, but they were all the wrong company and all going to Edinburgh. A policeman went to William Street and persuaded a coach driver to transport the eight stranded Scots back over the border. (*Scarborough Evening News*)

———— • ◆ • ————

1975: A destructive fire on this day burned down the Olympia building on Scarborough's Foreshore Road. For eighty years the building echoed the changing trends in seaside entertainment – after its opening as a 'Fisheries Exhibition' on May 31st 1895, it housed a roller skating rink, cinema, military billet, ballroom and amusement arcade. (Ed. Bryan Berryman, *Vintage Scarborough*, Hendon Publishing Co., 1976)

July 30th

1252: A Patent Roll with this date, and in the thirty-sixth year of the reign of Henry III, granted certain duties for the benefit of Scardeburgh (Scarborough) to construct a port using timber and stone. It read:

The King to his Bailiffs and Burgesses, and other good men of Scardeburgh, greeting. Whereas we have understood by an inquisition, which we commanded to be made by our Sheriff of Yorkshire, that it is for the benefit of our town of Scardeburgh, to make a certain new port with timber and stone toward the sea, whereby all ships arriving there, may enter, and sail without danger, as well at the beginning of flood, as high water. We have granted you in aid of making the said port, that from the day of the Assumption of the Blessed Mary, in the thirty sixth year of our reign, to the end of five years next following, ye may take in the said port of every merchant's ship coming hither sixpence, every time it arrives with merchandise; of every fisherman's ship there coming with fish, fourpence; and of every fisherman's boat there coming with fish, twopence. And we will that ye take the aid custom as is aforesaid. But the said term of five years being completed, the said custom is wholly to cease and determine.

(books.google.co.uk)

JULY 31ST

1312: On this day, Henry Lord Percy's custody of Scarborough Castle was formally ended by an order from King Edward II for his arrest. Some six months earlier, the King had handed custody of this important coastal stronghold to William le Latimer, but Percy refused to surrender it. In April, Edward II passed custody to Piers Gaveston, but he was immediately besieged there by the forces of Henry Lord Percy and the Earls of Pembroke and Warenne. Shortage of provisions forced him to surrender within a fortnight before he gave himself up with promises of safe conduct. As he was being escorted back to the South of England, Gaveston was seized by the Earl of Warwick and beheaded. It was his involvement in this violent series of events that led to the order against Lord Percy. (www.british-history.ac.uk)

———— • ◆ • ————

1963: It was announced on this day that a new laundry, costing £60,000, would soon be brought into service for hospitals in the Scarborough, Bridlington and Malton area. It had been built in the grounds of St Mary's Hospital, Scarborough, and twenty-eight staff would be based there under the manager, Mr Robert Wrigley. (*Scarborough Evening News*)

AUGUST 1ST

1881: The Central Tramway Company Scarborough Limited began to operate the cliff railway on this day. Built by George Wood of Hull, it was unique in using steam-powered winding instead of the water-balanced hydraulics used by other funiculars. As drivers had no view of the cars, they made use of marks on the rope to indicate the car positions. In 1910 the tramway was converted to electric drive. The line extends to 254ft and was originally built on a concrete, cast-iron and wrought-iron viaduct at a total cost of £10,358. In 1932, the railway was overhauled with the installation of a new electric motor and re-laid track and a further round of refurbishment, at a cost of £90,000, was marked by the unveiling of the town's 50th heritage plaque on July 13th 2012. (transportheritage.com)

1969: Paul Tonkinson, radio presenter and television personality, was born in Scarborough on this day. After attending Scalby School, his early media work included contributions to a range of Radio 4 comedy programmes, including *Loose Ends* and *Weekending*, as well as *The Paul Tonkinson Show* on *London Live*. Television credits include *The Stand Up Show* and *Michael McIntyre's Comedy Roadshow* for BBC, and Channel 4's *Big Breakfast*. (en.wikipedia.org)

AUGUST 2ND

1922: An article published on this day in the *Scarborough Mercury* by S.F. Yeoman read:

> Speaking of 'tall' scores and big drives, the best drive I ever witnessed on the cricket ground at Scarborough was one by Wells-Cole, which went clean over the chimney pots of houses in Trafalgar Square. I also witnessed C.I. Thornton in 1896 when he made no fewer than eight drives out of the ground, most off A.G. Steel. One of them soared clean over the Trafalgar Square houses.

(*Scarborough Mercury*)

———◆·———

1942: Lieutenant Colonel Sir Frank Brook took the salute for a march of Scarborough's Special Constabulary today, that took place on the town's cricket field at North Marine Road. During the Second World War, the number of Specials was kept at 302 members and they were trained in anti-gas measures, first aid and dealing with high explosive bombs and incendiaries. (Richard James Percy, *Scarborough in the 1930s and 40s*, Hendon Publishing Co. Ltd, 1990)

AUGUST 3RD

1944: Harry W. Smith, Scarborough's Borough Engineer from 1897 to 1933, died at the age of seventy-seven on this day. During more than three decades as head of this department, he was instrumental in creating several of the town's impressive collection of parks and gardens, as well as overseeing construction of the Marine Drive. Early schemes to lay out bowling greens and tennis courts in Alexandra Gardens were followed by work on the Peasholm area during 1908, which saw the creation of a willow pattern plate scene with a boathouse, café, bridge and floating bandstand on a man-made lake. An official opening followed in July 1912, and during the 1920s a rustic walk was added through a valley planted with a range of trees and flowering shrubs. Further features in Peasholm Park included a waterfall and oriental-style pagoda.

On his retirement in 1933, Harry Smith explained that he had extended the coverage of public pleasure gardens in the town from 55 acres to around 350 acres, and had spent in the region of £1 million of ratepayers' money. On December 21st 2006, a plaque was unveiled at his former residence, no. 41 Westbourne Grove, to celebrate his service to the town. (Scarborough and District Civic Society in Conjunction with Scarborough Borough Council, *The Scarborough Heritage Trail, Part 2: South Cliff and Spa, Crescent and Town Centre, North Bay,* 2nd Edition, 2009)

August 4th

1648: This date marked the beginning of a final siege of Scarborough Castle during the English Civil War. By this time, however, Royalist forces defending the ruined clifftop fortress were exhausted and further weakened by sickness and a shortage of rations. Worsening weather conditions added to defenders' difficulties and the castle was back under parliamentary control by December 19th of the same year. An order of parliament in July 1649 ordered the castle's demolition, but following its reprieve it was used as a prison for opponents of parliamentary forces. (*Scarborough Castle: An Illustrated Guide, With a Short History of the Castle from Earliest Times*, Ministry of Works, 1960)

———— ◆ ————

1908: On this day, John Allan Richardson was born. During his career, which spanned thirty-two years, in Scarborough Cricket Club's first XI, he built a reputation as one of Yorkshire's most accomplished amateur players. His working life as a farmer and auctioneer restricted his appearances for Yorkshire County Cricket Club to just seven matches between 1936 and 1947, but this tall, powerfully built batsman contributed enormously to the success of Scarborough CC. He scored six consecutive centuries in 1938 and captained the club for twenty-four years, up to 1959. He died in Scarborough in April 1985. (en. wikipedia.org)

AUGUST 5TH

1718: A Scarborough-based collier under the command of Captain Allotson Bell left Newcastle on this day, during a period when ownership of this type of vessel was heavily concentrated in Whitby and Scarborough. Captain Bell owned property in Scarborough's East Sandgate and his family had become wealthy through the town's maritime trade. (www.scarboroughsmaritimeheritage.org.uk)

◆

1933: The Scarborough Aviation Display took place on this day, at Ganton Aerodrome on the south-west side of the town. Private aircraft arrived from many parts of the country to participate in a range of competitions, and official guests included the Mayor and Mayoress of Scarborough, the Lord Mayor of Hull and Mayors of Middlesbrough and Wakefield, as well as Kathleen, Countess of Drogheda, who opened the display. Scarborough's Rose Queen was the focus of much attention, and there was considerable interest in the Cierva Autogiro, the so-called 'windmill machine', which rose into the sky and then hovered at 2,000ft. (Richard James Percy, *Scarborough in the 1930s and 40s*, Hendon Publishing Co. Ltd, 1990)

AUGUST 6TH

1874: Frederick Dade was born on this day at Crescent Villa, Scarborough, into a family with strong artistic links. His parents had recently moved to the seaside town where his father, also named Fred, had joined the photographic and portrait company of Oliver Francois Xavier Sarony. Tragically, his father died shortly before Frederick was born, and so Sarony organised a public appeal to assist his widowed mother, who now had seven children to bring up alone. Almost £100 was raised through the appeal and this eventually helped Frederick and his older brother to pursue artistic careers.

At the age of sixteen, both Frederick and his brother were living with their mother at no. 30 West Bank, and the census of 1891 lists him as an 'art student'. His career followed a similar course as many other contemporaries, with tuition under Albert Strange, head of the Scarborough School of Art, and he was named among the school's prize-winners in 1891 and 1892. A number of Frederick's coastal scenes, including *Moored Sailing Boats*, are exhibited along with others by his brother, Ernest, in London's National Maritime Museum. Several of these young artists were founder members of the Scarborough Sailing Club, which was later renamed Scarborough Yacht Club. (Anne and Paul Bayliss, *Scarborough Artists of the Nineteenth Century, A Biographical Dictionary*, Anne Bayliss, 1997)

AUGUST 7TH

1879: The Scarborough Cliff Bridge Company marked the opening of their Grand Hall on this day, with a performance of Haydn's Grand Oratorio, *The Creation*, for which Miss Anna Williams, Mr Edward Lloyd and Mr Bridson had been specially engaged. The conductor was Herr W. Meyer Lutz and the concert also featured the band and chorus of the Scarborough Choral and Orchestral Union. Architects for the building were Verity & Hunt of no. 27 Regent Street, London, and Verity came with an esteemed reputation for having played a part in designing the Albert Hall and the Victoria and Albert Museum, along with press reports of a 'high position as an architect in the Italian style'. Central to Verity & Hunts's Grand Hall was a 'well' on the ground floor, which accommodated the seated audience at a level some 3ft lower than the rest of the floor area. Beyond the 'well' was an area allocated, along with the balcony, to the popular Victorian activity of promenading. Space was also available for an organ but this was ruled out on grounds of cost. A formal opening ceremony was delayed until all the building work was complete in the following summer. (Meredith Whittaker, *The Book of Scarborough Spaw*, Barracuda, 1984)

AUGUST 8TH

1768: During the early evening of this day, three excise officers intercepted a farm wagon on the turnpike road between Scarborough and Malton-at-Ayton. The two men in charge of the cart resisted attempts by the officers to carry out a search, and drew pistols as a struggle broke out. One of the excise officers was fatally injured by a gunshot, and although the two smugglers escaped from the scene the other two officers recognised them. They were named as Joseph Haines, a shopkeeper from Hackness who fired the fatal shot, and his accomplice Valentine Bailey from Broxa.

A search of the wagon uncovered 30 half-ankers of Geneva, 240lb of tea and a small amount of coffee; the Excise Board offered an immediate £100 reward for information leading to the arrest and conviction of the two men. Both were brought to justice and Haines was soon convicted of the murder of the excise officer, John Smith. He was executed at York before the end of the year, while Bailey was imprisoned in the city's jail. Seven years later he petitioned for release as his family were suffering 'Dearly for his folly as they are now kept at the goodness of the parish'. (*Smuggling in Yorkshire 1700-1850* by Graham Smith)

AUGUST 9TH

1964: On this day, the Beatles made a second visit to Scarborough, performing at the town's Futurist Theatre (following an earlier appearance on December 11th 1963). During the day, a crowd of about 2,000 fans gathered outside the venue, but police officers kept traffic moving along the Foreshore. Some holidaymakers on the nearby beach joined the growing throng outside, a number of them left to find a quieter place, but some remained unconcerned in their deckchairs or continued paddling in the sea and riding donkeys.

As the 'Fab Four' arrived at the theatre, forty police officers caused a distraction at the front of the building and allowed the group's black limousine to draw up undetected in a side alley, beside the stage door. The car door next to the theatre would not open and it was left to John Lennon to open the opposite door, before scrambling over the bonnet and into the building. It was such a quiet entry that they had to appear briefly at a window before fans would accept that they were inside. Surprise visitors to the show were Bessie Braddock MP, who paid a backstage visit to wish her fellow Liverpuddlians good luck, and eight-year-old Kevin Monkman, who was allowed to watch from the stalls. (www.yorkshirecoastradio.com)

AUGUST 10TH

1914: A DFW Arrow 154 aircraft was taking part in the *Daily Mail* Circuit of Britain Race when a technical problem forced it to make an emergency landing on the Scarborough racecourse. The biplane had left the Southampton area at 6 a.m. and passed Ramsgate and Yarmouth, en route for Aberdeen. Upon landing at Scarborough, the pilot was initially arrested, as it was thought that the aircraft was German. However, it was soon realised that it had been requisitioned by the UK government and he was released from the army barracks on Burniston Road. After minor repairs, the aircraft rejoined the race and finished in second place. (www.yorkshire-aircraft.co.uk)

1943: Scarborough railway station was the scene of a serious accident today, involving two trains at Platform 5. The late-running 9.05 express from Hull was wrongly routed by the signalman and collided with the 11.18 stopping train, which was about to depart. Four passengers in the first coach of the stopping train – all soldiers – were killed, while eight others received serious injuries and another twenty-two suffered minor injuries. Nobody on the express train was fatally injured. (en.wikipedia.org/wiki)

2011: On this day, it was announced that Scarborough Sub Aqua Club had won the prestigious Heinke Trophy award, for having done the most to further interests of its members and the British Sub Aqua Club (BSAC). (www.bsac.com)

AUGUST 11TH

1688: A most curious incident took place in a Scarborough church today. The town's mayor, Thomas Aislabie, left his pew and, with stick in hand, marched up the aisle before seizing the clergyman, Mr Noel Boteler. He then caned the bewildered minister as he stood at his reading desk. The cause of this incredible assault was Mr Boteler's deliberate failure to read out a declaration from the King, on the question of liberty of conscience. He saw this order as a means of furthering the spread of Roman Catholicism at the expense of Protestantism. Mr Boteler soon won support for his action, most notably from a Captain Ouseley, who requested that the Mayor meet him to explain his unacceptable conduct. When there was no reply from the Mayor, Captain Ouseley enforced his demand with a group of musketeers, who unceremoniously tossed Mayor Aislabie in a blanket so that he was left 'revolving and bumping, rising and falling', held by the soldiers 'as though he were no weight at all'. This public degradation prompted the Mayor to head for London and the Royal Court, but Captain Ouseley had already made representation to plead for the King's gracious pardon and the matter was dismissed. (www. gutenberg.org)

August 12th

1822: On this day, His Majesty King George IV approached Scarborough on his journey northwards to Edinburgh, and the castle battery fired a royal salute. By the late seventeenth century, the castle garrison had been reduced and defences were in a state of disrepair until the mid-1700s, when the Jacobite rebellion prompted construction of a barrack block. A few years earlier, a small building had been purpose-built as accommodation for the master gunner serving the castle batteries. (John A. Goodall, *Scarborough Castle, North Yorkshire*, English Heritage, 2000)

———◆———

1872: Today saw the charity of William Benjamin Fowler approved at York and administered by the municipal charities' trustees, for the benefit of poor women in the parish of Scarborough. The trust consisted of £3,587 8s 10d, with the official trustees producing a yearly income of £89 13s 8d, which in 1906 was distributed monthly in alms to widows and spinsters, in sums of 3s to each recipient and about £30 in coal to the deserving poor. (www.british-history.ac.uk)

———◆———

1880: Royal assent was granted to the Scarborough and Whitby Railway today, to revive the powers of the 1871 and 1873 Acts and to extend deadlines relating to the purchase of land and completion of the railway. (*The Scarborough and Whitby Railway* by J. Robin Lidster)

AUGUST 13TH

1857: The Scarborough district was badly affected by flooding, which destroyed many buildings and caused considerable damage to St Mary's Churchyard in the town. A few miles to the east, a house in the grounds of Hackness Grange, which was occupied by William Smith, land steward to Sir John Johnson, was also destroyed. (www.scarborough.co.uk)

———◆———

1896: A menu published for meals at Scarborough's Crown Hotel on this day provides a fascinating insight into the range and quality of food available at this establishment in the late Victorian era. Breakfast offered fish dishes such as bloaters, kippers, fried whiting, dried haddock or salmon cutlets, which featured along with sausage and bacon, grilled ham, kidneys or lamb cutlets and, of course, eggs, which could be served boiled, fried, poached or scrambled. Then there was an assortment of cold meats such as chicken, ham, tongue and roast beef. Luncheon courses included a selection of potages, poisson, entrees, roti and entrements and there was a similarly impressive array of options for dinner. Following its opening on June 1st 1845, the Crown Hotel had set out to draw custom from the ranks of nobility and gentry, with lists of guests published in local newspapers. (*The Crown Hotel: 150 Years of Hospitality*)

AUGUST 14TH

1848: An anonymous visitor to Scarborough wrote in his diary for this day:

> This place was very full for there were four special trains from various parts on the same day – a most foolish thing. The railway brought in at least 3,500 people . . . and . . . Went in a fly to the station where the scene baffles all attempts at description – the confusion was altogether unnecessary but there was no attempt at forethought on the part of the railway officials – Mary and Emma tumbled down in the rush and scramble and Mary hurt herself a good deal. We went and returned in 2nd class carriage ... Upon the whole the journey was very well performed and clear of any accident – and all, I think, were well satisfied. The train must have paid the railway company well. If I should ever travel by a special train I will learn to go at the time named for starting – not before. The crushing is over and you are certain to be in time.

(Janice Anderson and Edmund Swinglehurst, *The Victorian and Edwardian Seaside*, Bounty, 2005)

———◆———

1900: Scarborough's Cliff Gardens opened to the public today, with design work carried out by the town's borough engineer and surveyor, Harry W. Smith. (Scarborough and District Civic Society in Conjunction with Scarborough Borough Council, *The Scarborough Heritage Trail, Part 1, The Old Town*, 2nd Edition, 2004)

AUGUST 15TH

1181: On this day, an annual Gablage Tax was levied on Scarborough households, with the amount based on the alignment of the property. People living in houses with a gable facing the street paid 4*d*, whilst those with house fronts facing the street had to pay 6*d*. (Ed. Julia Skinner, *Scarborough: A Miscellany (Did you Know?)*, Francis Frith Collection, 2006)

———•◆•———

1253: A royal charter allowed a trading festival at Scarborough, which started on this day (Assumption Day) and lasted until September 29th (Michaelmas Day). It was centred on the sands, but spread into the narrow streets and alehouses of the old township and attracted merchants from all parts of Europe, the Baltic region and the Ottoman Empire. Noise and colour was added by minstrels, fortune tellers, quack doctors and dentists during the six weeks of the fair. It flourished for more than 500 years before festivities were held for the last time in 1778, but in recent years it has been celebrated in the ballad 'Scarborough Fair' by Simon and Garfunkel. (Ed. Julia Skinner, *Scarborough: A Miscellany (Did you Know?)*, Francis Frith Collection, 2006)

———•◆•———

1945: VJ Day was celebrated in Scarborough today, amid rainy conditions that did not prevent street parties taking place. Bands provided musical accompaniment around the town, with the Royal Signals Band taking pride of place in the garden outside the Grand Hotel. Signal flares were lit, bonfires blazed brightly and at 9.30 p.m. Scarborough's Mayor ignited the ancient beacon on the castle walls. (www.mistoftime.co.uk)

AUGUST 16TH

1825: By her will, on this date, Mrs Eleanor Cockerill bequeathed her residuary estate to trustees upon trust to invest the same and pay the income to the vicar and churchwardens, for distribution every Christmas amongst poor widows residing in Scarborough. The total residue was invested in £1,684 4s 2d Reduced Stock, now New Consols (consolidated annuities) producing £42 2s a year, which in 1906 was distributed to 359 poor widows, in sums varying from 1s to 4s 6d, with the amount decided upon according to age. The stock is standing in the bank books in the names of the persons appointed for the purpose by the Charity Commissioners in 1867. (www.british-history.ac.uk)

* * *

1839: The opening of Henry Wyatt's Gothic Saloon at Scarborough's Spa was celebrated today, by a public breakfast attended by 'most of the fashionable visitors to the town and many of the respectable inhabitants'. Following the discovery of a natural spring by Elizabeth Farrow in 1626, visitors had been drawn to the Spa for its supposed healing properties. Wyatt's new saloon was located on a rock and concrete platform overlooking a new Spa promenade, above the spa wells, and the ceremonial breakfast was followed by dancing and fireworks. (www.mick-armitage.staff.shef.ac.uk)

AUGUST 17TH

1883: The enlarged premises of the Scarborough Dispensary were officially reopened by William Barry, Mayor of Scarborough and President of the Dispensary on this day. Local architect John Petch had added another storey to the Elders Street premises, at a cost of £450. This included a male and female ward, which increased accommodation from five to fifteen beds. A lift enabled patients to be transferred directly to the wards without being removed from stretchers, and improved accommodation for the housekeeper and nurse had also been incorporated.

Official proceedings got underway on August 17th at St Mary's parish church, where the Archbishop of York, William Thompson, preached a sermon before dignitaries. Guests then moved to Elders Street for a service of dedication in the male ward. (Anne and Paul Bayliss, *Scarborough Hospital and Dispensary: The First Fifty Years, 1852-1902*, Anne Bayliss, 2006)

———◆———

1942: On this day, wartime contingencies saw the introduction of dried egg, supplied in either a red and silver tin or waxed carton stamped with an image of the lend lease eagle. Both containers were said to hold the equivalent of twelve pure eggs at a cost of 1s 9d and the mixture had a life of about two months. After adding water – the process of reconstitution – it had to be used immediately. (Richard James Percy, *Scarborough's War Years, 1939-45*, Sutton Publishing Ltd, 1992)

AUGUST 18TH

1941: On this day, Scarborough's fire-fighting services were absorbed, along with other fire brigades, into the National Fire Service. Local officers had tackled serious fires on a number of occasions, including a blaze that completely gutted the Spa Grand Hall in 1876, a twenty-four-hour episode dealing with a fire at Hackness Hall in 1910, and an inferno that caused £70,000 of damage in the Queen Street/Market Street area during February 1915, but wartime air raids had placed increasingly serious demands on local resources. During March 18th and 19th 1941, Scarborough's fire service was put under enormous pressure and reinforcements were summoned from Middlesbrough and Northallerton. (S. Foord, *Scarborough Records*)

———— ◆ ————

1953: James William Booth died at Scalby today, after spending more than fifty years on the east coast. He was born in Manchester in 1867 and studied at the city's art school, before being elected a member of the Manchester Academy of Fine Arts and the Royal Cambrian Academy of Art. After moving to Yorkshire, Booth was an active member of the Staithes Group, and many of his landscapes, seascapes and portraits were exhibited at the Royal Academy between 1896 and 1935. (Anne and Paul Bayliss, *Scarborough Artists of the Nineteenth Century, A Biographical Dictionary*, Anne Bayliss, 1997)

AUGUST 19TH

1768: News of the violence involving smugglers in the Scarborough area some ten days earlier was reported in the *London Gazette* on this day:

> Whereas it has been humbly represented to the king, that His Majesty's Commissioners of Excise have, by letters from their officers at Scarborough dated the 9th of August, received an account of a murder, having been committed on John Smith, late officer of excise, who together with other officers, had seized a quantity of run goods . . . His Majesty, for the better discovering and bringing to justice the persons concerned in the said murder, is hereby pleased to promise His most gracious pardon to any one of them (except the person who actually committed the said murder) who shall discover his accomplice or accomplices in the same murder, so that he or they may be apprehended and convicted thereof.

(*London Gazette*)

———— • ◆ • ————

1940: During the hours of darkness on this day, enemy aircraft were active in skies over Scarborough for several hours, and for the first time, yellow-coloured parachute flares were used to illuminate possible targets. Sixteen high explosive bombs were dropped at Scalby, while other bombs fell into the sea and some fifty incendiaries burnt in fields. (Richard James Percy, *Scarborough's War Years, 1939-45*, Sutton Publishing Ltd, 1992)

AUGUST 20TH

1820: A smuggling run was intercepted by Revenue officers during the hours of darkness on this day, at a time when Scarborough was attracting visitors for its 'Spaw' waters and shoreline bathing machines. While a lugger from Flushing dropped anchor off the town, a small boat pulled alongside to unload 4½ gallon half-ankers of gin in kegs and row them ashore.

The Revenue officers were almost certainly acting on detail supplied by an informer, as they emerged from hiding to seize the contraband goods. After hiring a cart they moved the kegs to the king's warehouse for safe keeping, but the local smugglers made their escape into the darkness. (*Smuggling on the Yorkshire Coast* by J. Dykes)

1880: This day marked the second day of a cricket match (played over three days) between an eighteen man Scarborough and District team and the Australian tourists. Both sides included notable cricketers, with the overseas stars including 'The Demon' F.R. Spofforth in their ranks. Controversy surrounded events on the pitch, with the Australians accusing Helmsley-based Joseph Frank of 'throwing'. The Scarborough side won the two-innings-a-side match by 90 runs as one of the tourists, Bonner, acknowledged Frank as the best bowler they had faced in Yorkshire. (Ian Hall & John Found, *Cricket at Scarborough: A Social History of the Club and Its Festival*, Breedon Books Publishing Co. Ltd, 1992)

August 21st

1887: James Paul Moody, Sixth Officer RMS *Titanic*, was born in Scarborough on this day. At the age of fourteen, he took up a seagoing career at Birkenhead on HMS *Conway* nautical training ship and then studied at London's King Edward VII Nautical School. He sailed on RMS *Titanic* on April 10th 1912 and was on watch with other officers when the ship struck an iceberg at 11.40 p.m. on April 14th. After helping to launch the lifeboats, James Moody was last seen jumping into the sea from the deck and became the only junior officer of the ship to die in the disaster. There is a marble plaque to his memory in the Church of St Martin-on-the-Hill and a brass plaque was unveiled by his niece at Scarborough lifeboat house in April 2002. (en.wikipedia.org/wiki)

———◆———

1917: The merchant vessel *Norhilda* (1175 gross tonnage) was torpedoed on this day, about 5 miles south-east of Scarborough, resulting in the loss of one life. Built in 1910 by Swan Hunter, it was owned by C. Tennant and Co. Ltd. (Arthur Godfrey and Peter J. Lassey, *Shipwrecks of the Yorkshire Coast*, Dalesman Publishing Co. Ltd, 1974)

AUGUST 22ND

1772: On this day, George Wheelhouse was born in Scarborough. He was baptised in the town, but there is little information about the next forty years of his life until mention, in 1814, of his occupation in Deptford. In the census of 1851, now aged seventy-eight, he was described as a distiller with a residence at Deptford Bridge and a household including James Leask, named as a distiller's clerk, and house servant, Maria Wells. Ten years later the census described Wheelhouse as a retired distiller. On August 12th 1863, at the age of ninety, he made a new will. With no close family members, he made numerous charitable bequests, as well as leaving a codicil (supplement to the will) with four figure amounts to each of his nominated executors and discretion over allocation of the residue of the estate. Beneficiaries included several hospitals in the London area, the British and Foreign Bible Society and the poor of the parish of Deptford, but there was also the sum of £250 for a lifeboat for Bridlington, £200 for the Scarborough Dispensary and 'The sum of £250 to be expended by my trustees in erecting forty-three dwellings for the poor of Scarborough and in paying the sum of £1 10s annually to the occupiers of such dwellings'. (deptfordmisc.blogspot.co.uk)

August 23rd

1872: Scarborough's Christ Church was consecrated on this day, by the Archbishop of York. Early English in style, the building costs amounted to about £8,000 and the exterior was faced with beautiful freestone provided by Sir John V.B. Johnstone, from the Hackness quarry. The whole building was renovated in 1874, when the east end was reconstructed and memorial windows were inserted. (*Ed. T.F. Bulmer, History, Topography, and Directory* of North Yorkshire, T. Bulmer & Co., 1890)

———•◆•———

1942: On this day, a large crowd assembled to watch a parade by members of the National Fire Service, which was held to mark the anniversary of the nationalisation of the Fire Service. More than 200 full-time and part-time firemen and women represented Scarborough Urban and Rural districts in the parade. (Richard James Percy, *Scarborough's War Years, 1939-45*, Sutton Publishing Ltd, 1992)

———•◆•———

2011: A group of Scarborough divers were celebrating on this day, after setting a unique world record. Led by Heath Samples, dive leader from the Scarborough branch of the British Sub Aqua Club, the four man squad had completed a Channel crossing in one hour relays using sea scooters, which managed speeds of up to 2 knots against powerful tides. Apart from earning a place in the Guinness World Record Book, the team also raised funds for Help For Heroes and Scarborough RNLI. (*Scarborough Evening News*)

AUGUST 24TH

1924: Thomas McCraith Foley, medical practitioner and local politician, died on this day. He was given a full military funeral in Scarborough, during which his coffin was carried on a gun carriage and the 'Last Post' was performed on a cornet alongside his grave. Born and brought up in Ireland, where he qualified in medicine, Foley then served as a surgeon on ships crossing the Atlantic between Britain and America, and even on the Sultan of Morocco's yacht, the *Alhassannee*. After settling in Scarborough during the 1880s, Dr Foley was based as a general practitioner in Queen Street and he also served as medical officer to the Scarborough Sanatorium and the King's Cliff Hospital for eye and ear diseases.

His involvement with local politics led to him representing the East Ward on Scarborough Council between 1907 and 1912, and in 1921 Dr Foley was elected as the ex-servicemen's candidate to represent the North Ward. Medical work with the armed forces saw him hold the post of Surgeon-Captain and then Surgeon-Major to the First East Riding of Yorks. Volunteer Artillery and with the outbreak of war in 1914 he served in the Army Medical Reserve. (Anne and Paul Bayliss, *Medical Profession in Scarborough 1700 to 1899: A Biographical Dictionary*, A.M. Bayliss, 2005)

August 25th

1930: Scarborough's North Cliff Lift began operations on this day. The new lift had an operating speed of 200ft per minute, with steel ropes driven by a 47 HP electric motor through worm gear to a shaft carrying an 8ft diameter rope wheel. Cars were identical to those operating on the St Nicholas lift, with the same green and cream livery, and total cost amounted to £8,283. From 1945, Scarborough had two municipally-operated cliff lifts and two in private ownership. (*Scarborough Public Library Factfile: Cliff Lifts*)

1956: Early on this day, the calm atmosphere at Filey Camp station was shattered when a train of ten coaches smashed into buffers at the end of platform 3. The locomotive had come from Hull and was linked to the coaches at Bridlington, but the fireman had neglected to attach the brake pipe to the locomotive, meaning that there was no continuous brake on the train. The first part of the journey from Bridlington was a climb to Hunmanby, but soon after this stretch the fireman realised his error and applied the hand brake while blowing the whistle to attract attention. Driver and fireman then leapt clear of the train before it hit the buffers at 25mph. There were no injuries and the station remained open. (www.yorkshirecoastline.co.uk)

AUGUST 26TH

1878: St George's Music Hall opened on this day, with William Morgan as proprietor. The building had previously seen brief periods of use as a theatre, and Morgan used his earlier experience as a theatre manager in Bradford to rejuvenate the seaside venue. When audiences did not reach anticipated levels he reduced prices to 1s 6d and 3d whilst still staging top-class shows, but Morgan was soon to move on. In 1879, he took over management of the Winter Gardens at Morecambe, before returning to take up permanent residence in Scarborough, when he and two friends bought the town's aquarium in May 1886. He was the town's mayor from 1902 to 1905.

There were unscheduled dramatic scenes at St George's Hall in 1881, when fighting broke out among Salvationists. Early in the year they had begun to hold meetings at the hall, and a local fisherman, named Mansfield, became such a staunch supporter of the Salvation Army that he was sent to Rotherham to take charge of a unit. However, it seems that Mansfield's standards soon lapsed and reports of his inappropriate lifestyle were relayed back to a meeting at St George's Hall. When the accused individual arrived at the building, mayhem broke out among Salvationists and it took truncheon-wielding police to restore order. (*Scarborough Library Fact File*)

August 27th

1896: This day saw a dramatic climax to a prolonged dispute between Cornish and Lowestoft fishermen, towards the end of the herring season. Trouble over the question of Sunday fishing had already spread through a number of other ports until Lowestoft men determined to settle the argument when herring fleets arrived at Scarborough. Hearing of the threat of violence, the Chief Officer of Coastguards summoned help from the Admiralty and two warships, HMS *Hearty* and HMS *Starling*, reached the port with an offer to send marines ashore to help civil authorities maintain law and order.

Scarborough's mayor declined the offer, but the naval vessels remained offshore as the Chief Constable made plans to deal with any disturbances. A large reserve force was based at the police station, and late on Saturday, August 26th a considerable number of Lowestoft men came ashore while the Cornishmen stayed on-board their boats. The situation remained calm for some time, but as a crowd of several hundred people gathered to hear speeches on the subject of Sunday fishing, a Lowestoft fisherman, named Martin, began a disturbance. At this point, the Chief Constable gave his officers orders to clear the street and disperse the crowd. (S. Foord, *Scarborough Records*)

AUGUST 28TH

1947: Local newspapers carried reports and photographs of tunny fish that had been landed that day at Scarborough. For around two decades, between the early 1930s and '50s, the town and Yorkshire coastline became an aristocratic playground, with wealthy visitors spending weeks hunting the fish that is also known as the bluefin tuna. The first tunny was caught off Scarborough in 1929 by steam drifter, the *Ascendant*, and an early visitor to the area was a big game hunter, Major Rowley. He lived on his boat during the summer months of 1931 and enjoyed the sport immensely, but failed to land a big fish. By 1934, news of catches of tunny at Scarborough was attracting rich and famous customers, and local fishermen enjoyed a useful sideline in taking visitors out on trips. During 1934, Baron Henri de Rothschild arrived in his 1,000-ton yacht, the *Eros*, and along with several well-known military officers there was a Greek prince who chartered a drifter for the summer season. It seems that the tunny fish were attracted to areas of the North Sea by large herring shoals, but when numbers of herring declined their main source of food was lost. (*Scarborough Evening News*)

AUGUST 29TH

1869: This was the third and final day of a highly unusual cricket match at Scarborough's Castle Hill Yard, between the town's cricket club and a team of Australian Aborigines. A report in the *Scarborough Post* stated:

> This interesting match between eleven members of the Scarborough Club and the same number of black cricketers from Australia was begun on Thursday in the Castle Yard. Notwithstanding the boisterous state of the weather, a large concourse of spectators assembled to witness the novel sight: and they were well rewarded, for some very good cricket as shown by the dark-skinned players.
>
> Aborigine team members were listed on the score-card by name and a colour, e.g. Twopenny, plain; Tiger, pink; Cuzens, white; Mullagh, blue; Peter, green; Dick-a-Dick, yellow; Charley, brown and Mosquito, magenta . . . and it seems that the colours were probably a belt or tie around the waist to make identification simpler for the scorers. The match ended in a ten wicket victory for the Aborigines who scored 148 and 53 for 0 wicket in reply to Scarborough CC's 90 and 109.

(Ian Hall & John Found, *Cricket at Scarborough: A Social History of the Club and Its Festival*, Breedon Books Publishing Co. Ltd, 1992)

AUGUST 30TH

1879: On this day, Oliver Francois Xavier Sarony, one of the most noteworthy photographers of the Victorian era, died at his home in Scarborough. Born in Quebec in 1820, he arrived in England during 1843 and first operated as an itinerant daguerreotypist from locations in Yorkshire and Lincolnshire, before moving to Scarborough in 1857. His studio, which Sarony named Gainsborough House, was designed by architects John and David Petch and included a gallery long enough to place the camera 40ft from the sitter with a direct north light. A report in the *Scarborough Gazette* described it as 'An establishment for carrying out photography to perfection', and it was here that Sarony invented and patented a range of technological innovations.

Much of his business was from the production of high quality photographs of paintings, using a new carbon process and photographic enlargements that were painstakingly completed by artists. By 1871, Sarony's studio was regarded as the largest photographic establishment in Europe, and following his death, after a long battle with diabetes, the business continued into the twentieth century under the name Sarony & Co. (Anne and Paul Bayliss, *Photographers in Mid-Nineteenth Century Scarborough: the Sarony Years, a History and Dictionary*, A. Bayliss, 1998)

AUGUST 31ST

1903: The official programme for the Grand Pier Pavilion in North Cliff at Scarborough for this day provides a fascinating insight into this type of entertainment venue in the Edwardian era. Lessees were named as The Van Biene Comedy Co., and sole managers as Edward van Biene and H.V. Woods. For the week beginning Monday, August 31st 1903, the performance was under the distinguished patronage and presence of Lord Hawke and members of Yorkshire County Cricket Club. Entertainment comprised The Northern Opera Company in Gems from the Light Operas (under the direction of Mr Richard Slater) and included artistes Miss Emily McNeill, Mr Tom Brierly, Miss Eleanor Taylor, Miss Lizzie Lancashire, Mr Charles Chadderton and Mr Eddie F. Hon, Humorist.

Two performances were staged daily at 3 p.m. and 8 p.m., with doors opening half an hour before the start of the show. Prices of admission ranged from 'Orchestra Stalls 2s, Stalls 1s, Pit Stalls 6d including pier toll. Pay at the pier gates. A few chairs are available at a charge of 3d each (Pay at the Pavilion).' The programme was printed by Marshall & Son, Royal Printing Works, Scarborough. (Cliff Hayes, *Greetings from the Yorkshire Coast: A History in Picture Postcards*, Printwise Publications, 1992)

SEPTEMBER 1ST

1666: George Fox, the founder of the Society of Friends, more commonly known as the Quakers, was released from imprisonment in Scarborough Castle on this day, with an official letter which read:

> Permit the bearer hereof, George Fox, late a prisoner here, and now discharged by His Majesty's order, quietly to pass about his lawful occasions without any molestation. Given under my hand at Scarborough Castle, this first day of September 1666.

The castle had served as a prison from the 1650s and Fox was detained in the Cockhyll Tower from April 1665 until his release almost eighteen months later, in what represented the longest of his many periods of imprisonment. He recorded his experiences in a journal: 'I had neither chimney nor firehearth. This being to the seaside and much open, the wind drove the rain in forcibly, so that the water came up over my bed and ran about the room that I was fain to skim it up with a platter' and also wrote that: 'The officers threatened that I should be hanged over the wall.' After contacting friends, his case was eventually referred to the King, who sanctioned his release. (Keith Snowden, *Scarborough Through the Ages: The Story of the Queen of English Watering Places*, Castleden Publications, 1995)

SEPTEMBER 2ND

1939: The outbreak of war had an immediate impact on places of entertainment, with the closure of Scarborough's Floral Hall on this day. Within forty-eight hours cinemas were also closed, but it was arranged that they would reopen on September 9th, between 2 p.m. and 9 p.m. Other contingencies resulted in some curious rulings, like the Olympia Ballroom for instance, which no one was allowed entry without a gas mask when it reopened on September 16th 1939.

The town's Pavilion Hotel was the first provincial venue to be granted an extension of the music and dancing license from 11 p.m. to midnight after the outbreak of war. Granted on September 29th, it was only allowed because the hotel had an air-raid shelter with the capacity to accommodate guests.

One month later, on October 2nd, a football committee was convened at Scarborough's Athletic Ground and took the decision to suspend all games for the whole of the war. A compromise wartime arrangement saw the establishment of a new amateur club, which was to be named Scarborough United. The intention was to maintain a representative local side and to continue inter-town fixtures. (Richard James Percy, *Scarborough's War Years, 1939-45*, Sutton Publishing Ltd, 1992)

SEPTEMBER 3RD

1804: A sea cut on the north side of Scarborough was opened on this day, in an attempt to reduce flooding problems on lower ground between Malton and Scarborough. William Chapman had produced a scheme for an overflow channel from the River Derwent at Everley to the sea at Scalby Mills. The completed 5 mile route had a bed width of 30ft and a fall of 135ft, with ten weirs and four road bridges. (M.F. Barbey, *Civil Engineering Heritage: Northern England*, Thomas Telford Ltd, 1986)

1998: On this day, Scarborough pleasure steamer the *Coronia* made a most memorable cruise, when forty-six members of Scarborough Merchant Navy Association left the town's harbour for a day trip to Whitby. The oldest passenger was ninety-three-year-old Captain Syd Smith, who had sailed the first *Coronia* to Scarborough from the builder's yard in 1935. After negotiating heavy seas, the steamer reached Whitby at 1 p.m. Three hours later all were back on-board and as the *Coronia* left Whitby there was a moderate swell. This soon increased with deep swells from the north-east, but the return trip was completed through the North Bay and into the harbour in just over two hours. A memorable day for the veterans, which was completed with a celebratory pint. (Tom Machin, *Scarborough's Coronia*, HPE Print, 2008)

SEPTEMBER 4TH

1851: A letter to the *Scarborough Gazette* on this day highlighted some personal rivalry during the planning stages for a Dispensary in Scarborough. Dr George Peckitt Dale led an initial meeting of medical professions some months earlier in February 1851, but during the summer months Dr Robert Thomas Elsam Barrington Cooke used columns of the *Gazette* to state he had raised £30 towards his proposal for a dispensary. He was reassured in a firm statement by Dr Dale on September 4th 1851 that the dispensary 'May be said virtually to exist', and that in excess of £200 had been raised with much more promised. (Anne Bayliss, Paul Bayliss and Alan Jackson, *Scarborough Hospital and Dispensary: The First Fifty Years, 1852-1902*, A.M. Bayliss, 2006)

————◆————

1917: On this day, Scarborough was attacked by a U-boat at about 6.45 p.m. After surfacing, the raider fired some thirty rounds at the town, leaving three people dead and five others wounded. There were many unlikely tales about the exploits of German submarines reported at this time, with one of the most incredible suggesting that a U-boat had landed on a remote stretch of shoreline, where the captain scrambled ashore and visited a local cinema. (Arthur Godfrey and Peter J. Lassey, *Shipwrecks of the Yorkshire Coast*, Dalesman Publishing Co. Ltd, 1974)

September 5th

1991: This was day three of a four-day Britannic Assurance County Championship cricket match at Scarborough's North Marine Road ground. A number of records were broken during one of the most memorable matches at this venue, when Yorkshire met their old Roses rivals, Lancashire. Match umpires had boldly stated that the pitch was suitable for staging a Test match, and this was borne out as batsmen accumulated large scores during the first three days. Yorkshire captain, Martyn Moxon, was declared out on the fourth morning of play, after becoming the fourth player to score a century, leaving Lancashire needing to score 343 in a minimum of 80 overs for victory. As Darren Gough tore into Lancashire's batting line-up they were reduced to 99 runs for 7 wickets, before Phil de Freitas smashed nine boundaries during an innings of fifty, including 28 runs in one over from Carrick – his dismissal left the score at 129–8. Ian Austin then hit the fastest century of the season in 61 balls. As the tea interval loomed, Dexter Filton was stumped and Lancashire still needed 132 runs for victory, but the addition of 80 runs for the next wicket saw the tantalising possibility of victory, only for Martin to be caught out at slip. (Ian Hall & John Found, *Cricket at Scarborough: A Social History of the Club and Its Festival*, Breedon Books Publishing Co. Ltd, 1992)

September 6th

1892: Dr Frederick Gervis Jackson died on this day, after playing a prominent role in local matters in Scarborough for more than twenty years. Until the late 1860s, he was a general practitioner in Barnsley and seemingly moved to the coast after retiring from medical work. By 1873, he was a prominent figure in discussions over plans to build a new bridge between St Nicholas Cliff and South Cliff, and in 1877 he was a member of the committee of the Scarborough Bridge Company, which managed the Spa. This building had been destroyed by fire in 1876 and plans for rebuilding the spa had been prepared by the company's architect, Charles Bury, only for Dr Jackson to wage a campaign in both the committee and the local press against the scheme. This led to Bury's plans being dropped and his fee considerably reduced. Dr Jackson then tabled a vote of no-confidence in the Spa Manager, Francis Goodricke, but his opposition was negated and the Spa's refurbishment was completed in June 1879. Dr Jackson was also a founding member and secretary of the Scarborough Club, St Nicholas Cliff and director of Scarborough Gas Company. (Anne and Paul Bayliss, *Medical Profession in Scarborough 1700 to 1899: A Biographical Dictionary*, A.M. Bayliss, 2005)

SEPTEMBER 7TH

1887: On this day, Edith Louisa Sitwell, the eldest of three children, was born to Sir George and Lady Ida in Scarborough. After an unhappy childhood with eccentric parents, she moved into a small apartment in Bayswater, London, during 1914. accompanied by her governess since 1903, Helen Rootham. She had been publishing poetry since the previous year, with her first work entitled *The Drowned Suns*. Between 1916 and 1921 Sitwell edited *Wheels*, an annual compilation of poems in conjunction with her brothers, Osbert and Sacheverell.

A fascination with links between poetry and music led to *Façade*, which was published in 1922 and set to music by William Walton. This was followed seven years later by *Gold Coast Customs*, a poem composed to the rhythms of the tom-tom and jazz music. Poems composed during the Second World War brought heightened public recognition, with *Still Falls the Rain* perhaps the best-known of these works. She also wrote a novel *I Live Under a Black Sun* based upon the life of Jonathan Swift (published in 1937) and two books about Queen Elizabeth I, as well as *English Eccentrics* (1933) and *Victoria of England* (1936). Edith Sitwell became a Dame Commander in 1954 and died on December 9th 1964. (en.wikipedia.org/wiki/Edith_Sitwell)

September 8th

1876: The beautiful Spa Saloon on Scarborough's South Bay was destroyed by fire on this day. Opened in 1839, the Spa was built with Gothic-style stone features, which were the work of Henry Wyatt. The fire was caused by the overheating of one of the building's gas lights. Archdeacon Blunt was directing a church bazaar in the large hall as the blaze took hold and the first indication of the fire was when molten lead was seen dripping from the roof, where Superintendent Pattison later had a very narrow escape from injury whilst coordinating fire brigade operations. Shortly before its destruction, Henry Redmore, Hull artist and regular visitor to Scarborough, completed a picture of the Spa which was, in 2011, expected to reach between £12-18,000 at auction. Work began on the New Spa Grand Hall in 1877 and it was opened to the public on August 2nd 1880. (www.ebooksread.com)

1939: Work got underway on this date to construct underground air-raid shelters at various sites around Scarborough. These included Albemarle Crescent Gardens, St Nicholas Cliff Gardens and Alma Square Gardens, and it wasn't long before local builders were advertising brick or concrete shelters for sale. (Richard James Percy, *Scarborough's War Years, 1939-45*, Sutton Publishing Ltd, 1992)

SEPTEMBER 9TH

1963: On this day, a theatrical Gala Night was held at Scarborough's Spa Ballroom from midnight to 4 a.m. It was attended by 900 people, who watched artistes from the town's summer shows give impromptu performances. As the proceedings began, the Mayor and Mayoress Alderman and Mrs W.H. Smith were piped in by the Scarborough Highland Pipe Band, which later played as accompaniment for the Scottish dancing. Frankie Vaughan was among the line-up of stars to perform and he also conducted a mock auction of articles, including some of his own belongings. (*Scarborough Evening News*)

———◆———

1963: Bob Southgate and a camera man from the BBC TV programme *North at Six* were on-board the Scarborough keelboat *Margaret Jane* that sailed back into Scarborough Harbour in the early hours of this morning, after a night at sea. After filming Filey Fishermen's Choir at Bethel Mission Methodist Church the previous day, they had put to sea to record overnight herring fishing before covering their subsequent sale. The trip proved successful in terms of the catch and Mr Thomas Jenkinson landed 'top shot' of the day with thirty cran of herring. (*Scarborough Evening News*)

SEPTEMBER 10TH

2012: On this day, *The Rise and Fall of Little Voice* began a six-day run at Scarborough's Futurist Theatre with a cast of well-known performers, including *Coronation Street*'s Beverley Callard, *X-Factor* finalist Ray Quinn and impressionist Jess Robinson. The show was produced by *Little Voice*'s original writer, Jim Cartwright, and represented a return to its roots for the storyline following Scarborough being chosen as the location for the film version of the play.

During filming in October and November 1997, local people were able to rub shoulders with some of the most respected names in the film industry, including Michael Caine, Ewan McGregor, Brenda Blethyn and Jane Horrocks. Several local landmarks were also featured and among these were the Foreshore, West Pier, the Leeds Hotel in West Sandgate and Castle Dykes, and the old Bottomley confectionery warehouse in Trafalgar Street West was used as the home of Jane Horrocks' character. Some local residents appeared as extras in the film and musicians also played active roles, with trombone player Tony Turner serving as musical associate to recruit local artists such as Dave Kemp on saxophone, Bob Scott on drums and George Bradley the conductor. (*Scarborough Evening News*)

September 11th

2001: A flat in one of Scarborough's most historic properties, The Belvedere in Esplanade, was advertised for sale on this day. Completed in 1885 for George Lord Beeforth, who became Mayor and Chief Magistrate for the district in the early 1900s, it was designed by William Petch. Building work took 112 men about three years to complete, during which time they installed a hot water radiator system for heating and a full electricity system.

The interior of the house had a number of striking features including a hallway with a fifteen-panel stained-glass window depicting Psalm 150, genuine Carrara marble Doric pillars and moulded archways, while a custom-built pipe organ was installed in the library, by Hills of London in 1885. (It is claimed to be the only one of its kind in the world.) Beeforth was so keen to maintain his privacy that he constructed a tiled tunnel under Esplanade to give access from Belvedere to an area of woodland overlooking the Italian Gardens. Following his death at the age of 105, Belvedere was owned by the Ohlson family between 1918 and 1980, and it was the next owner, George Bowser, who converted the imposing building into six flats. (*Scarborough Evening News*)

SEPTEMBER 12TH

1871: A two-day match which proved to be of vital importance to Scarborough Cricket Club, played between Lord Londesborough's XI and Scarborough Visitors (C.I. Thornton's XI), was completed at Castle Hill on this day. Since 1863, the cricket ground at North Marine Road had been rented at a cost of £15 per annum, but few improvements had taken place and it still resembled little more than a meadow, with no boundary fence or proper provision for collecting entrance payments.

Ground conditions at Castle Hill Yard posed different problems too, which included high winds that sometimes led to iron bails being used on the stumps, and there was a conflict of interest with the Army who owned the land and often required it for rifle shooting practice. As a direct result of this match, Lord Londesborough applied considerable pressure for Scarborough Cricket Club to improve facilities, both on and off the field, and above all to find a new ground. Robert Baker, the club's first paid secretary, also influenced the decision to develop the ground on North Marine Road.

A further result of the 1871 match at Castle Hill was the start of games between Yorkshire and Middlesex, with the first taking place at North Marine Road in September 1874. (Ian Hall & John Found, *Cricket at Scarborough: A Social History of the Club and Its Festival*, Breedon Books Publishing Co. Ltd, 1992)

SEPTEMBER 13TH

1895: The Channel Fleet visited Scarborough on this day. A crowd of about 100,000 people cruised around the ships and went on-board the *Royal Sovereign*, the *Empress of India*, the *Repulse*, the *Resolution*, the *Bellona*, the *Halcyon*, the *Blenheim* and the *Speedy*. Celebratory parties were held for officers and men around the town, and after the fleet left on September 18th, there were reports of court cases involving crew members who had jumped ship. (W.H. James, *Scarborough Sailing Club, Scarborough Yacht Club: A History*, The Walkergate Press Ltd, 1976)

1996: The *Scarborough Evening News* carried a feature on this day about the town's last jail, which stood on an area of the council depot beside Dean Road. This forbidding building contained thirty-six cells for men, in addition to the twelve women's cells, and punishment cells in the basement with the intention of holding prisoners in solitary confinement for most of each day. Some inmates would have been put to work in the kitchens and laundry, but for those sentenced to a term of imprisonment with hard labour, time was in the stone-breaking yard. Meals were typically one pint of oatmeal gruel for breakfast, a pound of bread for dinner and a further pint of gruel for supper. Scarborough's jail was closed after just a dozen years in operation. (*Scarborough Evening News*)

September 14th

1941: The quiet setting of a Sunday evening was shattered on this day, when a single enemy aircraft came in from the east to swoop low over Scarborough. Air-raid sirens remained quiet, but local people gathered to watch as the raider droned over the town. One of the two bombs released exploded on the pavement outside properties on Prospect Mount Road, leaving numbers 1, 2, 3 and 4 devastated, as well as shattering a gas main, which fired a column of flames 40ft into the night sky. Occupants of the roadside houses were fortunate to escape serious injury, but an old bathing machine hut in one of the gardens was totally destroyed. The other bomb fell close to railings at the side of Woodlands Ravine Bridge, where it blasted out a large section of roadway and showered debris on the nearby railway line. A passing family were blown off their feet and were taken by wardens to an air-raid shelter for first aid treatment, while an empty pram was blasted into overhead power lines. The only fatality of the raid was a thirty-one-year-old woman, who died instantly in the explosion on Prospect Mount Road. (Richard James Percy, *Scarborough's War Years, 1939-45*, Sutton Publishing Ltd, 1992)

September 15th

1882: On this day, the Scarborough School of Art was opened by the town's MP, William Caine, with a £200 government grant and support from the South Kensington School of Art. Albert Strange was appointed as headmaster, and seventy-five part-time students, paying course fees of one guinea for twenty lessons, were accommodated at No. 1, Haddo Terrace, Aberdeen Walk. A management committee dealt with administrative matters and until 1920 the college was financed by fees and subscriptions.

During 1884, the School of Art was moved to larger premises at the junction of Vernon Place and Falconer's Road, where a former medical baths was adapted at a cost of £500. Opened by Geoffrey Howard, MP on August 1st 1884, the School of Art was self-financing for the next thirty-five years, until it was taken over by the Scarborough Corporation as a secondary school. On May 10th 1941, the School of Art building was destroyed in an air raid and three days later classes were transferred to part of the former Scarborough Girl's High School on Westbourne Grove. The main section of the building was already occupied by the Scarborough Technical Institute, to which the Art School had been affiliated since 1940. (*Scarborough Evening News*)

September 16th

1939: Len Hutton, one of Yorkshire and England's finest ever batsmen, married Dorothy Mary Dennis at Wykeham near Scarborough on this day. Born in Pudsey, near Leeds, on June 23rd 1916, he made his debut for Yorkshire at the age of seventeen and was mentored by Bill Bowes and Hedley Verity in his early seasons of county cricket. Hutton first played for England in 1937 and scored 364 against Australia in only his sixth Test match.

By the time the Second World War broke out he was established as one of England's leading batsmen, but an arm injury caused him to alter his batting style. During the post-war period, Hutton resumed his role as one of this country's finest batsmen, with his cautious style built around a sound defence. He captained England's Test team between 1952 and 1955, with a record of eight Test wins, four losses and the others drawn, but mental and physical exhaustion saw him retire from first-class cricket during the 1955 season. He was knighted for his contributions to cricket in 1956 and became a Test selector, journalist and broadcaster. Sir Leonard Hutton became Yorkshire CC President in 1990, but died a few months later in September 1990, at the age of seventy-four. (www. enotes.com)

September 17th

1963: The Royal Air Force Fylingdales Station was officially opened on this day, in a ceremony attended by senior officers of the RAF and US Air Force Systems Command. The early warning station was completed at a cost of £43 million and was under the control of RAF Fighter Command. RAF Fylingdales represented a joint British–US project, which completed the chain of three early warning stations providing a radar curtain for Western Europe, with the other two stations based at Thule in Greenland and Clear in Alaska. Construction work had taken over three years and completed the £350 million network of early warning systems.

At the opening there were official denials of any truth in a claim published by the *Daily Express* that Russian trawlers, submarines or aircraft outside the 3-mile limit could jam the scanners housed within the three 'Golf Balls', which according to spokesman, Group Captain Betts, represented 'The most complex and sophisticated defence system in the Western World'. In 1994, the 'Golf Balls' were replaced by the Solid State Phased Array Radar and on September 17th 2003, the 40th anniversary of the station becoming operational, a fly-past was provided by a Spitfire from the Battle of Britain Memorial Flight. (*Scarborough Evening News*)

SEPTEMBER 18TH

1837: Richard Wilson, a Scarborough shipowner and benefactor, died on this day. He had combed successful business ventures with generous support for a range of organisations and institutions in the town. Among other initiatives, he set up the almshouses, Wilson's Mariners' Homes (originally named Wilson's Mariners' Asylum) on Castle Road, and before his death Wilson selected fifteen trustees to administer the almshouses and their charitable fund. A set of rules were drawn up to ensure that all residents of the properties were 'of decent, orderly and sober character' and due to the careful scrutiny of applicants by the trustees, there were few reports of improper behaviour by residents.

However, a case that involved Mary Hodgson was considered at a meeting of the trustees on Wednesday, May 3rd 1848. Mary, aged seventy-seven, and her husband William, seventy-three, had been personally chosen as residents by Richard Wilson in June 1837, but trustees were appalled to hear Michael Almond, the resident of almshouse 13, complain about the 'Disgusting, drunken behaviour of Mary Hodgson'. Their immediate response was to arrange another meeting for May 5th in order to interview Mr and Mrs Hodgson, along with the almshouses' warden. Matters came to a head and the warden was severely reprimanded, while the Hodgsons left the almshouse on July 24th to live at the nearby Union Workhouse. (*Scarborough Evening News*)

SEPTEMBER 19TH

1960: On this day, building and engineering students were the first batch of students to move into the Scarborough Technical College buildings on Scalby Road. During January 1961, all remaining classes were transferred from the Technical Institute and School of Art to the completed building. Plans for the £400,000 Technical College had been approved at the end of February 1956 and work got underway in June 1958, with Messrs Gleeson Ltd. of Sheffield as the main contractors. The 15 acre site, at the junction of Scalby Road and Lady Edith's Drive, was designed to accommodate 300 full-time and 1,800 part-time day and evening students, and the first principal was Alec Bell. Scarborough Technical College was officially opened on October 30th 1961 by the Archbishop of York, Dr Donald Coggan. The original building has changed very little in the last fifty years, although all of the facilities have been modernised to a high standard, but the external character of the building remains unaltered. Additional buildings have been added in the form of a sports hall, learning resource centre and business centre. Now known as Yorkshire Coast College, it is part of the Grimsby Institute Group. (*Scarborough Evening News*)

SEPTEMBER 20TH

1864: On this day, the foundation stone of a third congregational church in Scarborough was laid by Lady Salt, wife of Sir Titus Salt, of Methley Park and Saltaire. Located in Filey Road, the South Cliff Congregational Church became a landmark within the town, as its tower and spire on the south-east corner soared to a height of 175ft. The cost of the building, which opened in 1865, amounted to £16,000 with space for 1,040 worshippers. (*Ed. T.F. Bulmer, History, Topography, and Directory of North Yorkshire, T. Bulmer & Co.,* 1890)

1870: The North Eastern Railway ran a cheap day excursion from Pateley Bridge to Scarborough on this day, as part of the Nidderdale Feast. A specially chartered train left Pateley Bridge at 6.00 a.m. and picked up passengers at other stations to Knaresborough, before continuing through to the east coast. Advertising posters also indicated that: 'The Return Train will leave Scarborough at 5.30 p.m. same day ... FARE THERE AND BACK Covered Carriages 3s Children under Twelve Years of Age Half fare ... NO LUGGAGE ALLOWED ...'

Railway excursions to Scarborough began just a month after the resort opened its railway station, with a 250-mile day trip from Newcastle. (K. Hoole, *A Regional History of the Railways of Great Britain. Volume 4, the North East*, David & Charles, 1974)

SEPTEMBER 21ST

1888: On this day, the 714 ton collier steamer *Haswell*, owned by J. Fenwick of London, left Sunderland bound for London, but as the vessel headed southwards a thick fog enveloped the Yorkshire coast. At 6.40 p.m., in extremely poor visibility, the *Haswell* collided with SS *Vinomona* off Scarborough and immediately began to take on water. The *Haswell* had been built as an iron vessel at Sunderland in 1861, at the yard of J. Laing, before it was then rigged as a three-masted schooner. Within a short time of the collision it had sunk to the bed of the North Sea. Crew members had little time to abandon ship, and they were pulled safely from the water by the crew of the badly damaged *Vinomona*. The next day they were landed at Sunderland.

Down the years, many of the shipping losses off Scarborough were the result of collisions, often in foggy conditions, and many other vessels that sank through sea unworthiness were involved in the coastal coal trade. During 1865 a total of 675 colliers were lost, and in the following year the *Lifeboat Journal* referred to 'floating coffins' and 'the rottenest and worst vessels that leave our coasts'. (Arthur Godfrey and Peter J. Lassey, *Shipwrecks of the Yorkshire Coast*, Dalesman Publishing Co. Ltd, 1974)

SEPTEMBER 22ND

1851: On this day, an annual ball was held in aid of the Funds of the Scarborough Dispensary and Royal Northern Sea Bathing Infirmary in the new saloon at the Spa, under distinguished patronage. The Dispensary opened in the Mechanics' Institute on Monday, January 19th 1852, and income was received from many different sources, with most coming in the form of annual subscriptions and donations. It was usual for dispensaries to appoint a person to collect local subscriptions and these collectors received commission on the total amount received, because of the onerous nature of the job. Collections were made in local churches after the preacher had delivered a sermon in support of the Dispensary. Members of the clergy received an allocation of dispensary tickets, relating to the size of their congregation's collection.

Income was also generated by special events, such as a lecture in 1852 by Father Allesandro Gavazzi, an Italian priest and social reformer, which raised £10. Two years later the owner of a steamship, the *Éclat*, organised a sea trip along the coast to Mulgrave Castle, near Sandsend, with half of the profits going to the Dispensary. (Anne Bayliss, Paul Bayliss and Alan Jackson, *Scarborough Hospital and Dispensary: The First Fifty Years, 1852-1902*, A.M. Bayliss, 2006)

SEPTEMBER 23RD

1931: Scarborough's lighthouse on Vincent's Pier was the focus of great celebrations on this day, as the town's Mayor, Alderman J. Butler, officially declared it to be working. Flags and bunting covered the structure during the ceremony, and the Mayoress unveiled a bronze plaque on the lighthouse tower to mark the occasion. The first documented evidence of a lighthouse on the pier dates from 1804, when a flat-roofed building with a brazier served to give warning of the water's depth in the harbour. Originally, light was supplied from tallow candles and oil lamps but gas arrived with Robert Nixon, who built a brick lighthouse on the site in 1806. Further building work saw the addition of a second level and by 1850 the domed top section had been added, from which a modern lighting system directed a beacon 9 miles out to sea. During the bombardment by German battle cruisers in December 1914, a shell struck the lighthouse tower and resulting damage meant that it had to be demolished to the first floor level. Fundraising events in 1930, held by the Scarborough Townsmen's Association, financed the rebuild. (Scarborough and District Civic Society in Conjunction with Scarborough Borough Council, *The Scarborough Heritage Trail, Part 1, The Old Town, 2nd Edition*, 2004)

SEPTEMBER 24TH

1942: Early on this day, an enemy aircraft flew low over Scarborough and fired rounds from a machine gun, along with cannon shells, across the township. It was reported that a sleeping woman in the area of St Leonard's Crescent suffered cuts to her neck and foot when bullets shattered her bedroom window. The residents of Colescliffe Road and Newlands Park Drive had a narrow escape when bullets raked tiles and shop windows above and below their first-floor accommodation. (Richard James Percy, *Scarborough's War Years, 1939-45*, Sutton Publishing Ltd, 1992)

1974: A Portuguese hotel worker appeared at Scarborough Court today, after attempting to leave Britain with £600, a number of Portuguese escudos, and large quantities of silverware and wine glasses that had been stolen from a local hotel and café. Mrs Palmita Paulina Neves da Costa Rodrigues had spent two years as a domestic assistant in Scarborough, before setting out for Lisbon, along with her husband and a female friend. When detained at Southampton, Mrs Rodrigues, who spoke limited English, admitted, 'I pinched them', after the goods were uncovered in her luggage. She was fined £25 for stealing the items from Eve's Café and given a conditional discharge for the theft of the cutlery that was also found during the search. The £600 was seized by customs and excise. (*Scarborough Evening News*)

September 25th

1851: A ferocious storm struck the Yorkshire coast on this day, leaving families anxious for the safe return of their menfolk. Local press reports spoke of their overwhelming relief when:

> On the Sunday afternoon, a week or more afterwards, one of the last missing boats arrived; we remember well, how, when the little vessel rounded the pier, and was safely entering the harbour, the hearts of all who witnessed its arrival seemed to swell with delightful emotion, which would fain have found utterance in a hearty huzza of welcome to the restored; but the bells of the venerated Saint Mary's reminded all, just at the time, of the fitting opportunity presented, to ascribe their gratitude for His mercies to Him who is indeed worthy to receive more than we can render.

(Scarborough Post)

———— • ◆ • ————

1916: Scarborough's trawling fleet suffered serious losses on this day, when eleven vessels from the port were sunk by a U-boat. According to reports, the U-boat skipper forced crews to abandon ship and then sank them all in turn by gunfire, apart from the *Nil Desperandum*, which had a bomb placed in the engine room. This dramatic episode left Scarborough with only three or four operational steam trawlers. (www.scarboroughsmaritimeheritage.org.uk)

SEPTEMBER 26TH

1974: On this day, organisers of a campaign to save Scarborough's Royal Opera House were collecting signatures for a petition, which was to be presented to the town's council before its next meeting two weeks later. They hoped to complete a petition with 25,000 signatures from townspeople, after only twenty-seven of the Opera House's 300 members had attended the last meeting. The Council's Policy and Resources Committee had earlier backed a plan by the Scarborough Theatre Trust for a new arts complex and refused a grant for the Opera House. (*Scarborough Evening News*)

2007: On this day, the Scarborough Borough Council announced its intention to purchase Scarborough FC's former ground at the McCain Stadium from the liquidators. However, it took until December 2008 for the purchase to formally go through. The club had been 'wound up' some three months earlier, on June 20th, but when the liquidators applied for the removal of a covenant that restricted the ground to sporting activities only, the council objected. Following the purchase there were several weeks of discussions, and the council voted to demolish the stadium on 13th April, before disclosing that Featherstone Rovers Rugby League Club had bought the east and west stands and removed them. Demolition was completed by the end of November 2011. (en.wikipedia.org/wiki)

September 27th

1993: This day marked the beginning of the Lady Chapel project at St Mary's parish church in Scarborough. When work was completed less than six months later, on February 6th 1994, there was a dedication service conducted by John Habgood, Archbishop of York.

It marked another phase in restoration work, following bombardment of the building during the Civil War, when it was used by parliamentary forces as a forward position for attacks on the castle. Canon fire from the castle had destroyed the splendid medieval choir and north transept areas, and some fourteen years after the bombardment, in 1659, the church steeple and bells collapsed. Within ten years, sufficient funds had been raised to rebuild the nave, St Nicholas aisle and the central tower, but it was almost 200 years later before Ewan Christian supervised further significant restoration work between 1848 and 1850. Large areas of wooden galleries and box pews were removed from the interior at that time, in order to restore the amount of available space. The clock in the central tower was positioned in 1856 and another major restoration scheme was completed during 1950. (Scarborough and District Civic Society in Conjunction with Scarborough Borough Council, *The Scarborough Heritage Trail, Part 1, The Old Town, 2nd Edition*, 2004)

September 28th

1860: On this day, John Hesp, three times Mayor of Scarborough, died at his home, no. 5 Westfield Terrace. Born at Knapton, near Scarborough, in 1792, he became a solicitor with an office in Tanner Street (now St Thomas' Street), and when His Majesty's Commissioners visited Scarborough to assess the need to reform the town's Corporation, he was one of three lawyers who challenged the Corporation's claim to be left unaltered. Reform was made and Hesp was elected to the first town council. Periods in office as Mayor followed in 1837-38, 1847-48 and 1852-53, and during his last mayoralty he officially opened Scarborough's new Market Hall. (Anne and Paul Bayliss, *Scarborough's Members of Parliament, 1832 to 1906: Scarborough's Mayors, 1836 to 1906: A Biographical Dictionary*, A.M. Bayliss, 2008)

———◆———

1861: Scarborough's new lifeboat was transported from the town's railway station to the lifeboat house today, where it was christened *Amelia*, after the daughter of the donor. Measuring 32ft long and 8ft wide the boat had ten oars and had cost £315. A total of eighteen Royal National Lifeboat Institute lifeboats were stationed along the Northumberland, Durham and Yorkshire coastline at that time. Sadly, the *Amelia* was in service for only two months before being wrecked off the Spa walls. (www.scarboroughsmaritimeheritage.org.uk)

September 29th

1688: Correspondence from London on this date stated:

> The Mayor of Scarborough and Captain Ouseley, who tossed
> the other in a blanket, were heard last night before the council:
> the Captain pleaded His Majesty's gracious pardon (which is in
> the press) and so both were dismissed.

The altercation between the town's mayor and the soldier
stemmed from the refusal by Mr Noel Boteler, a Protestant
minister, to read out a declaration for the liberty of conscience
in church. This led to the Mayor assaulting the churchman, as
an incredulous congregation looked on. Captain Ouseley then
ordered the Mayor to meet him the following day to explain
his conduct and although the Mayor initially failed to arrive,
a subsequent confrontation ended with the Captain and his
fellow soldiers tossing the Mayor in a blanket. The incident
resulted in the Mayor's office being replaced with two bailiffs on
November 16th 1688, due to his unpopularity. (Keith Snowden,
*Scarborough Through the Ages: The Story of the Queen of
English Watering Places*, Castleden Publications, 1995)

1933: Reports of the Annual General Meeting of Scarborough
Ladies Lifeboat Guild stated that there was an increase of
membership numbers, from 146 to 157, as well as financial
growth. In his address, Lt-Col. Salterthwaite spoke of it as a
model lifeboat station with excellent relations between the
committee, crew and lifeboatmen. (*Scarborough Mercury*)

September 30th

ANNUALLY: The Golden Ball in Scarborough's Quay Street was one of the town's oldest inns, and each year, on St Jerome's Day, 'prime old ales' were produced in a brewery on the site. Before the fourteenth century, incoming tides reached Quay Street, which formed the edge of the harbour and housed the Town Hall, custom house and post houses. Most of the custom at inns located in this area came from local fisherman and visiting sailors, but, before it was demolished by the local gas company and rebuilt at a nearby location, The Golden Ball was a venue for Corporation dinners.

St Jerome's Day was also the time for electing many of the Corporations positions, as well as new bailiffs. This was carried out at a meeting in the Common Hall by forty-four members, who represented Scarborough's ruling body for about 600 years; new members had to be invited from within this group. The bailiffs held positions of considerable power and prestige within the town and following their twelve months in office, they could then serve the next year as coroner or attempt to gain re-election. (*The Scarborough News*)

OCTOBER 1ST

1971: A press article released on this day raised the intriguing prospect that a former KGB spy had stayed at Scarborough some four months earlier. Mr Stuart Leslie, managing director of the women's underwear manufacturers Firth & Wilson, reported that a Russian trade representative who had been in the town on June 2nd and 3rd, was in fact the Oleg Lyalin, who had now defected. His theory was supported by Mr Peter Robinson of the Victoria Hotel, where the Russian stayed after signing in as 'O.A. Lialine', giving the address no. 32 Highgate, London. They were even more convinced of the Russian's true identity after seeing an identikit representation which matched the man they had met, and both men remarked on the fact that he spoke perfect English.

Mr Leslie had found his visitor to be charming company when he showed him around the town and lunched with him. Friends who were introduced to him remarked on the tremendously firm grip of his handshake. The Russian declined to dine out in the evening, explaining that he had other people to see, and as the mystery deepened it was revealed that he had initially booked in for one night at the Victoria Hotel, but in fact stayed two. (*Scarborough Evening News*)

OCTOBER 2ND

1971: Fifteen-year-old Melanie Jones had two reasons to celebrate when she was interviewed by local news reporters on this day. She had just returned from an international guide and scout camp in Sweden, where she represented her company and girl guides all over the country, when she was awarded her Queen's Guide badge. She was presented with her award by Mrs J.A. Thompson, the Scarborough division commissioner, at a special harvest supper. Afterwards, Melanie spoke to her fellow girl guides and showed colour slides of her trip to Sweden. She explained that the first nine days of her trip were spent with a Swedish family on the west coast, who took her to their holiday home on Tjorn Island, adding that it was very common for Swedish families to have both a home in town and one elsewhere for holidays. She described her time spent in both locations and after this explained how she moved on to a camp near Gothenburg, where she spent a week sharing with two Rumanian guides and one Swedish guide. The first night was quite an experience, she recalled, as all the theory she had learned about camping was put to the test when it poured with rain and the tent fell down. (*Scarborough Evening News*)

OCTOBER 3RD

1903: John Dale, a prominent local citizen during the second half of the nineteenth century, died at his home, Netherbank, following a lengthy period of illness. Born in Lancaster in May 1832, he was based on the west coast until poor health resulted in his retirement during 1882. During his working life, he had been a regular visitor to the Scarborough area, and in 1883 a York-based architect, James Demaine, designed Netherbank on Filey Road as a permanent home for John Dale and his wife, Lydia. He was soon involved with charitable causes in the town and after becoming secretary of the Charity Organisation Society in 1885, he demonstrated impressive organisational skills which led to better record keeping and an extension of the premises. His involvement with charities also included the Prevention of Cruelty to Children and Society for Prevention of Cruelty to Animals. As President of the Hospital Board during the early 1890s, John Dale played a key role in choosing and financing a new hospital for the town, which opened in 1893. It was probably this project that persuaded him to serve as Mayor in 1892-93. (Anne and Paul Bayliss, *Scarborough's Members of Parliament, 1832 to 1906: Scarborough's Mayors, 1836 to 1906: A Biographical Dictionary*, A.M. Bayliss, 2008)

OCTOBER 4TH

1802: On this day, the attractive village of Brompton-by-Sawdon, near Scarborough, was the setting for the marriage of Lakeland poet William Wordsworth to Mary Hutchinson. Mary was the daughter of a local farmer and lived at Gallows Hill Farm, just outside the village. Wordsworth stayed at the farm before their wedding which was conducted by Revd John Ellis at All Saints' Church at Brompton. The church dates back to the fourteenth and fifteenth centuries and has Grade 1 listed building status. A copy of the marriage certificate of William and Mary is displayed within the church. (Arthur Mee, *Yorkshire North Riding*, Hodder and Stoughton, 1941)

———◆———

1917: The German U-boat, *UB41*, sank following an explosion off Scarborough on this day. It had been commissioned into the German Imperial Navy on August 25th 1916 and sank a total of eight ships during thirteen patrols in the North Sea. These included the *William Cory & Son* and SS *Harrow* during early September, before attacks on SS *Ceveney* and SS *Clydebank* about a month later. At that time it was the only U-boat known to be in the area, and the explosion that destroyed the vessel was caused by either an English or German mine. All crew members were lost. (Arthur Godfrey and Peter J. Lassey, *Shipwrecks of the Yorkshire Coast*, Dalesman Publishing Co. Ltd, 1974)

OCTOBER 5TH

1929: On this day, Fred Feast, well-known film and television actor, was born in Scarborough, where he later attended Graham School. After achieving the rank of sergeant in the Parachute Regiment where he was a physical training instructor, Feast appeared as a variety artist at the Windmill Theatre and had a series of jobs before landing a role in *Coronation Street*. He played the character of Fred Gee from 1975 to December 1984 and then took minor roles in *All Creatures Great and Small* as well as *Family at War*, *Nearest and Dearest* and *Emmerdale Farm*. Feast even made a brief foray into local politics, before his final film role in 1999 as pigeon-fancier Arthur, in *Little Voice*. He died in a Bridlington hospital in June 1999. (www.corrie.net)

———— • ◆ • ————

2000: Mecca Bingo Club on Albemarle Crescent at Scarborough was given Grade II listed building status on this day. Completed during the late 1920s, the former Capitol Cinema retains its elaborated classical decoration. Soon after it opened in 1929, the building was wired for sound and it became a permanent bingo venue in 1977. (www.britishlistedbuildings.co.uk)

OCTOBER 6TH

1799: When a boat was spotted in difficulty just to the north of Filey Brigg, a group of local Scarborough men, led by John Harwood, launched a coble boat and rowed some 4 miles to the stranded vessel. They were able to rescue the crew members and complete the difficult journey back to Scarborough. Such incidents only strengthened calls for a lifeboat to be stationed locally, and during 1800, meetings were held and a lifeboat committee appointed. It was resolved that there would be twelve men in each crew and that the lifeboat should not be launched without the agreement of at least one member of the committee. By August 1801, funds totalling £212 1s 6d had been raised, so the committee paid five guineas for plans and the boat was constructed by Chris Smith at a cost of £129 5s, with an extra £17 7s for cork. First coxswain of the unnamed Scarborough lifeboat was John Harwood, who had played a crucial role in the rescue on October 6th 1799. (www. scarboroughsmaritimeheritage.org.uk)

———— • ◆ • ————

1830: On this day, the Scarborough Cliff Bridge Company's Annual General meeting instructed their York-based committee to lease collection of tolls on the bridge. This arrangement had caused endless problems since its opening in 1827. (Meredith Whittaker, *The Book of Scarborough Spaw*, Barracuda, 1984)

OCTOBER 7TH

1947: A violent explosion at about 9.10 a.m. on this day shook buildings around Scarborough. Some two years after the end of the Second World War, local people could still recognise the sound of an exploding mine and several fishing vessels immediately left the harbour to offer assistance. Distress signals from the stricken vessel, the 1,771 ton collier *Betty Hindley*, enabled the rescuers to reach the scene and attach tow ropes. The intention was to haul the *Betty Hindley* back to the South Bay, but the following day the stricken vessel ran aground about three quarters of a mile from Scarborough harbour and soon became a total wreck. The initial explosion had left one man dead and two others, including Captain Cole, severely injured. After breaking in two on the seabed, some 40ft below the surface, the bows were left intact and projecting about 25ft from the bottom. The *Betty Hindley* was owned by Stephenson Clarke of London, the oldest British shipping company, and they arranged for parts of the wreck to be disposed of by salvage contractors, but the location of the remainder of the wreck remains popular with divers and fishing trips. (Arthur Godfrey and Peter J. Lassey, *Shipwrecks of the Yorkshire Coast*, Dalesman Publishing Co. Ltd, 1974)

OCTOBER 8TH

1899: Richard Fell Steble, a major figure in Scarborough's public life during the late nineteenth century, died on this day at his home, Ramsdale Bank on Belmont Road. Born and brought up in north-west England, he qualified as a solicitor in 1858 and practised in Liverpool, where he served as a city councillor for fourteen years from 1867 and as mayor in 1874 and 1875. Following a move to Scarborough in 1881, Steble entered public life and served as a Liberal councillor in 1885 before accepting the office of mayor in 1891.

His mayoral year was characterised by a series of hospitality events, which included a Christmas party for 700 elderly poor at the Grand Hotel, popular concerts in the circus on St Thomas' Street, with as many as 2,000 spectators, and gatherings of local cabmen, railwaymen, bath-chair men and their families. Steble served as a magistrate for Scarborough and also for the North Riding, and his involvement with local organisations included helping to establish the Scalby and Newby Agricultural Society. He had been president of Scarborough Hospital in 1888, and in 1901 his widow presented the hospital with a Röntgen X-ray machine in his memory. (*Scarborough Mercury*)

OCTOBER 9TH

1888: On this day, bloodhounds Barnaby and Burgho, owned by Mr Edwin Brough of Wyndgate, near Scarborough, were put through their paces in a London park, as the search for Jack the Ripper intensified. A few days earlier, Mr Brough had been contacted by Metropolitan police officers about the possibility of employing the bloodhounds in manhunts and he immediately brought Barnaby and Burgho to the capital. He explained to journalists that training began when the dogs were just four or five months old, with short runs of about 100 yards on grass surfaces and upwind. When they were twelve months old the hounds were taught to go across country and practise crossing roads and brooks. Their first trial in the capital was at 7 a.m. in Regent's Park where they successfully tracked a young man, who had been given a fifteen minute head start, for almost a mile. Another exercise took place on the same evening in Hyde Park, with the hounds again on a leash, and a further trial was held the following morning, with Sir Charles Warren acting as the hunted man. The chief commissioner seemed pleased with the results, 'though he did not express any definite opinion'. (*London Daily News*)

OCTOBER 10TH

1940: At around 9 p.m. on this day, a single enemy aircraft flew low over the Castle Hill area of Scarborough and dropped a mine on rows of houses in the Potter Lane and Short's Gardens area. The explosion blasted a huge crater measuring 60ft across and 30ft deep, causing massive devastation. Five houses were completely destroyed and 500 others were damaged, out of which seventy-one had to be demolished among the twenty-four streets. Four people died in the raid but, thankfully, larger numbers of injuries and fatalities were averted because many local residents were at a Spitfire Dance at the Olympia Ballroom on the Foreshore, and others were at a whist drive at a local church hall. Rescue and demolition squads worked through the night to bring out the dead and injured. Many of the casualties were taken to St Mary's Hospital on Dean Road, while others were taken to makeshift facilities at St Sepulchre Street Centre, where they had to be washed in dustbins. The damage to terraced properties in Short's Garden was so severe that the street was completely cleared and later rebuilt as Castle Gardens. (Richard James Percy, *Scarborough in the 1930s and 40s*, Hendon Publishing Co. Ltd, 1990)

OCTOBER 11TH

1824: A Sunderland brig, the *Hebe*, foundered in Scarborough's South Bay on this day, but her crew of seven were safely rescued by the town's lifeboat. Designed by Robert Skelton, the lifeboat measured 28ft in length and 9ft across the beam, with ten oars. Silver medals were awarded to lifeboatmen James Fowler and Smith Tindall, in recognition of their gallant conduct during the rescue. (www.scarboroughsmaritimeheritage.org.uk)

———— •◆• ————

1946: The Scarborough lifeboat, *Herbert Joy II*, was purchased by Alexander Joy in 1931 in memory of his brother, Herbert, who was lost overboard from a yacht. Perhaps its most noteworthy rescue took place on this day, when the 850 ton steamer *Glamorganbrook* sprang a leak and began to sink off Robin Hood's Bay. The ship carried fifteen lifebelts for its fifteen crew members, including the captain, but sadly, there was one more passenger on-board this fateful day. The captain had invited his wife on the voyage and when they abandoned ship at 4.30 a.m. he passed his lifebelt to her. The ship's captain was the only loss as the *Herbert Joy II* pulled the fifteen survivors from the water and brought them safely to land. (Arthur Godfrey, *Scarborough Lifeboats*, Hendon Publishing Co. Ltd, 1975)

OCTOBER 12TH

1910: Angelina Geller, one of a number of notable artists based in Scarborough during the late nineteenth and early twentieth centuries, died on this day. She was born in St Pancras, London, and was the daughter of William Overend Geller, a successful portrait painter from Bradford who had moved to the capital in 1833 to develop his career; her early training was probably arranged by him. She worked mainly with oils and watercolours and during 1865-66, while still in her early twenties, Angelina had two paintings exhibited by the Royal Academy.

At some point in the next few years, William Geller moved with his wife, Angelina and her older sister Margaretta, back to premises on West Parade in the Falsgrave district of Scarborough, where he worked as an artist and engraver. Angelina and Margaretta remained in the town after their father's death in August 1881, and in Scarborough directories for 1890, 1892 and 1902 Angelina is listed as an artist. Most of her exhibited paintings featured flowers, but she described herself as a 'certified portrait painter' in the 1891 census, when her home address was recorded as no. 21 West Bank, Scarborough. (Anne and Paul Bayliss, *Scarborough Artists of the Nineteenth Century, A Biographical Dictionary*, Anne Bayliss, 1997)

OCTOBER 13TH

1933: On this day, the first in a series of ten lectures on the local history of Scarborough was given in the museum by Professor C. Gill, MA LittD. Gill was Head of the History Department at Hull University College, in conjunction with the local Philosophical and Archaeological Society, and he pointed out that:

> The first written history of this part of the country was at the time of the Romans . . . At that time there were large spaces of wasteland and the country was sparsely populated . . . some historians claimed that invaders might wander about for a fortnight without seeing anyone . . . The inhabitants of the East Riding were rather more developed than those of the north and had a certain amount of trade with Ireland and possibly Northern Europe.

Meanwhile, the latest in a series of University Extension lectures on *Chemistry and Modern Life* by Professor F.G. Tryhorn dealt with 'The Birth and Death of Modern Science' and traced the main steps in the development of modern chemistry as one of the most important sciences of the present day. The next lecture would deal with *Chemistry and the Production of Energy*. (*Scarborough Mercury*)

OCTOBER 14TH

1910: On this day, the *Scarborough Mercury* reported on birthday celebrations for local resident, Mrs Ruth Stoney Smith, who had reached the grand age of ninety. A large number of family members had gathered at the elderly lady's current residence, no. 31 Raleigh Street, and these included her twelve children whose combined ages totalled 500 years. Mrs Smith, who had been widowed for thirty-eight years, was the last surviving member of an old West Riding family with the name of Stoney. She had been born and raised in the remote wastes of Upper Nidderdale under the shadow of the mountain Great Whernside.

Smith was said to still be in full possession of her faculties and could recall how poor members of the community were provided for in her early days. Needy folk were billeted on farmers in the parish, who were obliged to give them food and lodging in return for work. When that arrangement was replaced by the Poor Law Amendment Act of 1834, the parish overseers had to take relief to the poor and a relative of hers, who did not care for that part of his duties, used to send Mrs Smith as the relieving officer, for which he used to buy her a new dress each year. (*Scarborough Mercury*)

OCTOBER 15TH

2011: This evening's performance was the closing night of Alan Ayckbourn's 75th play, *Neighbourhood Watch*, at Scarborough's Stephen Joseph Theatre. The five-week long world premiere also happened to be the 300th play the theatre had commissioned, and was written by the prolific playwright about a year earlier, during the autumn of 2010. The production, which featured a cast of eight, assumed a considerable amount of poignancy during rehearsals in August 2011, when its themes of an apparent collapse of law and order in the UK was reflected in four days of rioting in several of the country's major cities.

Following the opening performance at Scarborough on September 8th, a press night held five days later drew all-round praise. After its initial run at Stephen Joseph Theatre the production went on a short run of in-the-round venues during late October 2011. *Neighbourhood Watch* transferred to 59E59 Theaters, based in New York, as an element of the Brits off Broadway festival, which ran until January 1st 2012. Returning to London, the world premiere production staged its 200th performance on April 25th, with the same company that had launched the play in Scarborough during October 2011. (neighbourhoodwatch.alanayckbourn.net)

OCTOBER 16TH

1940: Tragedy struck the Scarborough fishing fleet on this day when 25-ton vessel the *Pride* was shattered in an explosion close to the harbour mouth. The mine, which caused the explosion, had been dropped from a German aircraft and all members of the *Pride*'s crew were lost in this disastrous episode. (*Shipwrecks and Smuggling on the Yorkshire Coast* by Arthur Godfrey and Peter J. Lassey)

———•◆•———

2008: At an awards ceremony held at No. 11 Downing Street on this evening, Scarborough was named as the nation's most enterprising place in the fourth annual Enterprising Britain competition. Scarborough was the representative for the Yorkshire and Humber region and was the best of twelve entrants that represented every region in the United Kingdom.

The Scarborough Renaissance Partnership submitted an entry for the competition in April 2008 and became regional winners during the following month, after beating competition from other Yorkshire towns including Leeds, Bradford and Rotherham. National judges travelled to Scarborough in June where they visited a range of projects and met some of the town's enterprising people, including the new tenants of the Woodend Creative Workspace and representatives from the Residents and Friends of Trafalgar Square. (www.scarborough.gov.uk)

OCTOBER 17TH

1840: On this day, St Thomas Church in Eastgate, Scarborough, was consecrated. This occurred some twenty months after a meeting of interested parties, held on March 23rd 1839, had decided that 'It is extremely desirable that a chapel should be built in the lower part of the town, principally for the accommodation of the poor.' Contributions already amounted to £1,400, including a grant of £300 from the Incorporated Society for the Building of Churches, 'On condition that 330 at least of the sittings be free and unappropriated. But we believe that a further sum of money is requisite to defray the debt which has been incurred.' (Solomon Wilkinson Theakston, *Theakston's Guide to Scarborough* 2nd edition, S.W. Theakston, 1843)

———◆———

1898: Benjamin Smith died on this day at his home, no. 4 Beulah Terrace, after a short illness. Born near Leeds in November 1808, he moved to Scarborough at the age of twenty-six on joining the brick-making company of John Barry. In 1850, he opened his own premises as a building contractor on South Cliff. He began his career in local politics in 1861, with the highlight of his career being his period in office as Mayor (1877-78). His stance as a total abstainer divided opinion at his inauguration banquet when alcohol was prohibited, and a highlight of his mayoralty was a visit by the Duke of Cambridge. (Anne and Paul Bayliss, *Scarborough's Members of Parliament, 1832 to 1906: Scarborough's Mayors, 1836 to 1906: A Biographical Dictionary*, A.M. Bayliss, 2008)

OCTOBER 18TH

1870: On this day, John Christopher Bell died in Scarborough, after working in the town as an artist for more than twenty years. Born in the nearby coastal town of Whitby, he is named in the Scarborough census and local directories from 1851- 1867, with addresses in York Place, St Nicholas Street and Albemarle Crescent. John Bell's works, which were exhibited in London (RBA) between 1857 and 1868, featured birds and animals and he specialised in portraying his clients' pet animals. (Anne and Paul Bayliss, *Scarborough Artists of the Nineteenth Century, A Biographical Dictionary*, Anne Bayliss, 1997)

———◆———

1960: Simon Dennis was born on this day, into a cricketing family. He was the son of former Scarborough captain Geoff Dennis and nephew of Sir Len Hutton. During his teenage years he developed into a fine left-arm bowler and represented the English Schools XI whilst attending Scarborough College. Appearances over seven seasons in the Scarborough First XI (from the age of seventeen) led to a call up for Yorkshire's county team, and during the 1983 season he took 52 wickets and was rewarded with his county cap. Unfortunately, Simon Dennis' progress was severely restricted by a rare blood disorder and, after being released by Yorkshire in 1988, he played for Glamorgan until his retirement from first-class cricket in 1991. (Ian Hall & John Found, *Cricket at Scarborough: A Social History of the Club and Its Festival*, Breedon Books Publishing Co. Ltd, 1992)

OCTOBER 19TH

1829: On this day, a poster for *Theatre Scarborough* stated that:

Mr Mitchell begs to state to the Nobility, Gentry, Visitors and Inhabitants of Scarborough that he has engaged the celebrated MR KEAN for four nights commencing on Monday, October 19th to appear in Shakespeare's Comedy *Merchant of Venice*. The part of Shylock by Mr Kean, Antonio, the merchant . . . Mr Fisher, Bassanio . . . Mr Marston, Gratiano . . . Mr Harding, Lorenzo . . . Mr Edwin, Salanio . . . Mr Jones, The Duke of Venice . . . Mr Christie, Old Gobbo . . . Mr Young, Launcelot Gobbo . . . Mr Garthwaite, Tubal . . . Mr Brown, Balthazar . . . Miss E Beswick, Portia . . . Mrs Fisher, Nerissa . . . Miss H. Watson, Jessica . . . Miss Beswick. A favourite song by Mr Edwin.

The whole to conclude with (first time) a new Farce in Two Acts, called The Man In The Moon or, The Bundle of Sticks. The Man in the Moon (on eccentric Planet, up to everything under the Sun) . . . Mr Mitchell, Salomon Wiseman (a newly discovered Northern Light) . . . Mr Young, Lawyer Quill (a fixed Star) . . . Mr Christie, Captain Grenville, alias Captain Hunter, alias Captain Sideral, a flaming comet strongly attracted by Venus . . . Mr Fisher, Joe Clump (a Yorkshire Satellite to the Man in the Moon and an unwilling Dabbler in the Stocks) . . . Mr Garthwaite. Boxes 4*s* Pit 2*s* Gallery 1*s*.

(C.R. Todd, Printer, Scarborough)

October 20th

1933: After forty-six years' service on the staff of Scarborough post office, Inspector C. Dawson of 60 Moorland Road, left his desk for the last time today. He had started work as a telegraph boy when the post office was situated in Huntriss Row and had been on the staff ever since. He was made a part-time postman in 1890 and full-time in 1893, before later rising to be head postmaster in 1894. In 1914, he became assistant inspector and in 1924 rose to his present rank. During his long and distinguished career, he had seen many changes and served under the charge of ten postmasters.

In 1887, telegraph boys received a token for every telegram delivered and this could later be exchanged for money. In those days, many more telegrams were sent owing to the scarcity of telephones and although boys had to walk rather than use bicycles, they still made plenty of money. This was especially the case when they had to deliver telegrams to fish buyers and salesmen on the West Pier during the herring season. (*Scarborough Mercury*)

OCTOBER 21ST

1874: On this day, Thomas Edwin Cooper was born at 44 Nelson Street, Scarborough. He showed a keen interest in buildings from an early age, and in his youth, he was apprenticed to the architects John Hall and Frank Tugwell, and after a period of overseas travel he joined the London firm of Goldie, Child & Goldie. A further move, in his early twenties, saw him return to Scarborough as a partner in the firm of Hall, Cooper & Davis, and local commissions included Westwood Higher Grade School (1897), Scarborough College (1898) and an extension to the *Scarborough Mercury* office (1913). His individual designs were used for the bandstand, Sun Court and Green Room on the Spa, and commissions for a number of buildings, including Hull's Guildhall and Marylebone Town Hall resulted, from his success in design competitions. Cooper's work in London included the Port of London Authority building (1912) and it is claimed that he designed more buildings in the capital than anyone since Christopher Wren. Edwin Cooper was elected Fellow of the Royal Institute of British Architects in 1903 and ten years later he was knighted. Other accolades followed, including election as a Royal Academician in June 1937, before his death in London some five years later. (Scarborough and District Civic Society, *Blue Plaques in Scarborough 1974-2010*, 2010)

OCTOBER 22ND

1825: Thomas Hinderwell, historian and philanthropist, died on this day and was buried in St Mary's churchyard at Scarborough. Born and brought up in the town, he attended Coxwold grammar school before spending twenty years as a seagoing man. In 1775 he returned to Scarborough and served on the town's Corporation over four periods, before retiring in 1816. Apart from his support for a range of local charities, Thomas Hinderwell is remembered for his *History of Scarborough*, which was first published in York in 1798. (Scarborough and District Civic Society, *Blue Plaques in Scarborough 1974-2010*, 2010)

———•◆•———

2005: The Scarborough Archaeological and Historical Society joined the Friends of Falsgrave Park today, to celebrate restoration of the park's well house, by following the route of the water supply from Princess Square to Falsgrave. The present well house, or spring head, is a small stone building with a stone-flagged roof and probably dates from the eighteenth century. Excavations at the site in 2001 uncovered older stonework which indicated an earlier structure, which could be the second Franciscan Spring dating from 1339. The Friends of Falsgrave Park had obtained Local Heritage Initiative funding to restore the building and to clear out the cisterns and inlet conduit, which then enabled the demonstration of how water was collected inside the well house before being piped to the town. (www.scarborough-heritage.org)

OCTOBER 23RD

1936: On this day, the *Scarborough Mercury* reported:

> In lovely autumn sunshine which enhanced the beauty of its situation, Scarborough's magnificent new 'Temple of Healing' was formally opened today by HRH the Duke of Kent whose second visit to Scarborough it was.

Total costs to build the Temple of Healing amounted to £135,000 and a plaque in the hospital's north entrance marks the occasion, which took place some twenty-eight months after the laying of the foundation stone on June 27th 1934.

In order to mark the 75th anniversary of the hospital's opening a local resident, Mrs Gillian Parsons of Filey Road, wrote a short story, *I'm Just Upside Down*, which features a time-travelling heroine who works at Scarborough Hospital in 1936 and goes on to make an appearance in the present day. Mrs Parsons has used the hospital since moving home to the town in 2004 and paid tribute to the tremendous work of the staff. She passed the short story to the hospital trust in the hope that copies would be published to raise funds, and the hospital's chief executive, Mike Proctor, used the 75th anniversary gathering to reflect on the dedication of loyal staff over that period. (*Scarborough Mercury* and *Scarborough Evening News*)

OCTOBER 24TH

1824: A most destructive north-north-east storm and tidal surge struck the east coast on this day, leaving hundreds of vessels wrecked along the coast, including a number in the Scarborough area. (Arthur Godfrey and Peter J. Lassey, *Shipwrecks of the Yorkshire Coast*, Dalesman Publishing Co. Ltd, 1974)

———◆———

1914: Paul Marny, a prominent artist and lithographer during the second half of the nineteenth century, died at Scarborough. He was born in Paris in 1829 and is thought to have worked as an apprentice painter at the Sèvres porcelain factory, and as a scenery painter at the Paris Opera. For a time, Marny worked with a French architect in Belfast but in about 1860 he was persuaded to move to Scarborough by the photographer and gallery owner, Oliver Francois Xavier Sarony. Although he is known mostly for his painting of the loss of the Scarborough lifeboat on November 2nd 1861, he also completed many landscapes and town scenes based on annual visits to French towns. In 1874, the *British Journal of Photography* reported that Paul Marny had patented a process for applying carbon printing to substances such as porcelain, and in 1891 he and his French wife, Claire, were living at 12 Royal Avenue in Scarborough. Following the death of his wife in July 1914, he moved briefly to Birmingham before returning to Scarborough in the final weeks of his life. (Anne and Paul Bayliss, *Scarborough Artists of the Nineteenth Century, A Biographical Dictionary*, Anne Bayliss, 1997)

OCTOBER 25TH

1731: Thomas Brown, an early member of the Methodist following in Scarborough, was born on this day. His memorial in St Mary's parish church states:

> In memory of Thomas Brown, one of the first members in this town of the people called 'Methodists' in connection with the Rev. John Wesley MA. He was a local preacher for 50 years and for 65 years a member of the society. Born October 25th 1731. Died June 2nd 1811.

(S. Foord, *Scarborough Records*)

1862: Thomas Weddell, doctor, businessman and mayor of Scarborough, died on this day at his home address of 7 Albion Place. Born in York in 1792, he had settled in the seaside town by 1821, where he built up his medical practice as surgeon to local military detachments and the Northern Sea Bathing Infirmary. In the first municipal elections of 1836, Weddell was elected as councillor for the North Ward and at the same time he was chosen as an alderman for a term of six years. He also held the office of Mayor from 1938-39 and 1844-45, as well as serving as a local magistrate. (Anne and Paul Bayliss, *Scarborough's Members of Parliament, 1832 to 1906: Scarborough's Mayors, 1836 to 1906: A Biographical Dictionary*, A.M. Bayliss, 2008)

OCTOBER 26TH

1869: As darkness fell on this day, large numbers of people gathered on vantage points south of Scarborough, and one onlooker described the scene:

> Great foaming waves were dashing against the cliff . . . the darkness was rent by a great meteor flash as a rocket rushed blazing out to sea . . . 200 yards distant a heavily laden schooner with a few pitch black sails still set was rolling fearfully on the rocks. Each successive wave broke right over the hull.

The unnamed vessel in distress was the South Shields-based schooner *Mary* which had started taking in water earlier in the day. After the ship's captain had made the decision to run for the shore, his ship ran aground to the south of the Spa after nightfall. The eyewitness described the rocket falling short of the stranded vessel, as did the next two as the strength of the wind drove them back. The drama increased as the rocket brigade ran out of projectiles and a rider had to be dispatched to bring more. The watching crowd lit a bonfire on the clifftop as the *Mary*'s crew clung to rigging. With provision of more rockets just before midnight, the ship's master and four crew members were brought to safety. (Arthur Godfrey and Peter J. Lassey, *Shipwrecks of the Yorkshire Coast*, Dalesman Publishing Co. Ltd, 1974)

OCTOBER 27TH

1880: On this day, a large storm developed at around noon and raged with such severity that it left a trail of damaged vessels trying to reach sheltered waters around Scarborough. In the teeth of the east-south-east gale, a brig struggled to enter the harbour, but was forced into shallow water in the middle of the bay. As the dramatic events continued into the next day, the lifeboat was able to get alongside to rescue the six crewmen. Soon afterwards, a 148-ton schooner, the *Black Eyed Susan* of Appledore, was forced towards land by the raging gale and grounded under cliffs on the south side of the Spa. Again, the town's lifeboat was able to edge alongside amid the turbulent waters and take off the five crew members.

Crowds of onlookers lining the seafront cheered as the lifeboat continued to transfer crewmen from stricken vessels to the safety of the shore. Two vessels attempted to reach the safety of the harbour, and crewmen on the brig *Maria*, of Yarmouth, managed to hurl a rope to rescuers on the pier, only for the fibres to split as it was edging to safety. A second ship, the *Glastry*, then smashed into the *Maria*, but this time ropes held and she was hauled safely into the harbour mouth. (Arthur Godfrey and Peter J. Lassey, *Shipwrecks of the Yorkshire Coast*, Dalesman Publishing Co. Ltd, 1974)

OCTOBER 28TH

1537: On this day, a truce was declared between rebels and forces supporting the King, during the Pilgrimage of Grace. This popular uprising had raised a revolt against the economic and religious policies of Henry VIII. From the outset, the constable of Scarborough Castle, Sir Ralph Eure, had declared his support for the King and his stronghold was besieged by locals. Following the declaration of a truce in York, hostilities in Scarborough were halted, but it was not long before a ship carrying supplies for the castle was taken by rebels and the blockade resumed. Sir Ralph retained control of the castle and was rewarded for his loyalty with guardianship of the building for the rest of his life. (John A. Goodall, *Scarborough Castle, North Yorkshire*, English Heritage, 2000)

◆

1880: During the raging storm on this day, a naked man was hurled with great force into the base of a cliff at Hayburn Wyke. At considerable risk to themselves, a local labourer, Ed Leadley, and PC Weedy, freed his body. A lone survivor from the wrecked Swedish vessel the *Arun* had raised the alarm but the three other crew members were drowned. All the victims were buried amid wreaths and flowers from local folk in nearby Cloughton. (www.scarboroughsmaritimeheritage.org. uk/sailorsgraves)

OCTOBER 29TH

2011: An exhibition of bibles was held on this day at St Mary's Church at Cloughton near Scarborough, to mark the 400th anniversary of the King James Bible. Worshippers had responded to a request to submit old and new editions, including copies of the book on CD. One of the books on display was a rare copy printed in 1725. St Mary's Church originally dated from 1831, but was heavily restored during 1889-90, and represented one of many locations across the UK and around the world that staged events and projects to mark the anniversary. Her Majesty the Queen had highlighted the importance of the anniversary when she opened the General Synod in November 2010. The Authorised Version of the Bible was commissioned by King James at the Hampton Court Conference in 1604 and completed seven years later. Celebratory events during 2010-11 were organised by the King James Bible Trust, whose patron is His Royal Highness the Prince of Wales. The 2011 celebrations were launched at Hampton Court and ended on November 16th 2011, with a service in Westminster Abbey. It was there, in the Jerusalem Chamber, that the final editing of the Bible was completed. (*Scarborough Evening News* and www.churchofengland.org)

OCTOBER 30TH

1914: The Scarborough lifeboat, the *Queensbury*, played a part in epic rescue attempts involving the hospital ship the *Rohilla* on this day. The converted liner had left Queensferry in Scotland a day earlier, bound for Dunkirk with 229 people on-board, but at 4 a.m. she struck rocks at Saltwick Nab, south of Whitby. Weather conditions were extremely poor and it was impossible to launch Whitby's no. 1 lifeboat from the harbour. The no. 2 boat, the *John Fielden*, was hauled from the harbour over the rocky foreshore and launched from the beach opposite the *Rohilla*, at 7 a.m. After considerable effort, five nurses and twelve men were rescued on the first trip and another eighteen men were safely brought ashore after a second attempt.

The *John Fielden* was badly damaged by this stage and other rescue boats were alerted. The Upgang lifeboat was lowered down cliffs, but was prevented from putting to sea by huge breakers, while the Scarborough lifeboat, the *Queensbury*, was towed to Saltwick Nab by a steam trawler. Darkness and a reef of jagged rocks around the *Rohilla* delayed a rescue attempt until the following morning, only for high seas to cause the *Queensbury* to return to Scarborough. It was the arrival of a motor lifeboat from Tynemouth that enabled further rescues from the *Rohilla*. (www.weetoddy.com)

OCTOBER 31ST

1636: On this day, Sir Thomas Posthumous Hoby presented a mace to the town of Scarborough. Sir Thomas was Senior Bailiff of the borough in 1610 and represented Scarborough in parliament from 1597-1603. A description of the mace by Brogden Baker states:

> The large mace of silver is a remarkably fine example, the shaft divided into lengths by massive knops, the bowl divided into compartments by semi-winged figures and foliage with the usual crowned emblems of the rose thistle fleur de lis and harp between the initials 'CR' and the open arches of the crown rising from a circlet of crosses, patee and fleur de lis with intervening balls and surmounted by orb and cross.

The mace, which has been altered after its initial presentation to the town, is carried by the Sergeant-at-Mace on ceremonial occasions. (S. Foord, *Scarborough Records*)

———•◆•———

1941: A mobile canteen was presented to the Scarborough Civil Defence Service on this day, by the District Regional Commissioner, Mr J. Lawson. It had earlier been a gift from the womenfolk of Southern Rhodesia to the Lord Mayor of London. (Richard James Percy, *Scarborough's War Years, 1939-45*, Sutton Publishing Ltd, 1992)

NOVEMBER 1ST

1801: On this day, a Newcastle-based brig, the *Aurora*, got into difficulties off Scarborough and the town's lifeboat was called into action for the first time. John Harwood, the lifeboat's first coxswain, and his crew rescued the seven crew members of the brig and brought them safely to shore. As a sign of their gratitude, the owners of the *Aurora* made a gift of five guineas to the lifeboat, and during the first year of operations similar donations were made by the owners of the brig *Experiment*, the brig *Assistance*, the hoy *Catherine* and two other vessels.

Moves to base a lifeboat at Scarborough had gathered momentum during 1880, with strong support from local people, such as Thomas Hinderwell, and fundraising events were held. A committee was chosen and it was agreed that there would be twelve men in each crew, with crews working in rotation and launchings were only allowed with approval from at least one member of the committee. By August 1801, funds raised amounted to £212 1s 6d and work began on a similar boat to Henry Greathead's *Original* of South Shields. Work was carried out by Chris Smith who charged £129 5s, plus an additional seventeen guineas for cork. (Arthur Godfrey, *Scarborough Lifeboats*, Hendon Publishing Co. Ltd, 1975)

NOVEMBER 2ND

1826: Scarborough's emergence as a popular resort during the late eighteenth and early nineteenth centuries was illustrated by the formation of the Cliff Bridge Company on this day. Founding members were twenty-six pioneers who met at the George in York, and at this initial meeting they appointed a Mr Outhett as Engineer, with a salary of £200 for supervising construction of the bridge. (www.discoveryyorkshirecoast. co.uk)

2011: The 150th Anniversary of one of the town's most noteworthy shipwrecks was celebrated in a special ceremony on this day. Five volunteers died during the rescue attempt involving a South Shields schooner, the *Coupland*, on November 2nd 1861. These included Lord Charles Beauclerk, who was a guest at the Crown Spa Hotel on the Esplanade. He was swept to his death in icy waters after he leapt into the North Sea, in a desperate attempt to save crew members of Scarborough's first RNLI lifeboat, the *Amelia*.

During a memorial ceremony, Lord Beauclerk's great-grandson, John Beauclerk, laid a wreath in memory of all five men, and Lord Beauclerk's grave was given a new headstone in recognition of his bravery. (*Scarborough Evening News*)

NOVEMBER 3RD

1935: Ernest Dade, artist and yachtsman, died on this day. His ashes were scattered from Scarborough pier. After moving from London to Scarborough, he began to sketch the harbour and its boats, before studying art in Paris and the South of France during the early 1800s. Dade exhibited in many London galleries, including the New English Art Club, before moving back to Scarborough where his work was widely displayed between 1889 and 1912. He usually painted marine, coastal and shipping subjects in oils and watercolours, but also worked in black and white. Ernest Dade was a founder member of the Staithes Art Group, and a founder member and first captain of Scarborough Yacht Club in 1895. He wrote specialist articles for *The Quarterly Journal of the Society for Nautical Research* on 'Trawling Under Sail on the North East Coast', in 1932 and 'Old Yorkshire Yawls', in 1933. (Anne and Paul Bayliss, *Scarborough Artists of the Nineteenth Century, A Biographical Dictionary*, Anne Bayliss, 1997)

———◆———

2008: On this day, it was announced that the Scarborough Building Society was to merge with the Skipton Building Society. Formed in 1846 as The Scarborough and North and East Yorkshire Building and Investment Society, it adopted the name Scarborough Building Society in 1903 and became the seventeenth largest in the United Kingdom. (*The Guardian*)

NOVEMBER 4TH

1902: A notice was published in the *Scarborough Evening News* on this day, regarding the formation of Scarborough Town Golf and Lawn Tennis Company Limited, with a capital of £1,500 in £1 shares. A meeting was planned for prospective members at the town's Cambridge Hotel, and when the meeting took place it was decided to form a golf club known as The Scarborough Town Golf Club, in order to distinguish it from the existing club at Ganton, which was then known as The Scarborough Golf Club. The Scarborough Cliff Lawn Tennis Club was also formed and the land for both clubs was rented from the Scarborough Corporation, with permission given to construct a pavilion, golf course and tennis courts. Original plans for a course, which would have extended from the present clubhouse towards Scarborough College, did not materialise, and the course was constructed along the Deepdale and Weaponess Valleys towards Eastfield. (www.soutcliffgolfclub.com)

———— • ◆ • ————

1914: The *Scarborough Pictorial* published an advert for the Boyes' Store's sale today, offering £300 of wool which was 'suitable for soldiers and sailors comforts'. Local shops bought in items specifically for this purpose as part of the war effort. The *Scarborough Pictorial* published photographs of soldiers and sailors who had volunteered for war service, along with poems and songs. (*Scarborough Pictorial*)

NOVEMBER 5TH

1895: Portrait painter Frank Reynolds died in Scarborough on this day. Born in London into a family of artists, he studied at the Royal Academy of Art before moving to Dublin, where he painted portraits and completed commissions for Cranfield, printer-seller and publisher. His work was exhibited in the Royal Hibernian Academy between 1860 and 1875; he then spent time in Brighton before moving to Scarborough sometime before 1890. He is listed as an artist in the Scarborough directory for 1890, and had an address in Oak Road in the 1891 census. (www.libraryireland.com)

***

2009: On this day, the Scarborough Maritime Heritage Centre opened in former shop building, no. 36 Eastborough, on a main route leading to the harbour. A group met in 2004 to investigate the possibility of establishing a centre, and two years later a committee was formed to seek out a base for two donated lifetime collections of over 50,000 maritime photographs, log books, certificates, harbour records and memorabilia. In the two years after its opening by the Mayor of Scarborough, Councillor Bill Chatt, the centre has welcomed over 6,000 visitors and is run by volunteers. (www. scarboroughsmaritimeheritage.org.uk)

NOVEMBER 6TH

1880: The disastrous storms at the end of October 1880 prompted an article that appeared in the *Scarborough Mercury* on this day. The article provided details of some of the graves to be found in Filey Churchyard for victims of earlier storms, which included the grave of John Cammish, aged sixty-eight, who drowned in Filey Bay on December 22nd 1824; his body was not discovered until February 5th 1825, at Flamborough Head. Other members of the Cammish family are also buried in this graveyard, including William Cammish who was also drowned at sea, in March 1851.

Another part of the article focuses on a less obvious area: 'While wandering over this churchyard, the eye is attracted by a small cross, in a secluded spot, graced by weeping willows, which points out where "strange sailors are interred".' This quiet commemorative corner was created to serve as a memorial to the loss of the Italian barque, the *Unico*, and its twelve crew members who drowned in the incident on January 16th 1871. The genuine sadness and sympathy felt by local people on these occasions shows through, as the article continues: 'Words are inadequate to tell the thoughts which cross the mind at the moment while reading this monument to the memory of those who perished so far from their native land.' (*Scarborough Mercury*)

NOVEMBER 7TH

1933: An interesting lecture was given in the Westborough Unitarian schoolroom on Jane Austen by Revd Rosamund H. Barker BD, recently appointed minister at Malton Unitarian Church. Miss Barker gave brief biographical details of Jane Austen's life and explained how her upbringing and surroundings reflected in her life and works. As a daughter of the manse, she spent most of her time at home in Hampshire or in Bath, with a brief schooling at Oxford, and her essentially quiet home life coloured her writings. Born in 1775, she lived through stirring times up to her death in 1817, but kept the themes of her novels traditional and did not delve too deeply into crime, passion or wickedness. Reverend Barker explained that although Austen knew society thoroughly, she only portrayed small parts of it in her work, which she did with considerable care. When she was sixteen, she had already filled a number of school copy books with her notes and writings, but her six main books were written at intervals from 1795 (when Austen was in her twenties), although they remained unpublished until 1811. (*Scarborough Evening News* and *Daily Post*)

NOVEMBER 8TH

1898: Mary, wife of Captain Thomas Gibson who was warden of Wilson's Mariners' Homes, died on this day. The single-storey block of almshouses in Castle Road, Scarborough, had opened in 1837, and Captain Gibson and his wife moved into almshouse No. 1 on July 2nd 1895. A fine set of character references led to his appointment as warden of the almshouses on November 25th 1896, and for almost two years, up until his wife's death, his performance in this post was exemplary. However, soon after his bereavement, Captain Gibson's lifestyle changed noticeably and he became a regular customer at the nearby Scarborough Arms. By 1904, he had gained a reputation in the neighbourhood as an habitual drunkard, which prompted the Vicar of Scarborough, Bishop Frederick Blunt, an ex-officio trustee of the almshouses, to call on the trustees to discipline Gibson for his 'disgraceful, unseemly insobriety'.

At a meeting on September 28th 1904, Captain Gibson was removed from his post, which brought an annual salary of twelve guineas, and was warned about possible eviction. It seems that he managed to maintain a more sober lifestyle until July 5th 1906, when he left Scarborough for an unknown address. (*Scarborough Evening News*)

NOVEMBER 9TH

1852: On this day, a Mayor's chain was presented to the Corporation by Mr John Woodall. The chain consists of a rose, the emblem of the County of York, alternated with ornaments of a medieval character and shoulder pieces bearing the inscription '*Sigillum Ville De Scardeburg*'. Attached to the collar, in the form of a pendant, is a badge which consists of the borough seal. On the reverse side of the badge is the inscription 'The gift of John Woodall Esq. to the Worshipful the Mayor and Corporation of Scarborough. November 9th 1852.' (S. Foord, *Scarborough Records*)

———◆———

1933: Two Scarborough men appeared in court on this day, charged with night-time poaching. James Dean, a gamekeeper, said he heard shots between 9 and 10 p.m. coming from the direction of Ruston cow pasture, and along with two other men he went to investigate. They met the defendants cycling down a lane, where they stopped and searched them and discovered a shotgun and six pheasants in their possession. Magistrates found the two men guilty and gave them a fine of 40s each, or prison for one month, as well as sureties of £5 each, or one of £10 for their good behaviour in the next 12 months. (*Scarborough Evening News* and *Daily Post*)

November 10th

2011: On this day, local newspapers reported that members of the Scarborough Maritime Heritage Centre (SMHC) were celebrating, after the group was awarded 'Heritage' status. This development followed a year of hard work by the centre's secretary, Faith Young, and the award was given by the Charity Commission. The centre had opened to visitors in November 2009 and in addition to staging regular public exhibitions, it also contains an impressive library and archive. Chairman of SMHC, Mark Vesey, attended the 4th National Maritime Heritage Forum in Chatham Dockyard on November 1st-2nd 2011, where it was reported that a study by the Association of Independent Museums (AIM) showed that maritime heritage contributes more than £100 million to the UK economy by attracting 8 million visitors each year and employing 2,300 people. Up to 5,000 volunteers contribute 'in kind' hours, equating to a value of over half a million pounds. Six volunteers from SMHC had recently attended training events staged by the Museums' Trust in connection with the Fears, Foes and Faeries exhibition, which was to open at the town's art gallery in March 2012. Volunteers had made oral history recordings of local fishermen and women about their superstitions. (*Scarborough Evening News*)

NOVEMBER 11TH

2011: An eighty-two-year-old Leyland Tiger bus was hauled onto a low-loader trailer and driven to London today, in readiness for its appearance in the Lord Mayor's Show the following day. Apprentices from Bluebird Vehicles had carefully restored the disused vehicle, for which some of them were rewarded with a place on-board during the parade. Other passengers on the bus included sixty-six-year-old Bernard Moment, who had come out of retirement to assist with restoration work, and representatives from the Welcome to Yorkshire organisation. Welcome to Yorkshire had been invited to enter the parade by the incoming Mayor of London, Bradford-born David Wooton, and in turn the organisation asked Bluebird Vehicles to provide a vehicle for the parade. The bus had the Welcome to Yorkshire logo emblazoned on its side during the procession. It was the first time that Scarborough had an entry in the historic event and only the second occasion that Yorkshire had been represented. In 2010, the Whitby steam bus the *Elizabeth* travelled the route and it returned a year later to represent the region alongside the Tiger in front of an estimated three million people who watched the parade. (*Scarborough Evening News*)

NOVEMBER 12TH

1871: This day marked Scarborough's first 'Dispensary Sunday'. The *Scarborough Mercury* announced that seventeen sermons would be preached on behalf of the institution at nine different churches, where special collections would be made. In the decade after the opening of the Dispensary (1852-62), church collections for its support fluctuated from £9 to £101, with an average of around £44. Initial moves towards a designated day began in August 1861, when the Vicar of Scarborough, Revd Whiteside, was invited to preach on its behalf at St Mary's parish church.

In about the same year, churches in Birmingham had begun fundraising on a specific Sunday, and even though the scheme proved successful, it was not until 1870 that the proposal was discussed in Scarborough. There was general agreement, but a body of opinion favoured allowing churches to choose their own Sunday. At a later meeting in September 1871, it was concluded that the second Sunday in November should be 'Dispensary Sunday'. The 1872 Dispensary Annual Report stated that total income during 1871 amounted to £488, of which more than £150 had been raised on this annual fundraising day. (Anne Bayliss, Paul Bayliss and Alan Jackson, *Scarborough Hospital and Dispensary: The First Fifty Years, 1852-1902*, A.M. Bayliss, 2006)

NOVEMBER 13TH

1836: On this day, Robert Cattle, Sheriff of York and 'projector' of the Scarborough Cliff Bridge Company (according to inscribed lettering on the foundation stone), sold his shares in the organisation to William Rowntree, a draper by trade. This sale brought his ten year connection with the enterprise to an end. In October 1826 he had written to the Scarborough Corporation to propose the floating of a company to build a bridge that would allow improved access to the Spaw from St Nicholas' Cliff. His efforts saw him become an honorary freeman, and committee members of the reconstituted company arranged 'free access to Robert Cattle Esq. and his family to the bridge and promenade at all times'. (Meredith Whittaker, *The Book of Scarborough Spaw*, Barracuda, 1984)

❖

1906: Scarborough's Forty Club staged a whole range of activities, including social gatherings and fundraising events, but its prime purpose was always to provide a forum for discussion and debate. In his paper to the Forty Club on this day, Mr Vasey 'Impressed upon members the importance of reading up matters for the subjects to come before them. He also recommended the members to read and inwardly digest literature, poetry and history as the only practical means of enlarging the vocabulary for public speaking.' (Alan Staniforth, *Scarborough Forty Club & Discussion Group: A Brief History: the '40' Club, founded in 1899*, Alan Staniforth, 2005)

November 14th

1902: On this day, the laying up dinner of the Scarborough Sailing Club was held in the town's Salisbury Hotel. According to reports, the highlight of the evening's proceedings was a summary of the popular raconteur, Albert Strange's cruising experiences. In his report, the club captain stated that there had never been a better feeling among members than at the present time, and that the abiding memory of the previous year's activities was the part the club had played in the Coronation festivities. (W.H. James, *Scarborough Sailing Club, Scarborough Yacht Club: A History*, The Walkergate Press Ltd, 1976)

1947: The formal opening of the Scarborough Art Gallery at Crescent House took place on this day, with a ceremony at the public library. In his speech, Mr A.C.M. Spearman MP mentioned current financial problems: '. . . for a period we shall have to forego some of the more hectic amusements of recent years and go back to the simple pleasures of our forebears . . . We have got an exhibition before us that will both interest and instruct.' Councillor N. Walsh, chairman of the Libraries Committee, proposed a vote of thanks and 'Hoped it would become a meeting place for Scarborough people. It would be one nail in the coffin of the criticism that Scarborough did everything for visitors and nothing for residents.' (*Scarborough Evening News*)

NOVEMBER 15TH

1897: Sir Sacheverell Sitwell was born this day at no. 5 Belvoir Terrace (then known as Belvoir House) in Scarborough. He was the younger brother of Dame Edith and Sir Osbert. Following education at Eton College and Balliol College, he served in the Grenadier Guards from 1916, before travelling widely in support of his siblings' literary presentations and his own research projects. He wrote more than 100 books on art, architecture, music and travel, up until his death at Weston Hall on October 1st 1988. He had two sons, Reresby and Francis, from his marriage to Georgia Doble in October 1925. A plaque in his memory was unveiled at Belvoir Terrace on November 15th 2004, by Sir Reresby Sitwell. (www. dictionaryofarthistorians.org)

1904: At a meeting of the Scarborough Forty Club on this day, a paper on 'Burns and His Times', delivered by Mr Pexton, was voted 'one of the best papers ever given'. (Alan Staniforth, *Scarborough Forty Club & Discussion Group: A Brief History: the '40' Club, founded in 1899*, Alan Staniforth, 2005)

1941: On this day, a single enemy aircraft circled above Scarborough for about ten minutes before dropping two bombs. One fell into the harbour and the other damaged properties in the Castle Dykes and interrupted a wedding ceremony at St Mary's Church. (Richard James Percy, *Scarborough's War Years, 1939-45*, Sutton Publishing Ltd, 1992)

NOVEMBER 16TH

1922: Dramatic events on this day in Scarborough's Bar Hotel helped Scotland Yard detectives to solve a mysterious murder case. St Nicholas Street and Newborough were crowded due to the election results being announced, when Inspector Abbott and Detective Nalton called at the hotel to interview a man who had been offering work to ex-servicemen in the local press. As they escorted Fitzsimmons, or Ernest Dyer as his real name proved to be, to his room upstairs he reached towards his chest. A struggle followed and a bullet fired from a revolver that had been in Fitzsimmons' pocket, killing the suspect instantly. At the inquest the coroner was unable to rule whether the gun was fired accidentally or deliberately, but he did draw attention to Fitzsimmons' murky past. The arrival of one of Scotland Yard's most senior detectives, Superintendent Francis Carlin, established a link with an unsolved murder; Ernest Dyer (Fitzsimmons) had been in a business partnership with an ex-soldier, Eric Gordon Tombe, who had mysteriously disappeared some seven months earlier. In a dream, Tombe's mother saw her son's body at the bottom of a well, and a subsequent search revealed his mutilated corpse at the bottom of a farmyard cess pool. Dyer was soon identified as the murderer. (S. Foord, *Scarborough Records*)

NOVEMBER 17TH

1903: On this day, the Scarborough Forty Club held a debate on the subject 'Are the working classes of this country injured by the policy of so-called "Free Trade"?' which was adjourned several times and continued over four consecutive meetings. (Alan Staniforth, *Scarborough Forty Club & Discussion Group: A Brief History: the '40' Club, founded in 1899*, Alan Staniforth, 2005)

———•◆•———

1906: A gathering of forty-nine men at the Albemarle Hotel in Scarborough established the Borough Bowling Club on this day, and fixed the annual subscription rate at 2s. This followed an earlier meeting on November 2nd 1905, when a resolution to form a club had not resulted as such. The town's links with outdoor green bowling extended back to at least the seventeenth century. The location where Scarborough's Mayor was once tossed in a blanket was named as The Old Bowling Green as early as 1688 and as visitors flocked to the Spa resort during the 1700s, outdoor bowls was played on a level stretch of turf between St Nicholas' Street and Huntriss Row. Increasing numbers of visitors meant there was a need for an improved green, and on August 2nd 1902 the town's mayor, William Morgan, opened Manor Road bowling green, which measured 36 yards by 46 yards with a crown of eight inches. (Jack Binns, *The Borough Bowling Club: the First Hundred Years 1905-2005*, 2005)

NOVEMBER 18TH

1882: Richard Cross, physician and surgeon, died on this date in Scarborough, where he had been based since 1840. Born in 1818 at East Heslerton Grange in Yorkshire, he later studied at Guy's Hospital in London and qualified as a surgeon in 1839. Some eight years after his move to Scarborough, Cross became a partner of a practice with Thomas Weddell in Queen Street, which continued first with Henry Wright and latterly with his son, Thomas Brown Cross, as partners. Cross served as Surgeon to the Royal Northern Sea-Bathing Infirmary, as well as the Medical Officer to the Ancient of Foresters Friendly Society, and Ordnance Surgeon for Scarborough, and in 1881 he was elected Fellow of the Royal College of Surgeons. He also played a leading role in public life, with election to the Scarborough Corporation in 1849, followed by continual re-election until 1862 when he was made an alderman. He was the town's mayor in 1860-61 and retired from civic activities in 1874. Cross was also a magistrate for the borough and a trustee of several local charities. He was given a military and civic funeral, which drew the largest attendance of townspeople to that date. (Anne and Paul Bayliss, *Medical Profession in Scarborough 1700 to 1899: A Biographical Dictionary*, A.M. Bayliss, 2005)

NOVEMBER 19TH

2000: Captain Sydney Thomas Smith MBE died on this day in Scarborough, after a lifetime associated with the sea. Born in Cooks Row in 1907, he was educated at Friargate School and Graham Sea Training School before joining the merchant navy at the age of sixteen. After rising through the ranks, he took his master's exam in 1936 and soon gained a reputation for daring exploits, which included rescuing prisoners of war from pro-Nazi Spain and transporting invasion forces into Africa, Italy, Burma and the D-Day landings during the Second World War.

On his return to Scarborough after the war, Captain Smith skippered vessels, including dredgers, along the east coast and he served as deputy harbour master from 1970 until his retirement in 1974. As an acknowledged expert on tidal matters he edited Olsen's *Fishermen's Nautical Almanac* for over twenty years and, as well as campaigning for cleaner coastal areas with Friends of Neptune, he was a trustee of Scarborough's Trinity House; a home for retired mariners in St Sepulchre Street. On September 2nd 2005, a bridge commemorating the life and work of Captain Smith, which connects the pier with the lighthouse, was officially opened by Scarborough's MP, Laurie Quinn. (*Scarborough Evening News*)

NOVEMBER 20TH

1899: Thomas Whittaker died at his home in Scarborough on this day, after a lifetime's service to the temperance movement, and a prominent role in local politics and the newspaper industry. Born in Grindleton in West Yorkshire in 1813, his family moved to Lancashire some ten years later, and at the age of twenty-two, Thomas Whittaker began his commitment to the temperance movement. In 1839 he first visited Scarborough to deliver a temperance lecture at the Methodist Chapel, Church Stairs, and ten years later he accepted William Rowntree's offer to run a temperance hotel in the Newborough area. During 1850 he was Vice President of Scarborough Temperance Society and went on to publish two books on the subject, as well as running his own paper, the *Watchman*, between 1867 and 1869. In 1875, Whittaker was a member of a consortium that bought the *Scarborough Mercury* and soon afterwards Thomas and his two sons took over sole ownership. In 1882, they began publication of the *Scarborough Evening News*.

Thomas Whittaker was elected to the town council between 1867 and 1873, and again from 1876 until his retirement in 1884. Between 1880 and 1881, he was Mayor of Scarborough, and his work for the temperance movement was highlighted by the British Temperance League at their annual conference in York during 1893. (Anne and Paul Bayliss, *Scarborough's Members of Parliament, 1832 to 1906: Scarborough's Mayors, 1836 to 1906: A Biographical Dictionary*, A.M. Bayliss, 2008)

NOVEMBER 21ST

1903: Scarborough's Promenade Pier was badly damaged today, when a strong north to north-westerly gale combined with a high tide to batter England's north-east coastline. Around 200ft of the pier's decking was ripped apart at the shore end, and an amount of ironwork along both sides of the structure was wrecked. Several windows in the café at the pier entrance were also shattered, leaving the total damage at around £200. During the storm, a number of anglers were trapped on the pier head and had to be rescued by boat.

Directors of the pier company considered making a storm claim against the Scarborough Corporation, on the grounds that the new sea wall had increased damage to the pier through a backlash of waves. It soon became clear, however, that the company lacked the finance to pursue such a claim, and during 1904 it was increasingly obvious that their attempt to promote the pier was doomed.

At an auction held on September 21st 1904, the pier was bought for the sum of £3,500 by the town's mayor, William Morgan, only for it to be totally destroyed by storms in early January 1905. (Martin Easdown, *Times of a Troubled Pier: a Brief History of Scarborough's Ill-Fated Promenade Pier*, Marlinova, 2005)

NOVEMBER 22ND

1851: On this day, a meeting held in the Scarborough Town Hall marked a major development in the provision of a dispensary for the local community. The initiative for such a venture had begun some nine months earlier, with a private meeting organised by Dr George Peckitt Dale involving five colleagues from the medical profession, and now attention was focused on a scheme to make use of rooms in the Mechanics' Institute building in Vernon Place (now Vernon Road). Originally opened in 1840 for the Order of Oddfellows, a friendly society, it was later renamed as the Hall of Commerce, before becoming the Mechanics' Institute. At the Town Hall meeting, a Dispensary subcommittee was set up and given a brief to reach agreement over suitable accommodation, with a maximum annual rent of £20 over not more than three years. The same working group was also charged with equipping the premises within a budget of £50, and an overall agreement was reached that the maximum salary of a resident apothecary would be £60, as well as provision of two rooms for his use with 'lights and coals'. The Scarborough Dispensary opened in the Mechanics' Institute building on January 19th 1852. (Anne Bayliss, Paul Bayliss and Alan Jackson, *Scarborough Hospital and Dispensary: The First Fifty Years, 1852-1902*, A.M. Bayliss, 2006)

NOVEMBER 23RD

1969: On this day, a dramatic and daring rescue by the Scarborough lifeboat resulted in the Maud Smith Award being given to Coxswain Bill Sheader. After the motor boat *Sheena* had capsized among dangerous outcrops of rocks in Scarborough's South Bay, it was Sheader's skilful navigation and considerable gallantry that enabled the rescue of a man from the sea. The Maud Smith Award was given for the bravest act of lifesaving carried out by a lifeboatman during 1969, and Coxswain Sheader shared it with Coxswain Eric Offer of the Dun Laoghaire lifeboat. (Arthur Godfrey, *Scarborough Lifeboats*, Hendon Publishing Co. Ltd, 1975)

———•◆•———

1971: Timothy Sheader, Bill Sheader's son, was born in Scarborough on this day. He grew up in the town and attended Wheatcroft School and Graham School, before taking up studies at Scarborough Sixth Form College. After graduating with a law degree from Birmingham University, he took up a career in the theatre industry and came to prominence with his appointment as Artistic Director at the Regent's Park Open Air Theatre in November 2007. His innovative approach to productions saw him pick up three Olivier awards in 2010, on behalf of the theatre, and a further award in 2011 for Best Musical Revival for his production of *Into the Woods*. (*Scarborough News*)

NOVEMBER 24TH

1488: Scarborough authorities ruled today, that any person having a vessel built or repaired at the 'Botehill' should not remove it without paying the bailiff 1s per week. (www.scarboroughsmaritimeheritage.org.uk)

❖

1816: Naturalist William Crawford Williamson was born in Scarborough on this day. For many years, his father was the first curator of the town's natural history museum and he was brought up in the company of scientific people, such as William Smith, the 'father of English geology'. At the age of sixteen he published a paper on rare birds of Yorkshire, and in 1834 delivered his findings on Mesozoic fossils of this home district to the Geological Society in London. After taking up a career in medicine, he continued research into aspects of botany, and when Owen's College was founded at Manchester in 1851 he became professor of natural history, with teaching duties covering geology, zoology and botany. Williamson continued in the chair of botany until 1892, before he moved to Clapham, where he died in June 1895. His research covered wide areas of fossil botany and he illustrated his work with his own drawings. (www.geolsoc.org.uk)

NOVEMBER 25TH

1793: James Cockshutt and a group of promoters met on this day, to hear news of his first survey report on a proposed canal from Scarborough to Malton. A further meeting was held on May 22nd 1794 to consider a revised route between the two towns but, like so many other similar schemes, it was not pursued. (www.jim-sheard.com/waterways)

———•◆•———

1925: Peter Jaconelli, who became known as 'the ice cream king of Scarborough', was born on this day. His father moved to the town from Scotland in 1933, and it was not long before he honed his skills in presenting ice creams. A spell of training as an operatic singer in Naples and at the Royal College of Music was followed by a return to the family business in Scarborough, where he expanded operations into restaurants, along with the distribution of ice cream and luxury desserts on a national scale. Weighing 21 stone and with a waistline measuring 50 inches, he became a prominent figure in local politics and as Mayor in 1970 he entered the Guinness Book of Records for consuming 42 oysters in 48 minutes, 42 seconds. He was also chairman of North Yorkshire and the county planning committee for many years. He died on May 15th 1999. (www.guardian.co.uk)

NOVEMBER 26TH

1866: John Barry, a prominent employer and former Mayor of Scarborough, died on this day and was buried in Scarborough Cemetery. Born in 1803 and baptised at St Mary's parish church on September 25th, he built up a highly successful building company, with projects ranging from work at Scarborough Spa in 1828 to Wilson's Mariners' Homes in Castle Road during 1836. After completing large contracts at Arbroath and Leith he returned to Scarborough in the mid-1850s and was elected as councillor for the North Ward, before becoming Mayor in 1859-60. His final major building contract was South Cliff Congregational Church (more recently St Andrew's Church), which opened in 1865. (Anne and Paul Bayliss, *Scarborough's Members of Parliament, 1832 to 1906: Scarborough's Mayors, 1836 to 1906: A Biographical Dictionary*, A.M. Bayliss, 2008)

1884: On this day, Liberal William Sproston Caine successfully fought a by-election at Scarborough against the Conservative candidate, Sir George Sitwell. He had failed to win parliamentary seats in Liverpool before moving his family to Scarborough, where he reorganised the local Liberal Party and success soon followed in the April 1880 general election. William Caine's main points of interest were temperance and India, and as the town's MP he was instrumental in founding the Scarborough School of Art; in the same year he laid a foundation stone for the local Salvation Army Barracks. He died at his London home on March 17th 1903. (Anne and Paul Bayliss, *Scarborough's Members of Parliament, 1832 to 1906: Scarborough's Mayors, 1836 to 1906: A Biographical Dictionary*, A.M. Bayliss, 2008)

NOVEMBER 27TH

1963: An experimental demonstration was carried out by the North Eastern Electricity Board (NEEB) at Wykeham on this day, whilst working on 11,000 volt live wires. A similar repair undertaken before now would have meant that 1,000 consumers in the Wykeham area would have had their electricity supply disconnected for the day, but on this occasion a mechanically-propelled 5-ton machine named Polecat, manned by a team of Newcastle-based engineers, was used for the first time in the area to demonstrate the 'live-line' technique. Polecat, which incorporated an insulated platform, was used to help replace a decayed wooden pole between Wykeham Church and Ruston village. Engineers from Harrogate, York, Whitby, Malton and Scarborough were invited to watch the experiment, and the District Manager of NEEB's Scarborough office, Mr J. Messenger, said the success of today's experiment and future experiments in the North Eastern area would determine whether the board were prepared to buy such a machine for use in the area. Another experiment at Wykeham earlier in the week involved workmen climbing poles in spiked footwear and using insulated poles instead of disconnecting wires and using ladders. (*Scarborough Evening News*)

NOVEMBER 28TH

1901: At a meeting of the Scarborough Forty Club on this day, Mr Whitehead gave a somewhat lengthy introduction to his paper on 'The Coming Education Bill' – it was moved and carried that the meeting be adjourned and that he be allowed three quarters of an hour in which to finish his paper the following week. (Alan Staniforth, *Scarborough Forty Club & Discussion Group: A Brief History: the '40' Club, founded in 1899*, Alan Staniforth, 2005)

———•◆•———

1933: On this day, Scarborough members of the Cyclists Touring Club (CTC) faced rain, hail and bright intervals. Six members left at nine o'clock in the morning on the club's tourist ride of 100 miles in eight hours, on a route that covered the greater part of the East Riding, including York, Market Weighton, Beverley and Driffield.

While the six riders were thus engaged, a more leisurely group, including four tandem pairs, enjoyed a ramble on the Wolds ending at Bishop Wilton, which was nestled beneath the edge of the Wolds, near Garrowby Hill. Lunch by a warm fire and a chat with some Hull CTC members passed a pleasant hour, before they proceeded to Millington Dale. They emerged from the dale at Huggate to hail and sleet storms, on the way to Driffield, but then were met with fair weather on the stretch to Carnaby near Bridlington, where they met the trial riders for the return journey via Reighton. (*Scarborough Evening News* and *Daily Post*)

NOVEMBER 29TH

1204: Figures included in pipe rolls for the period between July 20th 1203 and November 29th 1204 show Scarborough's total taxable trade as £330 5s 7d. Much of the port's trade was in codfish and at the beginning of the thirteenth century a tax of one fifteenth was imposed on all imports and exports of sea-borne trade. During the same period, Whitby's total trade amounted to just £3 0s 0d, while trade through the port of Hull had reached £5,170 15s 7d. (Keith Snowden, *Scarborough Through the Ages: The Story of the Queen of English Watering Places*, Castleden Publications, 1995)

———◆———

2011: On this day, it was announced that a temporary giant statue on Scarborough's Marine Drive was to stay in place, after local resident Maureen Robinson bought it for £48,000 as a present for the town. The steel structure, *Freddie Gilroy and the Belsen Stragglers*, showed a miner who was one of the first soldiers to liberate the Bergen-Belsen concentration camp in Germany at the end of the Second World War. The figure was the work of Durham artist Ray Lonsdale, who took three months to complete it using Corten steel, which Antony Gormley used for *The Angel of the North* at Hartlepool. (*The Yorkshire Post*)

NOVEMBER 30TH

1843: Plans for a railway linking Scarborough with York were submitted on this day, with support from George Hudson, 'the Railway King'. Earlier proposals for this line had met opposition from people such as George Knowles, who published a pamphlet in 1840 condemning the planned railway. He claimed that the town had 'No wish for a greater influx of vagrants, and those who have no money to spend. Scarborough is rising daily in the estimation of the public as a fashionable watering place on account of its natural beauty and tranquillity, and in a few years more the novelty of not having a railroad will be its greatest asset.'

Work on the line was approved and Hudson appointed Robert Stephenson as engineer for the 42-mile route, which included twenty-five bridges. When the line opened on July 7th 1845, Scarborough Station had an unfinished roof and no goods shed, but the two platforms with four tracks between them were in place. The main station building comprised a large central booking office, superintendent's room, a second-class waiting room, toilets, a porter's room and a store room. (Mike Hitches, *Steam Around Scarborough*, Amberley Publishing, 2009)

DECEMBER 1ST

1688: On this day, the Earl of Danby wrote to the Prince of Orange that he had seized Scarborough Castle, which 'Contained a very good magazine and put in a garrison'. Since the 1650s, the castle had operated as a prison, which housed inmates such as George Fox (during 1665-66), and the adjacent town was considered to be of sufficient military importance to be kept in a state of defence until the treaty of Nimeguen in 1678. However, King James II did not maintain a regular garrison and it was stated 'That a good office and two companies of militia would be sufficient to hold it if the Dutch descended on the Yorkshire coast'. Rebels in the locality were, for the most part, pardoned in 1690, and in the event Scarborough and its castle played no part in the overthrow of James II. No measures were taken to improve or repair defences. Subsequent military surveys continue to mention the castle and Arthur, Viscount Irwin, was appointed governor in 1694, but it was not until the Jacobite Rebellion of 1745 that efforts were made to restore the castle's ruined walls. (www. victorianweb.org/history/Glorious-Revolution)

DECEMBER 2ND

1921: The close-knit nature of North Yorkshire's fishing communities perhaps inevitably provided any number of surprising links. However, it was on this particular day that local newspaper the *Scarborough Mercury* focused on 'a remarkable coincidence'. Two local couples, Mr and Mrs Gray and Mr and Mrs Thomson, celebrated their fiftieth wedding anniversary on the same date, both had lost a parent at sea and both had nine children. Mrs Thomson's father, Charles Harwood, was a shipwright by trade and he was drowned in a coble that was put to sea to pilot a vessel in the bay. Mr Gray had seen his father, who was a pilot based at Whitby, lose his life after his coble filled with water. As he attempted to swim ashore he was crushed against the pier.
(*Scarborough Mercury*)

———— • ◆ • ————

1963: It was announced on this day that Miss H. Smith, Assistant District Commissioner for Wolf Cubs and Cubmaster to the 46th Westborough Scout Group, had been awarded the medal of merit for outstanding services to scouting. She became Assistant District Commissioner in 1962 and was only the third person in the Scarborough area to be awarded the medal. Two senior scouts, David Williamson, aged seventeen, and Michael Hunt, sixteen, were presented with the Queen's Scout Badge at the same meeting. (*Scarborough Evening News*)

DECEMBER 3RD

1830: Frederick Leighton was born in Vernon Road, Scarborough, and educated at University College School, London, before studying art at various locations in Europe, including Florence and Paris. Returning to London in 1860 he was based in Holland Park Road and was elected President of the Royal Academy on November 13th 1878. Leighton's sculpture, *Athlete Wrestling with a Python* – completed in 1877 – was credited with stimulating a renaissance in contemporary British sculpture known as the 'New Sculpture', and his paintings represented Britain at the 1900 Paris Exhibition.

Knighted in 1878, Leighton was created a baron eight years later and received a peerage in the New Year's Honours List of 1896. He was the first artist to receive such an honour, but died on the following day. Earlier, when the Scarborough School of Art was founded in 1882, he had sent a message of good wishes on 'The vitality and spirit manifesting themselves in my beautiful native town in the cause of artistic education.' (Anne and Paul Bayliss, *Scarborough Artists of the Nineteenth Century, A Biographical Dictionary*, Anne Bayliss, 1997)

———— •◆• ————

1939: Following the declaration of war, sirens were positioned around the town and the first test was held at 2 p.m. on this day. (Richard James Percy, *Scarborough's War Years, 1939-45*, Sutton Publishing Ltd, 1992)

DECEMBER 4TH

1849: Valentine Fowler was born at Filey on this day. After working briefly in Leeds during his teenage years, he moved to Scarborough, where he worked at his uncle's water company before setting up his own highly successful business as an auctioneer and valuer. Fowler was first elected to the town council in 1881 and on many occasions following this, serving for a total of thirty-two years. During 1894-5, he was elected as Mayor of Scarborough and during this term of office he approved four 'Health Lectures to Women' in February 1895 by Mrs Dr Longshore-Potts. In 1896, he was appointed as a Justice of the Peace for the borough of Scarborough, and during a second term as Mayor in 1907-8, a highlight was the opening of Marine Drive in August 1908, by HRH the Duke of Connaught. Valentine Fowler died on August 20th 1918 at his home in Scarborough. (Anne and Paul Bayliss, *Scarborough's Members of Parliament, 1832 to 1906: Scarborough's Mayors, 1836 to 1906: A Biographical Dictionary*, A.M. Bayliss, 2008)

1859: On this day, a new workhouse was opened on land between Dean Street and Victoria Street, with some ninety occupants made up of men, women, children and families of all ages. Designed by York-based architects George and Henry Styan, it had cost £12,000 to complete. (Colin Waters, *Scarborough Then & Now*, The History Press Ltd, 2011)

DECEMBER 5TH

1933: 'The December and Christmastide illuminations have come into operation with a general effect that was very pleasing and undoubtedly surpassed any other previous illuminations at Scarborough.' Various shopping districts had selected their own colour schemes and this produced a good deal of variety between one district and another. Of the five shopping areas, two – the Falsgrave and Victoria Road/Castle Road efforts – had arranged official opening ceremonies. Mr F.C. Whittaker switched on the Falsgrave lights and said the thoroughfare had been transformed into a veritable fairyland. The effect produced by thousands of vari-coloured globes was striking in the extreme and there were many commendatory remarks from the crowd which had gathered in spite of the cold weather. Mr Whittaker reminded the crowd that the seasonal lights began only two years ago and he hoped the event would grow.

A crowd of several hundred people also gathered at the junction of Victoria Road and Castle Road, where Councillor Jackson switched on the street illuminations. Addressing members of the public by loudspeaker he said that some other districts had copied their 'diamonds', but urged his audience not to venture away from this area. (*Scarborough Evening News* and *Daily Post*)

DECEMBER 6TH

1894: On this day, mystery surrounded the loss of the 1,234-ton steamship, the *Richmond*, after it crashed into rocks at the base of cliffs near Hundale Point. It was making the journey from Rotterdam to the Tyne, under the part ownership of Thomas Leinster, who had absconded while awaiting trial on a charge of setting fire to the vessel some nine months earlier – the ship was insured for several thousand pounds. At a subsequent Board of Trade enquiry it was alleged that the *Richmond*'s captain, while under the influence of alcohol, had shouted to the second engineer 'Open the sea cocks and let's all go to hell' while the ship was travelling at seven or eight knots. All members of the crew were safely rescued by the Burniston Rocket Brigade. (Arthur Godfrey and Peter J. Lassey, *Shipwrecks of the Yorkshire Coast*, Dalesman Publishing Co. Ltd, 1974)

2011: An exhibition entitled 'Celebrations of the Sea' opened on this day at Scarborough Sea Life Park, in which images of media and sporting personalities were projected into the aquarium's tanks among the centre's resident sharks, eels and tropical fish. Proceeds from the exhibition were donated to the Shipwrecked Mariner's Society, which supports retired and impoverished seafarers in UK. (*Scarborough Evening News*)

DECEMBER 7TH

1901: On this day, Sir Charles Legard, Conservative MP for Scarborough from 1874-1880, died of heart failure at the town's Royal Hotel. Born on April 2nd 1846, he pursued a military career before leaving the army to manage family estates and take up a career in politics. His success at the 1874 election has been largely ascribed to the splitting of the Liberal vote among three candidates, but his term in office was plagued by controversy and he was bottom of the poll in the 1880 election. During the last two decades of the nineteenth century, Legard continued to be active in Scarborough politics, as well as serving as a magistrate and member of the East Riding County Council. He was also a patron of the town's football club and patron and trustee of Scarborough Cricket Club. (Anne and Paul Bayliss, *Scarborough's Members of Parliament, 1832 to 1906: Scarborough's Mayors, 1836 to 1906: A Biographical Dictionary*, A.M. Bayliss, 2008)

———◆———

1906: Workmen began to demolish Scarborough's Revolving Tower, which had attracted controversy since plans were passed by the council on September 13th 1897. It was one of four similar observatory towers built by Thomas Warwick, but after an initial amount of success it fell into disrepair, and a benefactor, Alfred Shuttleworth, paid for its removal. (*Scarborough Fact File: Warwick Revolving Tower*)

DECEMBER 8TH

1945: The final troop train of the war years (1939-45) left Scarborough station on this day at 10.00 a.m., heading for Richmond. Remaining troops left the town later by ordinary passenger trains, and the departure of this last troop train signalled the end of a huge number that had been specially arranged to carry not only troops but also tanks, Bren gun carriers and other equipment during the war years. (Richard James Percy, *Scarborough's War Years, 1939-45*, Sutton Publishing Ltd, 1992)

———— •◆• ————

1954: During late afternoon on this day, Scarborough lifeboat, the *ECJR*, had been launched in atrocious weather conditions to escort several fishing boats back to sheltered water in the harbour. After five hours at sea, the lifeboat was about to enter the harbour when the crew were informed that one more boat, the *Rosemary*, was still at sea. While turning around to go back the lifeboat was struck by two freak waves and capsized, throwing crewmen into the swell. As the lifeboat righted itself some of the missing men were pulled back on-board, but three lifeboatmen, Coxswain John Sheader, Second Coxswain John Cammish and Signalman Frank Bayes, died in the incident during which all the other boats entered the harbour safely. An annual memorial service is held to mark this tragedy. (*The 200 year history of Scarborough RNLI*)

DECEMBER 9TH

1902: On this day, the first service was held at a new chapel in Scarborough's Manor Road cemetery. Plans for a chapel were made in February 1873, but in April 1876 it was reported that work on the chapel and a bridge had been postponed owing to the cost of iron and other building materials. Work was eventually carried out during 1901-02. (www.scarborough. gov.uk)

1951: At 11.15 a.m. on this day, Scarborough lifeboat, the *ECJR*, answered a distress call from a Dutch coaster, the *West Kust*. The lifeboat had an operational radius of 63 nautical miles at full speed and had been brought to the town earlier in the year. It was specially designed for use from tidal harbours, and within 14 minutes the lifeboat was at sea. Coxswain John Sheader was able to navigate the *ECJR* towards the Dutch coaster by rockets fired from vessels close to it, about 19 miles off Flamborough Head. Heavy swell made it difficult to manoeuvre alongside, but bowman Frank Dalton and Second Mechanic Thomas Mainprize were able to board and assist the *West Kust*'s ten crewmen onto the lifeboat. Sadly, Frank Dalton suffered fatal injuries as he returned to the *ECJR* and along with the two other lifeboatmen, he was posthumously awarded a bronze medal. (www.scarboroughmaritimeheritage.org.uk)

December 10th

1963: A press announcement on this day reported that a centuries-long wait for a water supply at St Martin's Church in Seamer should soon be over. The cost of connecting water to this large building had been estimated at £120 and a recent 'gift day' at the church, supervised by the vicar, Revd W.R. Bosham, had raised £200. This amount would cover installation of a water supply as well as leaving £30 for a wash basin and fittings in the vestry, and the remaining balance going towards church expenses. (*Scarborough Evening News*)

1963: A report on a meeting of the Scarborough and District Archaeological Society was issued on this day. It summarised a lecture by Mr W. Varley, in which he stated that Iron-Age hill forts were the most significant feats of engineering in this country before the Roman legions arrived. From about 350 BC, for around 400 years, hundreds of these defensive earthworks were erected from Sussex to Cornwall, and northwards to the Welsh Marches and the Irish Sea, where they would protect trade routes for supplies of copper from Ireland and tin from Cornwall. There was less need for such encampments in East Yorkshire, he added, where the Parisi tribe was more aggressive in using chariots and cutting swords, as well as already trading peacefully with the Romans. (*Scarborough Evening News*)

DECEMBER 11TH

1963: On this day, the Beatles played at Scarborough's Futurist Theatre as part of their autumn tour. Even hours before their appearance large numbers of teenagers were strolling about outside the venue. When the 'Fab Four' arrived in a large black saloon at 4.30 p.m. there was only a handful of fans around, but they still had to sprint into the theatre, where Mrs Peter Jaconelli served them platefuls of steak, mushrooms and chips (apart from Ringo Starr, who had beans and eggs). Both shows of that day were performed to capacity audiences and the second house was a sea of scarves, hats and waving arms, and a plea that jelly babies should not be thrown fell on deaf ears as they cascaded to the stage. During the second house, as the Beatles belted out the song 'Twist and Shout', around 600 screaming teenagers surged forward from the stalls and had to be held back from the stage by policemen and theatre staff. A St John's Ambulance brigade official reported that twenty girls had passed out momentarily. At the close of the show, crowds surged for the exit to catch sight of the band leaving, but they were disappointed for as soon as the curtain began to fall the Beatles sprinted out of the theatre to a ready and waiting car, on Bland's Cliff. (*Scarborough Evening News*)

DECEMBER 12TH

2011: On this day, organisers and exhibitors were reflecting on the success of the Arts Festival that had just ended, held in a former Sandside boatyard close to Scarborough's seafront. Professional and amateur artists displayed their work as part of a celebration of Scarborough's vibrant art scene and a competition encouraged youngsters to get involved with art. Displays and stands exhibited work from many of the twenty-three galleries across the borough of Scarborough, but most attention focused on the dramatic designs created in steel by Ray Londsdale. Five of his sculptures were on display with pride of place taken by *Freddie Gilroy and the Belsen Stragglers*, which depicts one of the first Allied soldiers to enter the Belsen concentration camp on its liberation in the Second World War. The sculpture shows the former miner, complete with cloth cap and overcoat, casually gazing out across rough North Sea breakers. Ray Lonsdale visited the festival and spent time in conversation with local resident, Maureen Robinson, who had generously acquired the sculpture on behalf of Scarborough. The competition for students was judged by international artist Clive Head, and the Mayor of Scarborough, Councillor John Blackburn, made presentations to artists. (*Scarborough Evening News*)

DECEMBER 13TH

1839: The foundation stone of the Wesleyan Centenary Chapel in Queen Street, Scarborough, was laid on this day by H. Fowler Esq., to mark the beginning of the Wesleyan Methodist movement a hundred years earlier. John Wesley, his brother Charles and several other students had formed a group devoted to study, prayer and helping the underprivileged whilst studying at Oxford during the late 1730s. As the movement gathered strength, John Wesley travelled widely and preached in 1759, 1761, 1764 and 1790 at an old chapel in St Mary's Street, which was replaced by the Centenary Chapel.

Work on the building was completed during 1840 and it opened for public worship on Friday, September 11th. Measuring 91ft in length and with a width of 66ft, there was space for in excess of 2,000 worshippers. J. Simpson Esq. of Leeds designed the interior, and the total cost amounted to £7,000 (of which £3,000 had been obtained by private subscriptions and collections at the opening services). Below the chapel were vestries, school rooms and accommodation for the chapel keeper. Renovation work to celebrate the chapel's jubilee was completed at a cost of £500. (Ed. T.F. Bulmer, *History, Topography, and Directory of North Yorkshire*, T. Bulmer & Co., 1890)

DECEMBER 14TH

1901: A 274-ton barquentine, the *Satellite*, was driven ashore during gale-force winds off Scarborough today. The three-masted vessel was first spotted at 5.30 a.m. making distress signals a mile east of the harbour, with her sails torn away, and by 7 a.m. she had been forced onto the beach by the storm. Local lifeboatmen were already in attendance and were able to transfer the eight crew members to the shore, although their task was made more difficult by wreckage from the *Boxer*, an earlier victim of the storms.

As the tide receded, the *Satellite* was left high and dry on the beach, apparently intact but before long heavy seas battered the vessel and she was sold as a wreck for £110. At the time of her loss the *Satellite* was owned by Filmer C. Baldwin of Dover and she was heading northwards to Hartlepool under the command of Captain Robert Dunn. The wreckage was purchased by a local fishmonger, who sold items such as ropes and pieces of equipment to local seamen, making a considerable profit. (Arthur Godfrey and Peter J. Lassey, *Shipwrecks of the Yorkshire Coast*, Dalesman Publishing Co. Ltd, 1974)

DECEMBER 15TH

1903: The Scarborough Forty Club met on this day, in a private room at the town's Balmoral Hotel in Westborough. The minutes record that:

> Mr Smith chose for his subject 'The Municipal Debt' in relation to which he delivered himself of some pertinent and forceful criticism. The members present appreciated the speakers' remarks notwithstanding the unfortunate break in proceedings during which time Mr Smith was urgently required to attend to an important business matter.

(Alan Staniforth, *Scarborough Forty Club & Discussion Group: A Brief History: the '40' Club, founded in 1899*, Alan Staniforth, 2005)

———◆———

1939: On this day, an unusual supper dish of macon and egg was served at Scarborough's Grand Hotel for the annual hospital gathering. This innovative dish was made from mutton, which was used as a substitute for bacon and cured in the same manner. As its popularity increased, local butcher J.L. Hopwood on Queen Street advertised it as the new mutton/bacon, and before long many of the town's butcher's and grocer's shops offered it for sale. With the outbreak of war, the Grand Hotel was requisitioned by the Royal Air Force as a billet for training wings, and anti-aircraft guns were mounted on the corner cupolas. (Richard James Percy, *Scarborough's War Years, 1939-45*, Sutton Publishing Ltd, 1992)

DECEMBER 16TH

1914: The full horror of modern warfare struck Scarborough during the early hours of this day, when German battlecruisers, the *Derrflinger* and *Von der Tann*, and lightcruiser, the *Kolberg*, appeared off the coastline. Just before 8.00 a.m., the *Kolberg* was sent south-east to lay a minefield off Flamborough Head, while the two battlecruisers opened fire on Scarborough's coastguard station and yeomanry barracks. They then sailed in a south-easterly direction along the coastline, whilst directing fire at the castle walls and the Grand Hotel; no one was injured, but considerable structural damage resulted in a repair bill of around £10,000.

The next target was the wireless station close to Falsgrave, but shells fell short and the battlecruisers then sailed north, still directing gunfire over the town, en route for Whitby. The bombardment of Scarborough lasted about forty-five minutes, with approximately 500 shells fired, leaving seventeen people dead, including fourteen-month-old John Shields Ryall. Panic drove local people from their homes, and the newly-recruited Territorials tended the injured at the town's railway station. This indiscriminate killing of innocent civilians outraged public opinion and 'Remember Scarborough' was used as a recruiting slogan for the rest of the war. (www.historyofwar.org)

December 17th

1869: On this day, there were dramatic scenes and a tragic outcome involving the barque *Highbury*, of South Shields. During the previous afternoon the vessel had been trying to reach its home port on the Tyne when a violent storm halted its progress north. As darkness fell, Captain Williams decided that the safest course of action was to seek shelter in Bridlington Bay, but at 5 a.m. on December 17th the ship's ballast shifted and the *Highbury* was driven, out of control, towards land. A short while later, between 6 a.m. and 7 a.m., she struck rocks below Scarborough Castle and immediately keeled over.

The ship's master and six crew members climbed the rigging and leapt from the mastheads on to cliffs, and from there they were able to scramble onto firm ground. Two other crew members lowered themselves over the boat's quarterdeck and attempted to wade ashore, only to be swept away by the rolling breakers and drowned. Their bodies were discovered on the shoreline later in the day, and by the following morning the oak-built *Highbury* had been smashed to pieces by the raging storm. (Arthur Godfrey and Peter J. Lassey, *Shipwrecks of the Yorkshire Coast*, Dalesman Publishing Co. Ltd, 1974)

DECEMBER 18TH

1953: A newspaper article on this day discussed recurring tales among local people about 'Hairy Bob', who allegedly lived in 'Hairy Bob's Cave' on the north side of Castle Hill. One correspondent, Mr T. Foster of no. 6 Moorland Road, maintained that the tales stemmed from the 1880s, when the son of a well-known Scarborough family, by the name of 'Bogg', left his home to live in a cave close by, that has a doorway and window and is often referred to by townspeople as 'Hairy Bob's Cave'. Another explanation came from Mr V. Harland in Sheffield, who recalled that his father insisted that the character was a former verger of St Mary's Church who could not 'hit it off' with his wife. The verger chiselled out the opening in the rock to form the window and door, in order to create a refuge from his spouse. (*Scarborough Evening News*)

1971: On this day, a Scarborough couple, Mr and Mrs William Cooper of no. 21 Victoria Street, celebrated their golden wedding anniversary. They first met while working for rival firms in the kipper-curing business on Durham Street, and Mrs Cooper recalled that in those days it was not possible to see from one end of the street to the other for smoke. (*Scarborough Evening News*)

DECEMBER 19TH

1963: A press report on this day described a concert the previous evening at Scarborough's Queen Street Central Hall.Members of the town's Amateur Operatic Society were joined by massed choirs and vocalist Jean Grayson to present 'A Night of Music'. The programme devised and conducted by Leslie Sturdy was in two parts. In the first half, 'Songs from the Shows', included items from *Bitter Sweet* and *Oklahoma*, while the second half consisted of 'Welcome to Christmas', as well as excerpts from Handel's *Messiah*. Profits from the event, which had been fully booked several weeks earlier, were to be shared between St John's Ambulance Brigade, the Council of Social Service and the British Red Cross. (*Scarborough Evening News*)

2011: On this day, news bulletins reported that six walkers had been rescued while tackling the Lyke Wake Walk – a 42-mile route across the North York Moors. After leaving Eller Beck the group became disorientated and two women in the party became ill due to the freezing temperatures. The party was unable to move from its location and became stranded in Jugger Ravine, between Fylingdales and Ravenscar. The Scarborough and Ryedale Mountain Rescue team received a call for assistance and an RAF helicopter located all six walkers and returned them to safety, transporting the two ladies that had fallen ill to hospital. (*Scarborough Evening News*)

DECEMBER 20TH

1910: At a meeting of Scarborough Forty Club on this day:

> Mr Yorke read a paper on the motor car . . . He stated that the invention of pneumatic tyres led immediately to the possibilities of the motor car which fourteen years ago was practically unknown . . . The major part of Mr Yorke's paper dealt with construction of the body of the car and samples of wood, leather etc. used for that purpose were handed round for inspection.

(Alan Staniforth, *Scarborough Forty Club & Discussion Group: A Brief History: the '40' Club, founded in 1899*, Alan Staniforth, 2005)

———•◆•———

2011: Performing arts students from Scalby School were given a major boost on this day, with the announcement of a significant sponsorship deal. Pupils were working hard in rehearsals for their four-day production of *The Wedding Singer* at the town's Stephen Joseph Theatre in February 2012, when it was revealed that the Scarborough company, Life's Energy, was backing the show with funding of £1,000. (*The Scarborough News*)

DECEMBER 21ST

2011: On this day, Heritage Minister John Penrose announced that the site of this country's oldest house, at Star Carr, was to be designated a scheduled monument, due to its rarity and archaeological importance. Located some 5 miles south of Scarborough in Flixton, the Star Carr is an early Mesolithic settlement and is extremely rare on account of the remarkable survival of organic material from that period found there, along with evidence of built structures. Mr Penrose commented that the diversity of finds at Star Carr and its history, which stretched back to 9,000 BC, were unequalled in British archaeology and represented one of the most important Mesolithic sites in Europe. The site was first discovered in the 1940s and has since attracted extensive research, which led to the discovery of a house in 2010, by a team of archaeologists from the universities of York and Manchester. They uncovered a 3.5 metre circular structure beside an ancient lake, as well as a well-preserved 11,000-year-old tree trunk, with its bark still intact and showing the earliest evidence of carpentry in Europe. Among other significant items discovered there were head-dresses, which are now on display in the British Museum. (*Scarborough Evening News*)

DECEMBER 22ND

1931: The Scarborough lighthouse officially reopened on this day, following destruction of the earlier structure in the bombardment by German battlecruisers during December 1914. This replacement lighthouse was originally fitted with a red light, but this caused some confusion and it was eventually replaced by a white light. It also had a foghorn which was operated during the Second World War as an air-raid siren. Scarborough's earliest lighthouse is believed to date from the beginning of the nineteenth century and it may be the same simple, 'flat' building of 1806, which had a single brazier on the roof. This was replaced by six tallow candles, and a few years later a tin reflector was installed behind them to increase illumination. In 1818 a copper reflector was put in its place, with a night-watchman employed to keep the candles lit. During 1844, the light tower was increased in height and the candles were replaced by gas lights. By the time of its destruction in 1914, electricity had been installed. (www.yorkshire-east-coast-unofficial-guide.com)

◆

1953: On this day, English Heritage gave Grade I listed building status to King Richard III House, on Quay Street Scarborough. Richard III ruled from 1483-85 and is reputed to have stayed here while visiting the town on naval business. (www.britishlistedbuildings.co.uk)

DECEMBER 23RD

1844: During the early nineteenth century, Scarborough's spa facilities attracted increasing numbers of visitors. Though incidents of unacceptable behaviour were infrequent, on December 23rd 1844 the Corporation committee was informed that 'some evil disposed persons had committed considerable mischief to the trees, shrubs etc. in the plantation' and had broken windows in the recently built gatehouse at the Crown entrance, as well as causing damage in other places. The committee's response was to offer a reward of £20 for information leading to apprehension of those responsible, and at their annual meeting in 1848, members had to consider action over 'The disorderly assemblages on the bridge and walk after dusk, more especially on Sunday evenings.' Intermittent reports of unacceptable behaviour included a statement during May 1862 that, 'In consequence of the unseemly conduct of the Misses Chambers on the Spa', the secretary had lodged a complaint with their mother, including a threat to refuse access in the future. When a local resident, Miss Mary Craven, who was known for her charitable works in the area, was caught 'purloining flowers from the grounds' she was threatened with further action if there was any repetition of this misbehaviour. (Meredith Whittaker, *The Book of Scarborough Spaw*, Barracuda, 1984)

DECEMBER 24TH

1851: An excursion handbill for this date advertised a cheap Christmas trip from Leeds and other local stations to Hull, York and Scarborough. Leaving Leeds:

> At a Quarter past 3 o'clock in the Afternoon . . . All the Carriages will be covered . . . In order to do this, the Second Class Fare has been withdrawn for these Trips . . . Fares to Scarborough and Back (from Leeds) 4s 6d Covered Carriages 7s 6d First Class . . . Passengers can return from Scarborough on Friday the 26th and Monday 29th by the regular train which leaves Scarborough at a Quarter to 10 . . .

The York and Scarborough branch of the York and North Midland Railway had opened on July 7th 1845, with celebrations on a grand scale at both Scarborough and York. Within a month, a cheap day excursion had been arranged from Newcastle; Scarborough's popularity as a resort and holiday centre increased dramatically. Excursion handbills soon began to follow a certain style and included a considerable amount of information on one single sheet, often with the woodcut of a train forming the header. These were soon followed by a whole range of guidebooks, leaflets and posters. (Robin Lidster, *Yorkshire Coast Lines*, Hendon Publishing Co. Ltd, 1983)

DECEMBER 25TH

1773: John Thurston, engraver and artist, was born in Scarborough on this day. His early career as a copperplate engraver began when he was articled to the established engraver, John Heath, but he later produced wood engravings and watercolours for book illustrations. Many works by poets and novelists in the first two decades of the nineteenth century were illustrated by Thurston, and in 1805 he was elected associate of the Old Watercolour Society. He died in Holloway on September 29th 1951. (Anne and Paul Bayliss, *Scarborough Artists of the Nineteenth Century, A Biographical Dictionary*, Anne Bayliss, 1997)

2004: On this day, the Scarborough lifeboat was launched at 4.35 p.m. following a call from the crew of a sinking fishing boat, the *Kerloch*, some 36 miles off shore. The Humber Coastguard escalated the incident to a 'Mayday' and called out a search and rescue helicopter from RAF Leconfield. On arriving at the scene, the helicopter lowered a salvage pump onto the boat's deck, and, after several attempts amid rough conditions, two lifeboatmen clambered aboard the *Kerloch*. Lifeboatman Andy Blackwell, a mechanic by trade, managed to restore some power to the vessel and they were able steer the boat safely back to Scarborough, escorted by the lifeboat. It reached Scarborough at 2.30 a.m. on Boxing Day, almost ten hours after the rescue began. (*RNLI: Scarborough Lifeboats*)

DECEMBER 26TH

1898: Having been previously played on Christmas Day, the Fishermen & Firemen's Charity Football Match was first played on Boxing Day of this year, a custom that has continued to the present day on South Bay Beach. The match is a primary fundraising event for the Fishermen & Firemen Charity Fund, which supports elderly and needy people throughout winter. The charity was initially set up to help the widows and orphans of five Scarborough fishermen, who were drowned when the trawling smack *Evelyn and Maud* was wrecked in late November 1893.

The *Evelyn and Maud* had sailed to Flamborough Head fishing grounds, where it was seen trawling at 4.30 p.m. on November 16th. A storm blew in two days later and when other boats headed for Scarborough, there was no sign of the *Evelyn and Maud*. Extensive inquiries over the next five days failed to locate the missing smack and after initial theories suggested a collision with another vessel, it was subsequently determined that she had most probably capsized whilst trawling in rough conditions. A memorial service was held at St Mary's Church on December 3rd 1893 for the five men lost at sea, and the Evelyn & Maud Fund was set up. By 1900 it had become the Fishermen & Firemen's Charity. (www.fishermenandfiremen.co.uk)

DECEMBER 27TH

1773: Sir George Cayley, 'The Father of Aeronautics', was born at Scarborough on this day. He spent some time at school in York, where he showed an early and keen interest in mechanics. Early projects included constructing a model helicopter at the age of nineteen, when he inherited the family estate. Cayley made some substantial improvements to the estate and allowed each capable labourer an acre of land under his allotment system (the land had an improved drainage system that enabled its use for pasture and the growth of cereals).

Cayley's mechanical skills soon focused on topics such as railway safety, heat engines, self-righting lifeboats, ballistics and the application of electricity as a motive power. In 1831, he was Vice President of the Yorkshire Philosophical Society when it helped set up the British Association for the Advancement of Science, and the following year he was elected as Liberal MP for Scarborough. In 1809, George Cayley had published a pioneering paper on aerial navigation and the culmination of his interest in aeronautics came in 1853, when his glider flew several hundred yards along Brompton Dale, with his coachman as pilot. He died at Brompton Hall on December 15th 1857. (Leonard Rivett, Jim Matthew & Derek Reginald Reed, *Yorkshire Genius: Brief Study of the Life, Work and Achievements of Sir George Cayley*, Yorkshire Air Museum, 1996)

DECEMBER 28TH

1835: On this day, the first elections since the passing of the Municipal Corporations Act were held in Scarborough. Under the terms of the legislation, Scarborough kept its original boundaries and was divided into two wards – north and south – each with nine seats on the new council. The electorate was comprised of 549 rate-paying adult residents, and seventeen of the eighteen seats were won by Liberal reformers. The only successful Tory candidate was John Woodall, and topping the poll in the North Ward was Samuel Byron, who had pursued the case for reform under the old corporation. Six of the new council members were selected to be aldermen and they were replaced by known reformers, including John Rowntree, the Quaker businessman.

The reformed system introduced more efficient aspects of administration, including monthly meetings with public reports, and the appointment of a town clerk and borough treasurer, who were not members of the council. Samuel Byron was elected as the first mayor of the reformed borough of Scarborough in January 1836, several years after leading the case for reform when Commissioners investigated the town's 'affairs of council governance'. (Anne and Paul Bayliss, *Scarborough's Members of Parliament, 1832 to 1906: Scarborough's Mayors, 1836 to 1906: A Biographical Dictionary*, A.M. Bayliss, 2008)

DECEMBER 29TH

1933: Many thousands of people, including, no doubt, large numbers of visitors, flocked onto the South foreshore and to vantage points on adjacent cliffs, to witness the night-time lifeboat launch towards a burning vessel, which was staged as a Christmastide spectacle. Fog, which had persisted for some days, prevented one of the principle items of the display – the bombing of the ship from an aeroplane – from taking place. The weather conditions meant that taking off and landing at the Scarborough Aero Club's Heslerton base was considered to be too great a hazard. It also curtailed the power of the illuminations on the sea, so that once the lifeboat was away it appeared in the ray of the searchlight as a ghostly image. A striking picture was presented as the lifeboat was run across the beach to the launching place. Powerful floodlights on the West Pier and Lighthouse Pier left the sands so brilliantly lit, that it was remarked that a football match could have been played within range of the lights. (*Scarborough Mercury*)

1941: The Edgehill area came under attack again today, when a lone enemy aircraft dropped bombs on allotments, causing damage to nearby houses. (Richard James Percy, *Scarborough's War Years, 1939-45*, Sutton Publishing Ltd, 1992)

December 30th

1925: William Boyes died on this day, after a highly successful lifetime as a businessman and politician in the Scarborough area. After establishing the family business during the 1880s, he was invited to stand for the town council during the following decade. As a Liberal candidate he was unsuccessful in 1895 when he was beaten by the established Conservative councillor, E.H. Gawne. However, he won four years later when he stood for a different ward. His business background attracted some humour, and one lampoon in a news-sheet, entitled 'The Man in the Moon', showed him at the door of his shop against a background of window stickers advertising an 'After Election Sale', with items such as 'damp squibs', 'hats for enlarged heads', 'rejected election addresses in assorted colours', and even 'a coat of many colours to suit politicians of any ward'. This period of service in local politics lasted nine years, but after a gap of ten years he was re-elected in 1919 and became Mayor of Scarborough in 1921. In November 1922, he was made an alderman on the day that his term as mayor finished; he set a record of being a councillor, alderman and mayor on the same day. A second term as mayor ended just a month before his death. (*Boyes: The Story of a Family Stores 1881-1981*)

DECEMBER 31ST

1909: Today's *Scarborough Mercury* reported proceedings at the town's Police Court, where Alfred Wilson, aged thirty-five, was charged with three cases of stealing goods from the *Eliza*, a Filey-based yawl. A crew member from the *Eliza* reported that the yawl had been moored in Filey Harbour and left secure on December 23rd. On his return, four days later, it was clear that the cabin had been broken open, but he mentioned it to no one else, and it was only when the vessel was put to sea that articles were found to be missing. When the *Eliza* returned on December 28th, the police were informed and PC Stockdale searched Wilson's coble. He found all the articles mentioned in the charge, apart from a compass and clogs, and, when arrested, the prisoner was wearing some of the stolen clothing. He claimed to have thrown the compass into the harbour and to have left the clogs in the churchyard; these items were soon revovered. The chairman of magistrates said that, 'although Alfred Wilson's last court appearance was some six years earlier, on a charge of drunkenness, he would have to go to prison for a month on each of the three charges'. (*Scarborough Mercury*)